Free to Die for Their Country

FREE TO DIE FOR

THE CHICAGO SERIES IN LAW AND SOCIETY

EDITED BY WILLIAM M. O'BARR
AND JOHN M. CONLEY

THEIR COUNTRY

The Story of the Japanese American Draft Resisters in World War II

Eric L. Muller

With a Foreword by

Senator Daniel K. Inouye

The University of Chicago Press

Chicago and London

Eric L. Muller is professor of law at the University of North Carolina, Chapel Hill.

The University of Chicago Press, Chicago 60637
The University of Chicago Press, Ltd., London

Printed in the United States of America

10 09 08 07 06 05 04 03 02 01   1 2 3 4 5

ISBN: 0-226-54822-8 (cloth)

Library of Congress Cataloging-in-Publication Data

Muller, Eric L.
Free to die for their country : the story of the Japanese American draft resisters in World War II / Eric L. Muller.
p. cm.—(The Chicago series in law and society)
Includes index.
ISBN 0-226-54822-8 (cloth : alk. paper)
1. World War, 1939–1945—Conscientious objectors—United States. 2. Japanese Americans—Evacuation and relocation, 1942–1945. I. Series.
D810.C82 M85 2001
940.53'162—dc21
2001027405

This book is printed on acid-free paper.

In memory of my grandfather,
Felix Muller

For my children,
Abby and Nina

We may lose the verdict,
but the verdict shall be man-made;
and with the passing of Time,
eternal truth and right
will come to light.
That is my firm belief.

—**George Ishikawa**
in a Wyoming county jail
early May 1944

Contents

Foreword

The period covered by the experience of the men whose stories are told in this moving account constitutes one of the darkest moments in the history of the United States. It was during a time in which our parents who were born in Japan were declared to be ineligible to become citizens of the United States.

It was a time when Americans of Japanese ancestry were designated by our Selective Service system as "4C"—enemy aliens. This designation was obviously the most feared. We were the enemy in the midst of America.

This was a period when 120,000 people were rounded up to be incarcerated in ten concentration camps located in some of the most desolate areas of our country. They were incarcerated because they were Japanese. No one ever accused them of sabotage or "fifth column activities" or treason.

In this climate of hate, many felt the necessity of stepping forward to volunteer for service in the military to prove their loyalty to the United States. These men for the most part carried out their military obligations with much courage and valor.

However, in this climate of hate, I believe that it took just as much courage and valor and patriotism to stand up to our government and say "you are wrong."

I am glad that there were some who had the courage to express some of the feelings that we who volunteered harbored deep in our souls.

—Senator Daniel Inouye

Preface

"And these," said the woman at the lectern, nodding toward a screen onto which an old black-and-white photograph was projected, "are the Nisei draft resisters from Heart Mountain." The speaker, a local historian in Laramie, Wyoming, was giving a public presentation about the history of the Heart Mountain Relocation Center, one of the ten concentration camps in which the U.S. government confined the Japanese American population of the West Coast during World War II. The photograph, which you will find near the middle of this book, was of several rows of young Japanese American (Nisei) men seated behind a heavy wooden table in a marble-walled federal courtroom in Cheyenne, Wyoming. Some seemed to twist awkwardly in their chairs; others sat ramrod straight. Some looked worried, some looked amused, a few looked bored, and some bore the look of smug defiance that only a man in his early twenties can produce in a courtroom. "They were tried as a group, all sixty-three of them," the historian explained. "It was the biggest mass trial in Wyoming history. And when they were convicted of draft evasion, they were all sent off to serve about three years in federal prison." Then she clicked to the next slide in her presentation.

My mind, however, stayed with the previous image. *Draft* resisters? Japanese American internees who were draft resisters? Could it be, I asked myself, that the U.S. government had dared to conscript Japanese American internees into the army after forcing them into internment camps on suspicion of disloyalty?

At the time I saw this photograph, I was finishing up my second year of teaching at the University of Wyoming College of Law in Laramie. The Japanese American internment was something I felt I knew something about. In my constitutional law class, I covered the Supreme Court's 1944 decision in *Korematsu v. United States,* upholding the constitutionality of the wartime internment of the Japanese Americans of the West Coast. In order to teach that case effectively, I had read about the escalating deprivations that the government imposed on those of Japanese ancestry, alien and citizen alike, in the wake of Pearl Harbor—the house searches, the arrests of community leaders, the curfews and the travel restrictions, and, of course, the wholesale eviction and incarceration of every person of Japanese descent from California, Washington, and Oregon.

This was a story that touched me deeply because it resonated with my own family history. I am the son of a Jewish refugee from Nazi Germany. In November of 1938, Gestapo officers ransacked my grandparents' Frankfurt home and then dragged my grandfather to Buchenwald. After his release from that concentration camp a few weeks later, he and my grandmother escaped with my father and my aunt, first to Switzerland and then, in April of 1941, to America. They settled in southern New Jersey on a chicken farm and were living there on December 8, 1941, when the United States entered the war against Japan and Germany. Ironically, my father and his family were transformed in that moment into "enemy aliens"—Germans in the eyes of the American government, even though as Jews they had long ago lost their German citizenship, not to mention any desire to advance the cause of the regime that was murdering Europe's Jews. And as enemy aliens, they were subject to some of the same restrictions that were simultaneously imposed on the West Coast Japanese Americans. Their farmhouse was searched by FBI agents, who discovered a pair of binoculars and seized it as contraband. Like the Japanese Americans of the West Coast, my grandparents were forbidden from traveling more than five miles from their home without government permission.

Because of these connections, I had delved a bit more deeply into the story of the Japanese American internment than many of the other topics I covered in my constitutional law class. But I had never heard of these Japanese American draft resisters. The only people I knew of who had resisted the internment in any way were the tiny handful of Japanese Americans—Gordon Hirabayashi, Minoru Yasui, Mitsuye Endo, and Fred Korematsu—whose cases had made their way to the U.S. Supreme Court. I also knew of Japanese American combat veterans from World War II, such as Senator Daniel K. Inouye of Hawaii, a man I greatly admired for his role in the Watergate investigation. But I had never thought about how Japanese Americans had gotten into the army. I suppose I assumed that they all volunteered. It was unthinkable to me that the government would have drafted them.

About a year later I saw that photograph again—this time in Washington, D.C., in a permanent exhibit at the Smithsonian called "A More Perfect Union," which presents the story of the Japanese American internment. I came upon the photograph about two-thirds of the way through the exhibit, just beside the entrance to a big room devoted to the Japanese American soldiers of World War II. Set in the middle of a small display about the draft, the photo immediately brought back the questions that had swirled through my mind the first time I saw it—none of which I was any closer to answering. Beneath the photo, however, was a card that identified the men in the photo as some of the *several hundred* Japanese Americans who had resisted the draft from inside the internment camps. This form of resistance was obviously a larger phenomenon than I had realized. I took out a piece of paper and jotted down the few details that the display offered about the resisters, resolving that upon returning to Wyoming I would head to the university library and read up on their story.

Back in Wyoming, I found plenty of books about the internment, and several about the Japanese American veterans, but not one about the draft resisters. Even the finest works on the internment, such as those of the historian Roger Daniels, devoted at most a couple of pages to the topic and spoke only of the draft resisters from Heart Mountain, to the exclusion of the more than two hundred young men from other camps who resisted the draft. Somehow, notwithstanding all of the public and scholarly attention that the Japanese American internment had received in the 1980s, with Congress's authorization of $20,000 redress payments to each of its surviving victims, and in the 1990s, with the novel *Snow Falling on Cedars* on the best-seller list and on the big screen, the story of the Japanese American draft resisters had gone untold for more than fifty years. There ought to be a book on this, I said to myself with a mix of amazement and frustration.

This is that book.

Acknowledgments

Of the many people I wish to thank for their help, advice, and support on the project that has become this book, two groups of people stand out. The first is my family. My wife, Leslie, gave me the space, time, advice, and love that I needed—not to mention several careful edits. My wonderful daughters, Abby and Nina, surrendered some time with Daddy so that he could go off and work on "that book about those men who didn't go to the war and went to jail." And without the love and support of my parents, Joan and Jim Muller, I would never have been in a position to undertake a project such as this.

The other group is the men whose story I tell. Much of the material in this book comes from my interviews, both in person and over the telephone, with the following Japanese American draft resisters. Any quotation of these men in this book comes from these interviews, except where I indicate otherwise.

- Gene Akutsu: Seattle, Washington, 20 February 1998; telephone conversation, 3 March 2000.
- Frank Emi: San Gabriel, California, 11 October 1998; Alhambra, California, 25 July 2000.
- Kazuo Hiromoto: Richmond, California, 9 January 1998.
- Takashi Hoshizaki: Los Angeles, California, 11 October 1998; Alhambra, California, 25 July 2000.
- Mits Koshiyama: San Jose, California, 10 January 1998 and 26 July 2000.
- Yosh Kuromiya: Alhambra, California, 12 October 1998 and 25 July 2000.
- Tom Noda: telephone conversation, 21 June 1999; Dixon, California, 15 June 2000.

- George Nozawa: Mountain View, California, 9 January 1998 and 16 June 2000; San Jose, California, 26 July 2000.
- Jack Tono: Chicago, Illinois, 24 October 1997.
- Jimi Yamaichi: San Jose, California, 16 October 1998.
- Frank Yamasaki: Seattle, Washington, 19 February 1998.

Many of these men welcomed me into their homes, where I also had the pleasure of getting to know Tomiko Hiromoto, Barbara Hoshizaki, Irene Kuromiya, Fusaye Nozawa, and Sadie Yamasaki.

I garnered very important background information from interviews and, in some cases, correspondence with Daniel Bennett, Lorraine Bennett, Bill Hosokawa, Norio Mitsuoka, Joe and Tee Norikane, Eleanor Jackson Piel, Paul Tsuneishi, Clifford Uyeda, William Wunsch, and Ken and Kay Yoshida.

The California Civil Liberties Public Education Program provided me with a generous grant that helped me turn a rough draft of the manuscript into the finished product that you are holding. This program and its energetic director, Diane Matsuda, provided me with a wealth of support, both financial and logistical.

Books such as this would be impossible without the assistance and expertise of archivists and librarians. I was especially fortunate to have the help of Mike Griffith of the United States District Court for the Northern District of California; Janis Wiggins of the National Archives and Records Administration (NARA) in College Park, Maryland; Aloha South of NARA in Washington, D.C.; Eric Bittner of NARA's branch in Denver, Colorado; Claude Hopkins in the San Bruno, California, branch of NARA; Carol Bowers and Lori Olson at the University of Wyoming's American Heritage Center; LaVaughn Bresnahan of the Wyoming State Archives; Susan Snyder of the Bancroft Library at the University of California at Berkeley; the staff of the Katherine R. Everett Law Library at the University of North Carolina School of Law, especially Tom French (now director of the H. Douglas Barclay Law Library at Syracuse University), Dave Solar (now at the library at Duke University's Fuqua School of Business), Steve Melamut, and Anne Klinefelter; and Tim Kearley and Debora Person of the George W. Hopper Law Library at the University of Wyoming College of Law.

A number of colleagues and friends were good enough to read and comment on all or parts of the manuscript while I drafted it. The book is much stronger for their efforts. Thanks to John Q. Barrett, Sara Sun Beale, Lou Bilionis, Caroline Brown, Bo Burt, John Conley, Roger Daniels, Joe DiMartino, Glenn George, Art Hansen, Arnold Loewy, Buck Melton, Bob Mosteller, Hiroshi Motomura, David Muller, Jim Muller, Duncan Murrell, Gene Nichol, John Orth, and Dan Peris. Joe Kennedy not only read the manuscript and provided insightful comments, but also offered much-needed inspiration at key stages of the project. I might still be staring at a blank computer screen were it not for him.

A number of colleagues on the faculty at the University of North Carolina School of Law offered other kinds of valuable assistance at various points: Gail Agrawal, Jack Boger, Brian Bromberger, Patricia Bryan, Marion Crain, Tom Kelley, Melissa Saunders, and Marilyn Yarbrough. I have gotten valuable help, advice, and encouragement of other kinds from Frank Abe, Ann and Alex Branden, Jeanne Holland, Stephen Kanovsky, Steve Lowry, Cliff Marks, Nick Philipson, Martha Radetsky, Maureen Ryan, Brad Saxton, Joel Selig, Roger Shimomura, and Mark Squillace.

I had research help from Mary Frasché in Chapel Hill, Matina Kilkenny and Don Tunison-Campbell in Eureka, David Stoddard-Hunt in Philadelphia, and Bob Faucher and Shannon Meacham in Boise.

Marilyn and Ira Tublin and Eric and Sari Tublin opened their homes to me while I was doing research at the National Archives in Washington, D.C. I enjoyed their hospitality after long days with the documents. In Los Angeles, Gary and Jenny Snegaroff offered me similarly comfortable and welcoming accommodations. In San Francisco, Ruth Radetsky and Edward Hasbrouck not only hosted me, but also provided all sorts of valuable suggestions on everything from where I should look for materials on draft resistance to how I should get to Mountain View during rush hour. They also both read the manuscript and provided me with valuable feedback.

Louis Fiset and Bob Sims both helped me sharpen my understanding of the situation in Seattle and Idaho.

John Tryneski at the University of Chicago Press has been enthusiastic, wise, and enormously helpful from the start of our working relationship.

Last, but certainly not least, are the institutions where I have had the good fortune to be employed while working on the book. The idea for the book was born in Wyoming, while I was on the faculty at the University of Wyoming College of Law. I got some important seed money in the form of a Faculty Growth Award from the university and several dispensations of funds for travel from then-Dean John Burman. In my current position at UNC–Chapel Hill, I received a University Research Council grant that helped subsidize some of my trips to the West Coast. Judith Wegner, my former dean at UNC, and Gene Nichol, my current dean, offered me breaks in my teaching load, financial support, a wealth of suggestions and contacts, and, perhaps most important, the strong sense that this was an exciting and worthwhile project—not just for me, but also for the University of North Carolina School of Law. I am indebted to both of them.

ONE UNTOLD PATRIOTISM

On the last day of spring in 1944, as American infantrymen began their assault on the Nazi-held port city of Cherbourg in northern France, the U.S. Army staged an induction ceremony for sixty-six new draftees in Idaho. In most ways, the ceremony was quite ordinary. The inductees, three abreast and twenty-two rows deep, marched into formation around a flagpole. Military music blared over a loudspeaker. Proud but worried parents and friends gathered around the new soldiers to listen to speeches of welcome and praise.

Only one thing was unusual about this ceremony. The army that was welcoming these new draftees was simultaneously guarding them and their families at gunpoint as potential subversives. The ceremony was taking place behind the barbed wire of the Minidoka Relocation Center in Hunt, Idaho. Minidoka was one of the ten concentration camps that the federal War Relocation Authority (WRA) set up in 1942 to house the nearly 120,000 "Nikkei"—people of Japanese descent—that the government had deported from the West Coast on suspicion of disloyalty in the wake of the Japanese attack on Pearl Harbor. The Minidoka draftees were all "Nisei"—American citizens born along the West Coast in the 1920s to the generation called the "Issei." The Issei were immigrants who had come to the United States from Japan around the turn of the century but had been forbidden by American law to apply for American citizenship because of their Asian origin.

Military service had been promoted to the Nisei as a precious opportunity to prove the loyalty and patriotism of all Japanese Americans—qualities that the Japanese attack on Pearl Harbor had sharply, even if unfairly, called into question. And Nisei loyalty was what the induction ceremony at Minidoka was designed to emphasize and celebrate. The chairman of the internees' community council pursued this theme in his welcoming comments to the draftees and the four hundred other internees in attendance. "We are mightily proud of you boys," said the Issei leader. "We know you will make good and we, and others, will point to your records; and we—all of us here—Issei and Nisei alike, will benefit by your records." After these opening remarks, the president of the Minidoka Parent-Soldiers Association presented each of the inductees with a Bible and a shiny metal cigarette case as good luck presents.

Then it was time for the swearing of the military oath. Lieutenant B. M. Harrington, a member of the army's Traveling Examining and Induction Board, rose to swear the boys in and to offer a few inspirational comments to the boys and their families about the task they were undertaking. "We in the American armed forces," the lieutenant said to the new troops, "are happy to welcome you Japanese among our ranks, even though your country, Japan, is at war with the United States." The crowd stirred uncomfortably: did the lieutenant not know that the draftees were all American citizens, not Japanese?

Harrington continued. "The fact that you young Japanese are willing to fight against your country," he stressed, "should prove to all that there are a few Japanese who are good Americans." The lieutenant expressed his hope that, at the end of the war, "all nationalities could live in peace in America" and then blundered to his conclusion, congratulating "you Japanese" for "making a splendid record in our Army, where you are welcomed and given all of the rights and privileges of any other citizen who is brought into the service."

Harrington's comments visibly sapped the crowd of its enthusiasm. "Doesn't he know we were born here and are citizens of the United States, not Japan?" muttered one young man. Exclaimed another: "Why doesn't that guy get next to himself and discover to what country we belong? We are no Japs."

A Minidoka administrator took Harrington aside after his speech and pointed out the lieutenant's errors: the Nisei draftees were Americans, not Japanese; they were leaving the camp to fight *for* their country, not *against* it; and the U.S. Army was as much theirs as it was Lieutenant Harrington's. Harrington accepted the suggestions and "agreed in good spirit to leave out such references in future induction ceremonies." But for the Minidoka internees, the insult had registered. One of the sixty-six young men turned his back on the assembly and walked away just before the oath was administered, joining in defiance the tiny handful of other young men from Minidoka who had decided to resist the draft rather than comply with it.[1]

In the scheme of things, Lieutenant Harrington's words were actually a petty indignity. The men and women in his audience, and their fellow internees at the nine other WRA internment camps, had suffered far more painful wounds by June of 1944 than Harrington's insensitive speech. Indeed, it would be safe to say that by this point in the war, the U.S. government had placed almost impossible burdens on them. About two years earlier, in March of 1942, the government had confined them to their homes from dusk to dawn as suspected subversives. Then the government rounded them up and warehoused them for the summer of 1942 in so-called assembly centers—filthy sheds hastily thrown up at local fairgrounds and racetracks. That fall the government loaded them onto trains and shipped them off for indefinite detention behind barbed wire in desolate camps such as Minidoka, the Heart Mountain Relocation Center in Wyoming, and the Tule Lake Relocation Center in California. Their crime was their ethnicity, and the government had made them pay for it with their livelihoods, their possessions, their liberty, and their dignity.

In January of 1944, the government demanded still more. It announced that it would begin drafting the very same Japanese American men it was jailing on suspicion of disloyalty. By early February, young men at the ten relocation centers began receiving notices directing them to report to their local draft boards for their preinduction physical examinations. They were to join the same army that had been guarding them for years, and that continued to aim weapons and searchlights at their parents and siblings.

This extraordinary government demand left these young men with no good choices. On the one hand, they could swallow their outrage at years of mistreatment and leave captivity to fight for someone else's freedom. To do this would mean more than risking their own lives; it would also mean leaving their families behind to uncertain futures as wards of a hostile government. On the other hand, they could give voice to their outrage and resist the draft. To do this was to risk prosecution, many more years of incarceration, and the lifelong stigma of a felony conviction.

Most of the young men in the camps, like the sixty-five Minidokans who were sworn in that June day by Lieutenant Harrington, choked back their resentments and chose to accept the draft as just another unwanted test of their patriotism. Many served bravely in Europe with the 442nd Regimental Combat Team, the racially segregated battalion for Japanese Americans that the army created for them. Some lost their limbs, others their lives.

Some of the internees, however, made the other choice and refused to comply with their draft orders. Usually, these were solitary acts of disobedience. At Minidoka, for example, nearly forty young men ignored their draft notices, each unaware that others were doing the same. At the Heart Mountain Relocation Center, on the other hand, draft resistance became a noisy and well-publicized political movement that led nearly ninety to resist. In all, more than three hundred Japanese Americans from the ten WRA camps refused to show up for their physical examinations or for induction. They pressed a simple moral question: if we are loyal enough to serve in the army, what are we doing behind barbed wire?

The government not only declined to answer this question, but also punished the resisters brutally for asking it. Through the spring and summer of 1944, agents of the U.S. Marshals Service came to their tarpaper barracks and arrested them on charges of draft evasion, carting them off to local jails to await trial. Their cases came to trial in federal courtrooms across the western United States in the summer and fall of 1944.

Many of the defendants were at least guardedly optimistic; they knew that if there was one branch of the federal government that might protect them, it was the federal courts. Their optimism was guarded because they knew it was wartime and they knew that they looked like the enemy. While the Japanese threat to the U.S. mainland had vanished by the summer of 1944, most of the country still shared the view of Japanese Americans that the military official responsible for their evacuation and internment had publicly voiced: "A Jap's a Jap."[2] As long as the war was still on, the resisters understood that they would have a hard time finding a sympathetic ear for their claim. But they viewed the federal courts as their best hope.

This was not entirely unrealistic. Franklin Delano Roosevelt had had twelve years to load the federal bench with New Deal liberals.[3] This is not to say that the federal courts in 1944 were the institution we now recognize them to be; the Warren Court had not yet been born, and the activist era in the area of individual rights that it would usher in was still in the offing. But it was not far in the offing. *Brown v. Board of Education,*[4] the most daring defense of individual freedom ever undertaken by any branch of the American government, was just a decade down the road. Already on the Supreme Court, beginning to find their judicial voices, were several of the eventual leaders of the Warren Court revolution. Decisions protecting the rights of Communists, blacks, labor unions, and unpopular religious groups were starting to appear with some frequency. The federal courts that would hear the prosecutions of the Japanese American draft resisters were in flux, moving from earlier, more timid times on matters of civil rights to the bolder ones that lay ahead.

The federal courts, however, failed the resisters dismally. With but one exception, the federal judges hearing the cases waved aside the resisters' attacks on the legality of drafting internees and ran shoddy trials that produced across-the-board convictions. This disappointing group of federal judges then sentenced the resisters to lengthy terms of imprisonment—most commonly two to three years, but sometimes as long as five—in federal penitentiaries such as Leavenworth and McNeil Island. The resisters traded in their years of detention as pariahs in relocation centers for years of incarceration as felons in federal prisons.

Only one federal judge saw the cases differently. Judge Louis E. Goodman of the Northern District of California dismissed the government's charges against the twenty-six draft resisters from the Tule Lake Relocation Center, saying that the decision to prosecute them was "shocking to [his] conscience" and a violation of due process.[5] The government did not appeal his decision, and so it might be said that the Tule Lake resisters won. But even these twenty-six winners ultimately lost: their prize for beating the draft evasion charges was a trip back to the barbed wire confines of their concentration camp.

This story is an untold chapter in the history of the American justice system. With the exception of Judge Goodman, the chapter is a bleak tale of callous judges and overzealous prosecutors. But the chapter is a depressing one in a larger sense as well because it is far from clear that the law would have enabled the courts to reach more satisfying results. Judge Goodman's decision was a good deal longer on courage than on careful legal analysis, and what little analysis there was pushed due process doctrine into uncharted—possibly unchartable—terrain. The cases of the Nisei draft resisters thus illustrated with unusual poignancy how law can deviate from justice.

The resisters' story, however, is not just a story about a failed judicial process. It is also a story of failure in the most elemental process of American life—the process of assimilation. The America that entered World War II was a nation that had long cherished the image of the patriotic resister: a colonist heaving tea into the waters of Boston Harbor, Patrick Henry rising to demand his freedom or his death, Thomas Jefferson penning the list of the Crown's offenses in the Declaration of Independence. This was part of what set America apart from the totalitarian regimes it was battling: good citizenship was not the preserve solely of the obedient. To the children of its Japanese immigrants, however, America would not extend the option of loyal protest. Through the force of the criminal sanction, it demanded that these young Japanese Americans prove their patriotism through unquestioning obedience to authority, ironically a trait more Japanese than American.

Ultimately, it was not only the federal government that demanded this of the draft resisters; much of the Japanese American community did, too. And herein lies the greatest and most painful irony of the resisters' experience. Notwithstanding its wartime demands, the federal government soon made amends with the Japanese American internees who resisted the draft. President Truman granted them a Christmas Eve pardon in 1947, removing from their records the stigma of their felony convictions for draft evasion. To this day, however, the resisters have not been pardoned by some members of their own community who see their wartime defiance as an act of disloyalty and betrayal. So powerful was the condemnation within the Japanese American community for years after the war that many of the resisters did not share their story of oppression even with their own children. Even today, almost sixty years after the resisters' federal court trials, the oldest and most prominent Japanese American civil rights organization has only just begun to overcome years of bitter internal conflict over apologizing to the resisters. And the sizable literature on Japanese Americans' wartime exile and incarceration almost completely omits the resisters' tale, focusing instead on those, like the sixty-five Minidokans "welcomed" into the army by Lieutenant Harrington, who said "yes" to the draft rather than "no."[6]

What follows is, in a double sense, a story of untold patriotism.

TWO UNEASY WELCOME

The young men in the camps who received their draft notices in the winter and spring of 1944 were all American citizens. They had been born in this country between 1909 and 1926. Their parents were Japanese immigrants who, over the preceding several decades, had arrived from Japan, often via Hawaii. They had settled at first in the large cities of the West Coast, and later in more rural areas, finding work on the railroads, in stores, and on farms.

These immigrants, called the Issei, were aliens, citizens of Japan. As is typical of first-generation immigrants, most of the Issei retained a sense of Japanese identity and preserved as much as they could of the language and culture of their native land.[1] But they remained Japanese citizens at least as much out of necessity as desire. Since 1870, American law had offered naturalization only to white people and to people of African descent; the Issei were neither.[2] It was legally impossible for any Japanese immigrant to become a U.S. citizen.

For the children of the Issei, called the Nisei, the situation was different. Section 1 of the Fourteenth Amendment says quite clearly that "[a]ll persons born . . . in the United States . . . are citizens of the United States. . . ."[3] Thus, American citizenship for the Nisei was not a matter of legislative grace; it vested at birth by constitutional command.

Yet Nisei citizenship did not arise simply by operation of law. It also arose by operation of the heart. For most Nisei, America was the only country they knew. Like so many children of immigrants before and after them, they quickly mastered the language and absorbed the culture of the American mainstream, often to the consternation of their parents.[4] They attended American schools, where they read the Constitution, memorized the Gettysburg Address, and learned American and European history. They jumped rope, played baseball, and joined the

Scouts. They drank Coca-Cola, went to their proms, and danced to the sounds of the big bands. Along with the rest of America, they struggled through the Great Depression and looked hopefully to Franklin Roosevelt's New Deal.

The Akutsus of Seattle were a typical Nikkei family. Kiyonosuke Akutsu came to America from Japan in 1907, in the words of his son Gene, on "an adventure, to see if he could make his millions and then head back home" to Japan.[5] After working various jobs for a few years, he returned to Japan to find a bride. There he met and married a young woman named Nao Fukui. He then returned, without her, to the United States, to set aside enough money to support her and a family. After several more years of labor, he called for Nao to come join him in Seattle, and she did so. Within a few years, the Akutsu family grew to four with the arrival of two sons—first Jim, in 1920, and then Gene, in 1925.

It became clear to Kiyonosuke and Nao Akutsu very early on that Jim and Gene were growing up in a very different culture from the one they themselves had known as children in Japan. When their boys were nine and four years old, Kiyonosuke and Nao did something that was not uncommon among Issei parents: they sent their sons to Japan to attend school and live with their grandparents. Those Nisei who handled this adjustment well and remained in Japan for much of their schooling became known by a different label—"Kibei"—upon their return to the United States.[6] Jim and Gene Akutsu, however, would not become Kibei because their time in Japan was a fiasco. Nine-year-old Jim, an outspoken leader-of-the-gang type and something of a fighter, clashed with everyone in his new Japanese environment. "Over in Japan," Gene explains, "you're supposed to be seen and not heard," whereas in this country the brothers had "started to do a little questioning." "We were not as controllable as the kids over in Japan," recalls Gene. After a month, the grandparents, having "found out what kind of kids we were," told Jim and Gene's parents that they wanted no part of them. They packed the boys up and sent them home to Nao and Kiyonosuke in Seattle.

Yosh Kuromiya, one of the draft resisters from the Heart Mountain Relocation Center, had an even shorter and less successful experience in Japan. His Issei mother took him there when he was five years old to visit his grandparents. Without toys or playmates, the little boy spent much of his time wetting his fingers and popping them through his grandparents' shoji screens. One day, he recalls, he "discovered a neat little sitting place—a little alcove . . . in the wall of the main room." The youngster "just removed the fat little statue and the smelly incense and . . . had a nice little space" all to himself. There he sat, arms folded, until his grandmother came into the room. She "muttered something harsh in Japanese, pulled me gently but firmly from my throne, and replaced the statue." He thought this was no major transgression, but after being put to bed on a futon that night, Kuromiya peered through the hole he had made in one of the shoji screens and saw his "mother kneeling, her face almost touching the floor," and his grandparents "towering over her, their faces red in righteous anger, threatening to send us back to decadent America in disgrace, all because of me."[7] It was already a good deal easier to take the Nisei out of America than it was to take America out of the Nisei.

The assimilation of the Nisei generation into American culture created some tension between Issei and Nisei. Often, for the Nisei, this tension showed up in the form of shame—shame of what they saw as their parents' marked foreignness and their insistence on clinging to old ways. "I was overzealous in my attempts to be accepted as an American," says Heart Mountain draft resister Mits Koshiyama. "For a while, I rejected everything Japanese. I didn't want to study Japanese, and I used to criticize my mother and father for using chopsticks. 'What are you eating rice every day for?' " Koshiyama would demand of his parents. When he grew older and had his own family, he softened somewhat in his anti-Japanese stance and today happily eats his rice with chopsticks. But most Nisei, he says, "were really ashamed of being Japanese" as youngsters.

Notwithstanding their efforts, even the most assimilated of the West Coast Nisei stood apart from the American mainstream in certain ways. Many lived in or near ethnic enclaves, such as Li'l Tokyo in Los Angeles or the Japantowns of Seattle and San Francisco, and associated primarily with others of Japanese descent. Most attended after-school programs in Japanese language and culture. As a result, most grew up with warm feelings for the language, culture, and food of their parents, as well as a healthy respect (if not always warm feelings) for the Japanese values of self-sacrifice, obedience, and stoicism that their parents instilled in them. Of course, in feeling these tugs from the land of their parents, they were no different from any other group that had ever tossed itself into the American melting pot. The country was full of people—even very prominent people named Joe DiMaggio, and Felix Frankfurter, and Fiorello LaGuardia—whose American pedigree was still new, but who were nonetheless American. The same was true for the Nisei.

This did not mean, however, that the American society into which the Nisei were born welcomed them with anything like open arms. Quite the opposite was true. Anti-Asian sentiment, having ebbed and flowed since the Chinese Exclusion Act of 1882, was on the rise again in the second and third decades of the twentieth century, when many of the Nisei were youngsters. This was especially true on the West Coast, where the success of many Issei farmers was the painful envy of many whites. Anti-Japanese propaganda decrying the "Yellow Peril," helped along by rising Japanese militarism in the Pacific, flooded the national consciousness.[8] Western states began passing laws barring the Issei from owning or leasing land. The few Issei wealthy enough to buy land tried to get around this proscription by buying land and titling it in the name of one of their Nisei children. But California outlawed even this practice in its Alien Land Law of 1920. Finally, in 1924, the national government succumbed to the demands of primarily West Coast nativist groups, such as the Native Sons and Daughters of the Golden West and the Japanese Exclusion League, and completely outlawed all further Japanese immigration.[9] These were decidedly unfriendly times for Americans with Japanese names and features.

The Nisei growing up in the twenties and thirties felt that unfriendliness. Yosh Kuromiya remembers being stopped at the front door of a white friend's house because he was Japanese. He and some other neighborhood children had been playing in pepper trees in the backyard and decided to go inside. Kuromiya, the only Nisei in the group, was at the back of the line as they filed in. But as he arrived on the landing, the screen door slammed shut and was locked. Kuromiya thought at first that it was just an oversight. He waited outside, assuming that "the other kids would say, 'Where is Yosh?' and come out after me. But nobody came. So I sat there for a while. And then after a while it just dawned on me that I wasn't wanted there. Because I was Japanese. I was the only Japanese, and I guess I would have been an embarrassment to them." This sort of incident was not isolated. Many Nisei can recall being excluded from their white classmates' birthday parties, or being forbidden from serving on the student council, or simply learning which parts of town were off-limits.

For some, the consequences of discrimination were more severe. When Monica Sone tried to get into a state vocational school, she was informed that the school admitted only six Nisei girls per year. Jimi Yamaichi and Tom Noda, both of whom would become draft resisters at the Tule Lake Relocation Center, had to vie for the two carpentry positions that their local trade school opened to Nisei applicants. The school would have accepted more, they were told, but with the labor unions refusing to admit any Nisei at all, the school saw little point in training young men for jobs they could not get.[10]

Life for the young Nisei in the 1920s and 1930s was thus something of a drama: the drama of American assimilation. Most Japanese Americans were struggling to find a way to honor their Japanese cultural legacy even as they reached to embrace the very different American culture in which they lived. But to mainstream America, the Nisei looked Japanese, not American. American culture, seductive as it was to the Nisei, often recoiled from their embrace. This made assimilation an unusually difficult process for the Nisei, one that produced a good deal of anxiety.

Not surprisingly, those insecure feelings surfaced quite visibly in the organization that a group of Nisei created in 1930 to advance the interests of American citizens of Japanese descent. The organization was (and still is) called the Japanese American Citizens League, or JACL. Its founders and early leaders were primarily members of the tiny Nisei professional class—doctors, dentists, lawyers, writers—who had already taken strides toward assimilation through their education and professional training. The elders of their generation, these Nisei wished not only to bolster their own somewhat tenuous position at the fringes of the American middle class, but also to improve the lot of the many thousands of younger Nisei who would be coming into the workforce in the 1930s and 1940s and would face rampant anti-Japanese prejudice and discrimination. However, their strategy for advancing the Nisei cause was decidedly—one might say anxiously—pro-American. Bill Hosokawa, an early JACL member and the primary Nisei chronicler of the Japanese American experience, described the founders' views in this way:

> These Nisei knew they were American citizens, but few others seemed to know or care. They were accustomed to having well-intentioned strangers ask: "When did you come to the United States? What is Japan like?" In their bull sessions the Nisei asked themselves: "What good is our citizenship? Are we going to live with the same discrimination that our parents experienced? What should we, as Nisei, do? Many admitted there had been times when they resented their Japanese blood because they felt it was a handicap in their efforts to become good Americans.[11]

The JACL's strategy was to prove to the rest of the nation that the Nisei were true and loyal Americans, free from the pull of any foreign allegiance: Japanese on the outside, American on the inside.

It was difficult for the JACL to attract much interest from the vast majority of Nisei struggling through the economically depressed 1930s. Many spurned the organization as little more than a country club for the well-to-do. Yosh Kuromiya remembers the prewar JACL as a "college-type, sophisticated social organization that was interested in establishing itself as elite—kind of a snob thing." "Possibly," he says, the group may have "had some political goals too, but that didn't seem to be promoted that much back then." Kuromiya never thought of joining the group; he recalls that he had "a distaste for it from the very beginning—the very idea that some people could think they were better than everyone else just because they went to college, or because their families had a little more money than everyone else." Kuromiya's memories here are undoubtedly a bit harsh; while the organization had a white-collar pedigree, by the late 1930s its membership, although small, did include Nisei laborers, farmers, and others with blue collars. Kuromiya was right, though, that the group in its early years focused rather more on the social than the political life of the Nisei.

That is not to say, however, that the JACL of the 1930s did nothing more than hold banquets and spin records. It also began, cautiously, to try its hand at lobbying. The welter of anti-Japanese legislation that was either on the books or up for debate during the JACL's first decade left the organization plenty of potential targets. The law for which it decided to lobby first says a great deal about the organization's views on how to become an American.

That law was an amendment to the naturalization laws that would permit Issei veterans of the U.S. Army to become American citizens. During World War I, some aliens resident in the United States offered to volunteer into the U.S. Army, and the army took them. One such volunteer was a Japanese immigrant named Tokie Slocum.[12] Slocum served valiantly in the trenches of France, made the rank of sergeant major, and inhaled so much lethal gas on the battlefield that he spent much of the rest of his life in and out of hospitals. Just after the armistice in 1918, Slocum applied by mail from Europe to become naturalized as an American citizen. He was availing himself of a recent veteran-friendly amendment to the naturalization laws that allowed "any alien . . . who has enlisted in or entered . . . the armies of the United States" to apply for immediate naturalization.[13] A federal judge granted Slocum's naturalization petition on the plain language of the 1918 amendment. But the court later had to cancel it on the basis of a Supreme Court decision holding that Congress did not intend the words "any alien" in the 1918 amendment to override the basic racial limitations of American naturalization law that reserved the privilege of citizenship to whites and people of African descent.[14]

Slocum was outraged to lose the American citizenship that he felt he had earned by risking his life for America in the trenches. Yet somehow his ire did not dim his commitment to America. Speaking at the JACL's first national convention in 1930, he made something of a spectacle of himself by "str[iding] up and down the platform to shout that 'if war comes tomorrow between Japan and the United States, I would be fighting for the Stars and Stripes.'"[15] Slocum burned to see the law changed. The JACL endorsed him and his cause, passing the following as its very first resolution at the 1930 convention:

> Whereas a large number of Japanese residents of the United States of America were induced to join the Army and Navy of the United States of America during the World War

> by promises made that those who received their honorable discharges would be granted citizenship,
>
> And whereas these World War veterans were denied American citizenship, contrary to the promises and inducements offered them,
>
> And whereas such action is both unfair and unjust,
>
> Be it now resolved that the Japanese American Citizens' League, meeting in Seattle, Washington, requests the attention of Congress to this injustice which has been done to these World War veterans who gave up their positions and careers and offered their lives in defense of our country.[16]

The JACL sent Slocum off to Washington to fight for his citizenship.

Slocum fought as valiantly in Washington as he had in France. He knew that Congress would be unlikely to pay much heed to him and the fledgling JACL, so his strategy was to enlist the support of groups that legislators would hear. He contacted old war buddies who had risen to positions of prominence with the American Legion and the Veterans of Foreign Wars, persuading them to join his cause.[17] This was a dicey move because the American Legion was no friend of the Japanese in America. It was a key member of the Japanese Exclusion League, which for years had been sponsoring and lobbying for anti-Asian legislation on the West Coast. Still, Slocum's extraordinary war record appealed to the veterans' groups, and they supported him.

Slocum was eventually rewarded for his efforts on behalf of the Issei veterans. In June of 1935, Congress passed and President Roosevelt signed the Lea-Nye Bill, which granted citizenship to about five hundred honorably discharged Asian World War I veterans, most of them Japanese.[18] Slocum and his fellow Issei veterans became American citizens for good. For the JACL, the Lea-Nye Bill was a double victory. The organization had shown to its Nisei constituency that it could do more than just plan a party. And it had also proven a proposition that would soon become one of its articles of faith: the straightest road to loyal American citizenship runs through a battlefield.

The JACL's lobbying achievements did manage to raise the organization's profile by the late 1930s. George Nozawa, who would go on to resist the draft at Heart Mountain, was impressed enough to join the group when he turned eighteen. He remembers tacking up the JACL's creed on the kitchen wall of his family's small farmhouse in Mountain View, California. That document, which purported to speak with the voice of all American citizens of Japanese descent, proclaimed that the Nisei "believe[d] in America's institutions, ideals, and traditions; . . . glor[ied] in her heritage; . . . boast[ed] of her history; . . . trust[ed] in her future." America's future, however—at least in the short term—would not prove itself worthy of the Nisei's trust.

THREE

INJURY

Pearl Harbor

The drama of Nisei assimilation turned to outright tragedy on December 7, 1941, when Japanese bombs fell on Pearl Harbor. The surprise attack incensed and terrified the American people, especially those on the West Coast who suddenly felt vulnerable to enemy raids or even an all-out invasion. Because Japan launched the attack while two of its envoys talked peace in Washington, the Pearl Harbor raid immediately confirmed in the public mind what many Americans already thought about "Orientals"—that they were sneaky, untrustworthy, inscrutable. Needless to say, the attack did nothing to advance the cause of Nisei assimilation. A panicked nation had little interest in drawing careful distinctions between the Japanese of Japan and the Japanese of America.

Some Nisei managed to take Pearl Harbor more or less in stride. Jack Tono, who would become one of the Heart Mountain draft resisters, was working alongside whites in a produce packinghouse that Sunday. "[W]e heard it over the radio," he recalls, "and we figured it was one of those things. It didn't hit us that bad, you know; we all got along good with everybody." That the enemy was the land of his parents caused Tono no special anguish; "[t]he only country we knew," he says, "was the United States." Later that day one consequence of the war did sink in for Tono—military service. "All being citizens," he remembers, "a bunch of us were talking that we eventually would have to go to the Army and defend the country, that was about the main thing."[1]

Yosh Kuromiya had a similar reaction. He was working at his family's roadside produce stand that Sunday morning. Some of his family's white neighbors who were regular customers approached Kuromiya to assure him that notwithstanding Pearl Harbor, "everything was going to be all right." The young man reacted with a touch of annoyance. "My reaction was, 'Of course it was going to be all right.' You know, I had no fear of [what had happened at] Pearl Harbor. Those were Japanese from Japan. They're different people. You know, I'm an American. Why are they laying this trip on me and assuring me?" It bothered Kuromiya that he "would be picked out as being related to the enemy."

More commonly, though, the Nisei reacted to Pearl Harbor with shock and disbelief. Mits Koshiyama, another of the Heart Mountain draft resisters, was with his sister, peeling garlic for planting, when word of Pearl Harbor came over the radio. They were stunned. Koshiyama told his sister, "I hope they know the difference between us and the enemy," and spent the rest of the day worrying that he would run into trouble when he returned to high school the next day. Another Nisei, Mary Tsukamoto, was playing piano for a Sunday morning church service when her husband burst in with news of the Japanese attack. Years later she recalled that "suddenly the whole world turned dark. We started to speak in whispers, and . . . we immediately sensed something terrible was going to happen. We just prayed that it wouldn't, but we sensed that things would be very difficult."

It did not take long for things to grow difficult. At first, it looked as though the Issei alone might bear the brunt of the government's reaction to Pearl Harbor. Between Sunday, December 7, and Wednesday, December 10, the FBI swept through the Japanese communities of Hawaii and the West Coast and arrested nearly thirteen hundred Issei men. The government was able to move quickly against the Issei because it had compiled lists of people it deemed potentially suspect in the months before Pearl Harbor. The government had been aided in this process by several Nisei leaders of the JACL, who wished to show their good faith by quietly fingering outspoken or influential members of their parents' generation. When the post–Pearl Harbor sweep actually occurred, though, it did not focus only on the outspoken and the influential. It touched virtually every Issei who had been active in Issei life—as business leaders, farmers, travel agents, Shinto and Buddhist priests, judo instructors, editors of the vernacular press, and the like.[2]

Among those apprehended in Seattle was Kiyonosuke Akutsu. Akutsu suspected no trouble the morning of December 8, 1941. Like many Issei, he had been somewhat active in Seattle's chapter of the Japanese Association of America, an organization that had been created by the Japanese consul in San Francisco in 1909 primarily to handle the Issei's dealings with the bureaucracy of the Japanese government. In its heyday, the Japanese Association had played a major role in Japanese-American society, albeit primarily an administrative one. By the mid-1920s, however, the Japanese Association began to fade from prominence in the community as the flow of new Japanese immigrants stopped completely with the ending of all Japanese immigration and the Nisei generation began its ascendancy. Other than his membership in this weakening organization, Akutsu's life offered little to draw the government's attention. He and his wife were reserved people who had kept a generally low profile in Seattle's Japanese community and who had never identified themselves as rabidly pro-Japan. Unlike many Issei homes, theirs was not adorned with a Japanese flag, and they displayed no picture of the Emperor. Thus, as Akutsu left home for his shoe repair shop as usual at 7:00 that Monday morning, he undoubtedly worried about the ominous turn of events in the Pacific, but he feared no immediate personal harm.

Later that day Jim Akutsu got a phone call from his mother. Nao Akutsu told him that agents of the FBI had appeared at his father's shop and announced that they would be taking him away for a period of time. "They want to take Dad away," Nao told her son, "so come on home and help me close up the store." When Gene Akutsu got home from high school that afternoon, he learned what had happened to his father. "The FBI had come down on us," he recalls, "and it really surprised the living daylights out of me." A few days later Kiyonosuke called his family, told them that he thought he was going to be sent away for a while, and asked them to bring him some of his personal belongings. Nao, Jim, and Gene brought his toothbrush and shaving kit to a downtown building and said a brief farewell to Kiyonosuke in a hallway under the watchful eye of an FBI guard. The next day he was shipped to a Justice Department internment camp for enemy aliens in Missoula, Montana. Gene, Jim, and Nao Akutsu did not see Kiyonosuke again for two years.

Most Nisei, of course, were only indirectly affected by the initial arrests of the Issei. They saw the leadership of their parents' generation decimated virtually overnight and were left to absorb the shock of that disruption, but were spared arrest themselves. As to their own futures, they therefore tried to remain hopeful. Frank Emi, who would later emerge as one of the leaders of the draft resistance movement at Heart Mountain, "didn't have an inkling that we ourselves were going to be bothered because we Nisei had been born here in this country and we were American citizens."[3] Mits Koshiyama similarly remembers that "[w]e [Nisei,] as American citizens, said, 'Oh, well gee, mom and dad may have to go'" into detention during the war. "But we're citizens and nothing like that's going to happen to us."

For a few weeks, public pronouncements by national leaders gave Koshiyama, Emi, and their fellow Nisei some reason for hope. For example, U.S. Attorney General Francis Biddle, a Pennsylvania blue blood with a strong sense of noblesse oblige, urged the nation to recognize that "[i]f we care about democracy, we must care about it as a reality for others, for Germans, for Italians, for Japanese. . . . For the Bill of Rights protects not only American citizens but all human beings who live on our American soil, under our American flag." Biddle was a corporate lawyer from Philadelphia who, in the early 1930s, had decided to leave behind his membership in the Republican Party and his years representing railroad interests, to line up as a Democrat behind Franklin Roosevelt's New Deal. As attorney general, Biddle would oppose, on jurisprudential, practical, and sometimes moral grounds, the massive impositions on the Nikkei that were later proposed and debated. These early words from the chief law enforcement officer of the land allowed the Nisei at least a bit of optimism.[4]

The Curfew

The year 1942 dashed the hopes of the Nisei, binding them (along with their Issei parents) in ever-tightening chains of confinement. The man wielding the chains was General John L. DeWitt, commanding general of the Western Defense Command, a huge region encompassing eight western states, including California, Oregon, and Washington. This post at the Presidio in San Francisco was the culminating assignment of a long military career for DeWitt. He had abandoned his studies at Princeton to join the army in 1898 so that he could fight in the Spanish-American War. After that, he never left the service, rising slowly through the ranks as he moved from one desk job to another, mostly as a supply officer. He was not highly regarded within the military. He was, in the words of Roger Daniels, the leading scholar of the internment, "a cautious, bigoted, indecisive . . . army bureaucrat."[5]

DeWitt's first move against the West Coast Nikkei was the curfew. On March 24, 1942, DeWitt issued an order confining all German, Italian, and Japanese aliens and all U.S. citizens of Japanese (but not German or Italian) ancestry to their homes between eight o'clock in the evening and six o'clock in the morning, and requiring them to get military leave to travel more than five miles from their homes.[6]

The dusk-to-dawn restriction had little practical impact on many of the Nikkei because most were struggling economically, working long days in shops or on farms, and had little reason to be out at night. As Mits Koshiyama recalls, "[O]ur social life was very limited before the war—we'd go to church, or a community picnic, or something like that. We weren't night people." Koshiyama remembers only one Nisei for whom the curfew had any significant impact, a champion bowler who made a few extra dollars for his family by setting pins in the evening at a bowling alley in Santa Clara. This young man broke the curfew to set pins and got stopped by the police for being out late. But when the police heard why he was out after curfew, they decided he was harmless and let him go.

The five-mile limit was, however, more burdensome. Those who lived in rural settings needed permission simply to go grocery shopping or get their hair done; truck farmers would often need a permit just to deliver some vegetables. For some of the Nikkei, though, this restriction was downright laughable. George Nozawa, for example, lived in Mountain View, California. The nearest offices where travel permission could be obtained were in Palo Alto and San Jose, both of which were more than five miles away. When news came that the Nozawa family was to be evacuated, George's Issei father wanted all of his children's teeth checked. Their dentist was in San Jose. "And so," Nozawa recalls with a chuckle, "we went to San Jose, over five miles, to get a permit to get there." Small wonder that World War II gave birth to the Catch-22.

In certain situations, however, the curfew was no laughing matter at all. Helen Murao was fifteen years old and living in Portland, Oregon, when the curfew order came into effect. Her twenty-year-old sister was sick with tuberculosis in a sanitarium in Salem, about fifty miles to the south. On April 24, Murao got a telephone call from Salem telling her that her sister's condition had worsened and asking her to come. Murao and her brothers immediately reported to the military office in Portland to request permission to travel to Salem. There they sat for four hours while military authorities placed phone call after phone call to determine whether their sister's situation really warranted an emergency visit and where the family would spend the night. Finally, they were granted permission to drive to Salem. When they arrived, their sister was dead. Devastated and furious, Helen Murao and her younger brothers then defied their orders to spend the night in Portland and returned to Salem immediately. "All I knew," Murao later recalled, "was that she was dead, and 'they' had done it. And I can't identify even now who I felt 'they' were. It was just, you know, me against everybody, and everybody else had done it to me, or to us." All Murao wanted to do "was get out of there, and I was very upset that nobody accorded us any kind of sympathy or any kind of human courtesy at all."[7]

Even when the practical consequences were not dire, as they were for Murao, the curfew nonetheless took a psychological toll on all of the Nisei. The race discrimination in DeWitt's order was not lost on them; they immediately recognized that they had to sit at home while the American-born children of German and Italian immigrants, many of whom were their school classmates, were free to walk the streets. Naturally, this overt discrimination offended and angered them, even when it did not make them change their daily schedules much.[8]

The Deportation and the Assembly Centers

Sadly, the curfew was just a prelude. At the end of March, General DeWitt issued his Public Proclamation No. 4, which forbade any person of Japanese ancestry in the western halves of California, Oregon, and Washington and the southern half of Arizona to leave those areas without military permission, in order "to ensure an orderly, supervised, and thoroughly controlled evacuation" from those areas, to be administered by the government. (Just a few weeks later General DeWitt added the eastern halves of California, Oregon, and Washington to the zone of evacuation.) This proclamation reflected a change in policy. For several weeks, the military had been encouraging Issei and

Nisei from those areas to leave their homes voluntarily for places of their own choosing in the interior. But it was hard for most of the Nikkei just to pick up and leave. All Issei bank accounts were frozen, few of the West Coast Japanese knew anyone to the east of the military zone where they were being urged to resettle, and wrapping up their affairs and disposing of their property took more time than the Nikkei had. Moreover, the handful of intrepid souls who managed to relocate on such short notice were encountering hostility in their new eastern and midwestern homes, and news of the hostility was trickling back to the West Coast. General DeWitt therefore converted the evacuation program from voluntary to mandatory: the military was to empty the West Coast of all ethnically Japanese people, aliens and citizens alike.[9]

General DeWitt had been empowered to take this drastic step about six weeks earlier, in mid-February, when President Roosevelt signed Executive Order 9066. That order authorized military authorities to designate "military areas" from which "any or all persons m[ight] be excluded" and to provide "transportation, food, shelter, and other accommodations [for such persons] until other arrangements are made."[10] The order cited as its basis the need for "successful prosecution of the war," and there is no question that the military authorities who pressed Roosevelt to sign the order saw a grave military threat to and on the West Coast. For months, the island nations of the Pacific had been falling like dominoes to Japanese forces. Australia had been shelled and was braced for a full-blown assault. The American military was preparing for an attack on the islands at the end of the Aleutian chain off Alaska. In these circumstances, General DeWitt thought it probable that Japan's forces would attack shipping in coastal waters, big cities along the coast, and vital defense and industrial operations. He also foresaw "[s]abotage of vital installations throughout the Western Defense Command."[11] Although little of what DeWitt feared ultimately came to pass, his worries about a possible Japanese attack were certainly understandable at the time.

Considerably less understandable was DeWitt's assessment that every person of Japanese origin, alien or citizen, threatened subversion. His reasoning for mass suspicion of all Issei and Nisei was unabashedly race-based. "The Japanese race," he argued, "is an enemy race." Although the Nisei, whom he conceded to be American citizens, had become "Americanized," their "racial strains" were "undiluted." For DeWitt, it "follow[ed] that along the vital Pacific Coast over 112,000 potential enemies, of Japanese extraction, are at large today." What was more, DeWitt saw "indications" that these legions of "potential enemies" were "organized and ready for concerted action at a favorable opportunity." Chief among these, argued DeWitt, was "the very fact that no sabotage has taken place to date"—a "disturbing and confirming indication that such action will be taken."[12]

Thus, DeWitt purported to know that sabotage by Japanese Americans must be imminent because none had yet occurred. What was this but the stereotyped image of the inscrutable and unscrupulous Oriental? To be sure, some Nisei—especially many of the several thousand Kibei, who had received some or all of their childhood education in Japan—must have reacted to the war with mixed feelings. A small number may have hoped for outright Japanese victory, others perhaps for a negotiated peace. But to indict the vast majority of the Nisei—the "Americanized" Japanese, as DeWitt saw them—the general had nothing to go on but his own racism-tinged belief that a Nisei's "racial strains," rather than his beliefs and experiences, determined his loyalty.

DeWitt was not alone in his views. Indeed, what the general said in his mid-February report recommending removal was, if anything, a toned-down version of what many lobbying groups, West Coast politicians, and widely read columnists had been saying for months. The call for exclusion of the Japanese from the West Coast came first and loudest from nativist groups and economic competitors who had long opposed all Japanese immigration. Local chapters of the Native Sons and Daughters of the Golden West busied themselves in January of 1942 passing and publicizing resolutions that demanded the removal of all ethnically Japanese people from the West Coast. This call was quickly picked up by white farmers' organizations with an economic axe to grind against their very successful Issei and Nisei competitors. Austin E. Anson, the managing secretary of the Salinas, California, Vegetable Grower-Shipper Association put it brutally:

> We're charged with wanting to get rid of the Japs for selfish reasons. We might as well be honest. We do. It's a question of whether the white man lives on the Pacific Coast or the brown men. They came into this valley to work, and they stayed to

> take over. . . . If all the Japs were removed tomorrow, we'd never miss them in two weeks, because the white farmers can take over and produce everything the Jap grows. And we don't want them back when the war ends, either.[13]

Politicians joined the chorus for exclusion. In mid-January of 1942, Congressman Leland Ford of Los Angeles urged "[t]hat all Japanese, whether citizens or not, be placed in inland concentration camps." He contended that "if an American born Japanese, who is a citizen, is really patriotic and wishes to make his contribution to the safety and welfare of this country, right here is his opportunity to do so, namely, . . . by permitting himself to be placed in a concentration camp." By complying with his own eviction, Ford argued, each Nisei "would be making his sacrifice and he should be willing to do it if he is patriotic and is working for us." Within a short time, most members of the West Coast states' congressional delegations were voicing similar views.

Most vicious of all were the newspapermen. Henry McLemore, a syndicated columnist with the Hearst newspapers, let the nation know that he was "for immediate removal of every Japanese on the West Coast to a point deep in the interior." And McLemore did not "mean a nice part of the interior either." The authorities should just "herd 'em up, pack 'em off and give 'em the inside room in the badlands. Let 'em be pinched, hurt, hungry and dead up against it." As if these words left any doubt, McLemore concluded with a confession that he "hated the Japanese. And that goes for all of them." Other editorialists and columnists filled the daily papers with similar views. Even Walter Lippmann, the dean of American newspaper columnists, came out for removing the Nikkei from the West Coast en masse, arguing that "there is plenty of room elsewhere" for Japanese Americans "to exercise [their] rights."

It was in this atmosphere of economic jealousy, political pressure, and ethnic hatred along the West Coast that General DeWitt reached his decision for mandatory removal. And thus the chains of confinement tightened a bit further around the Issei and Nisei. Beginning on March 29, 1942, when DeWitt's Public Proclamation No. 4 took effect, the military began notifying the Nikkei in neighborhoods up and down the West Coast that they must register with the Wartime Civil Control Administration (WCCA), a military agency DeWitt had hastily set up to administer their deportation, and then prepare to be removed for "temporary residence elsewhere." Neither the duration of "temporary" nor the location of "elsewhere" was disclosed. But the deportees soon learned, to their horror, that they were to be put up in shabbily constructed fairground shacks and in filthy, urine-stained racetrack stables in or near the major cities of the West Coast. These were the concentration camps the WCCA euphemistically called "assembly centers," and they became home to nearly one hundred thirty thousand people—60 percent of them U.S. citizens—for the summer of 1942.

There was little talk among the Nikkei about refusing to comply with the removal program. Most understood that they were up against the power of the federal government during wartime and that resistance would be pointless. Moreover, every Nisei had grown up hearing his Issei parents recite the phrases *shikata ganai* and *gaman suru*—"it can't be helped" and "just endure it." It was thus a virtue, or at least a feature, of Japanese culture to accept what could not be changed. It was also a virtue of Japanese culture not to do things that draw the attention of others: "The nail that sticks up," explained the Issei to their children, "gets hammered."

In addition, the Japanese American community lacked a leadership that might have counseled resistance. Most of the Issei community leaders had been rounded up just after Pearl Harbor and were locked away in Justice Department internment camps in the spring of 1942. Their absence from the community created a leadership vacuum that the JACL began to fill. But the JACL, intent on proving Nisei loyalty, was of no mind to counsel resistance. Quite the opposite was true. Once the government decided upon mass deportation—a step the JACL had at first politely opposed, at least for the Nisei—the JACL quickly pledged to the government fully to support the removal plan and to help in making the process go as smoothly as possible.[14] JACL President Saboru Kido summed up the JACL's position in a speech he delivered to an emergency meeting of the organization in March of 1942:

> We are going into exile as our duty to our country, because the President and the military commanders of this area have deemed it necessary. We have pledged our full support to President Roosevelt and to the nation. This is a sacred promise which we shall keep as good patriotic citizens. . . . "We also serve" must be our badge of courage in these trying

> days, for we also serve, each in his own way, this country of which we are so fond. What greater love, what greater testimony of one's loyalty could any one ask than this, leave your homes, your business, and your friends in order that your country may better fight a war?[15]

Within a short time, Kido and the JACL would dream up greater testimony of loyalty—the idea of leaving Nisei bodies on the battlefields of that war. But for the moment, the JACL was content to present compliance with deportation as the ultimate wartime sacrifice.

The typical family was given several weeks' notice of the date when they would be required to leave their homes for the assembly centers, although some families had as little as a few days. They were also told that they could bring with them only what they could carry. Naturally, these circumstances threw the deportees into a panic. Those who owned property had to sell it instantly or try to brainstorm a way of making mortgage payments with no stream of income, and from an unknown destination. Farmers were forced to leave produce rotting in the fields, harvest it before its time, or find someone to look after it in their absence. Families searched frantically for scarce storage space for a lifetime's worth of valuables, heirlooms, and household goods. Countless families found no such space and simply abandoned their possessions. Many of the lucky families who found storage space returned to the coast years later to find their storage areas ransacked and their belongings stolen.

Rather than abandon or stash their goods and property, some tried to sell them. But even the least sophisticated of buyers understood that this was no seller's market and profited handsomely from their neighbors' distress. Tom Noda, one of the Tule Lake resisters, remembers the forced sale of his family's property as the most difficult chapter in his family's entire internment story. "My dad, he worked for fifty years, with a lot of sweat," says Noda. "Built a home for us and bought a ranch, and in twenty-four hours, bingo—everything lost." Noda's father was forced to sell his twenty-acre farm, a three-year-old ranch house, and the family's truck to a dairy farmer for an even ten thousand dollars. "That was the saddest part of the whole thing," Noda recalls.

Some families who were able to drive themselves to the camp's gates, rather than being trucked in by the WCCA, hoped that by doing so, they might manage to bring some more of their belongings with them than the "only what you can carry" rule permitted. But they were wrong, and they, too, lost everything. Yosh Kuromiya and his family, for example, had to report to the assembly center at the Pomona racetrack in southern California. Because it was just a few miles from their home, the Kuromiyas loaded up a flatbed truck with their belongings and drove it to the gate. At the gate, though, they were told to grab what they could carry in their hands and leave the truck behind. They took a few suitcases and went inside. For a few days, they could see their truck through the fence, with their goods piled high under a lashed-down tarp in the back. Then, one day, the truck simply disappeared. They never saw either the truck or their belongings again.

George Nozawa reported to the WCCA for deportation with his Issei father and three older sisters at nine on a May morning in San Jose, California. (His mother, who died just before the war, was spared the ordeal.) There they learned they were to be taken by train to the Santa Anita racetrack outside of Los Angeles, several hundred miles away. It was a long ride, and they did not arrive at the racetrack until 10:30 at night. Because it was too late for them to be assigned barracks, they spent the night on the train. They stayed up until two or three in the morning, peering out the windows at the searchlights and armed sentries and worrying about what morning's light would reveal.

They were awakened at seven the next morning by the banging of tin plates in an assembly center mess hall that was next to the train. They straggled from the train and saw the spectacle of one of the largest racetracks in the country transformed into a sprawling concentration camp. The enormous parking lot was full of barracks, as far as the eye could see. The members of the Nozawa family were quickly assigned to their barracks and told to get in line for mattresses. Nozawa and his father soon spotted the line, and when they reached the front of it, a worker handed them five big empty bags and said, "These are your mattresses." "What do you mean, 'these are our mattresses'?" asked the younger Nozawa. The worker explained that if they walked around the corner of the barrack, they would find a pile of straw. That was what went in the bags. They found the straw pile and together began filling a bag. After filling one bag they grew disgusted, dropped the others on the ground, and walked away to take a look at their accommodations.

Opening the door to Unit U-11-6, the Nozawa family saw a stark square room about twenty feet by twenty feet with huge gaps between the walls and the roof that opened onto the rooms of their neighbors on either side. Privacy was out of the question; already they could hear their neighbors' conversations from the five other rooms up and down the long barrack. The décor was spartan: two small windows in the back that did not open, another one by the door, a bare light bulb, and five army cots. The barrack had no plumbing; the Nozawas and the nearly nineteen thousand other deportees at Santa Anita shared six latrines. Lines at the washbasins were so long during the day that the elder Nozawa often went to shave at midnight. The barrack also had no kitchen; everyone ate in the mess halls. Quietly, the Nozawas did their best to settle in to their new home.

A day or two later George Nozawa got an order to show up for work on a production line at the assembly center that was weaving camouflage netting for the army. Nozawa had mixed feelings about beginning work so soon. On the one hand, in the weeks leading up to his deportation, he had been doing farmwork for fifty cents an hour, and his family certainly needed the money. On the other hand, he had just arrived in camp, and his family—especially his aging Issei father—was still rather disoriented and in need of his help. Nozawa and a couple of his friends went to the administration building to ask for a delay. "We just got here," they told the administrator. "We don't even know where the latrine is yet." The administrator's response was sharp: "You'd better stop this complaining, or you'll end up on the blacklist in no time." Nozawa did not know what the "blacklist" was—indeed, to this day he does not know—but it certainly did not sound like a list he wanted to be on.

The administrator added that Nozawa and his friends would be paid for their work. "How much?" they asked. "Eight dollars." At this, the Nisei brightened. "Eight dollars a day—that's a dollar an hour, twice what I was just making on the outside," Nozawa thought. But then the administrator clarified that the wage was eight dollars per *month.* "Gee," Nozawa remembers thinking, "do you think Uncle Sam can afford that?"

Within a week or two, Nozawa heard a few Nisei talking about taking a trip over to "the zoo." He did not know what this was, and so followed along. What he found depressed him. The zoo was a border of the camp that ran along part of the town of Arcadia, California. It was an old, deserted neighborhood, with windblown streets and boarded-up storefronts. The WCCA had placed a large cyclone fence along the edge of the Santa Anita racetrack to mark the perimeter of the camp. This was the place where internees originally from the Los Angeles area would go to receive visitors—white friends and neighbors who would come to spend some time with the interned Nikkei. The fence, which stood between the internees and their visitors, gave the zoo its name. "I didn't know whether we were the chimpanzees or they were," recalls Nozawa of his one visit to the zoo. But when he saw those outside the fence forced to deliver care packages to their friends on the inside by hurling them over the fence, Nozawa decided he had seen enough and walked away.

Nozawa soon discovered that the zoo was not the worst of it. About a month after arriving, he was at work, stringing camouflage netting, when a friend referred to someone who lived "over in the stables." Nozawa did not know what he meant. So on a Sunday, Nozawa and his friend took a walk over there. Nozawa was stunned to see families "[a]ctually living in a horse stable." "Most families," he recalls, "had one whole stable," which consisted of a front room with two small windows, in which the parents typically slept, and a smaller windowless room in the back, where the children slept. But couples and small families had it even worse: the stables were partitioned to accommodate two horses, and often "couples and small families had to share a stall and live on either side of the partition." To make a horse stable habitable, the WCCA "raked the bottom reasonably flat and rolled it with a hand roller or something to pack it down a little. Then they put [down] asphalt, which was only about an inch thick, so the legs of the cots eventually poked through." Conditions were hardly sanitary because "the floors and walls were pretty well saturated with horse urine and all that horse hair." Even today Nozawa can barely contain the emotions that well up with these memories—his horror at what he saw, his anger over what good and innocent people were made to endure. "That's the only time I walked through there," he remembers, his words coming slowly and his eyes moist. "I never went back. I couldn't believe it."

The deportees spent the entire summer of 1942 in the fourteen WCCA assembly centers in Oregon, Washington, California, and Arizona. Working either alone or with camp management, they managed to create at least the semblance of a normal life, with medical and dental clinics, school programs for the children, skeletal community government, athletic events, and home-grown entertainment. Most Nisei and some Issei busied themselves in the running of the centers, doing mess hall duty, custodial work, construction and repair, and other work for menial pay. The assembly centers were, in effect, small Japanese American cities behind barbed wire, and it was up to each city's "residents" to make the city run.

The Relocation Centers

From the start, though, the assembly centers were understood to be temporary. The whole idea of the deportation, of course, was to remove the Nikkei from the West Coast, and yet all of the assembly centers were in the zones from which the Nikkei were supposed to be removed. Thus, even while the WCCA was setting up the assembly centers in the early spring of 1942, the government was hard at work trying to figure out where the deportees would go after their temporary sojourns in the assembly centers. This was the problem of the War Relocation Authority (WRA), a civilian agency that President Roosevelt created by executive order early in March of 1942. The man Roosevelt chose for the job of running the WRA was Milton Eisenhower, a New Deal liberal and Ike's younger brother. His agency's mission was to take over from the army's WCCA the long-term supervision of the West Coast's Nikkei.

Eisenhower took over the helm at the WRA at a time when the military was still hoping that its program of voluntary removal might take care of the problem. Within a week or two, however, the military reported to Eisenhower that the voluntary program was a disaster and must be abandoned in favor of forced removal. The WRA director, horrified by the moral and logistical problems of such a plan, searched desperately for some solution short of shipping more than one hundred thousand people to concentration camps in the interior, but came up empty-handed. He soon faced the cold fact that mass deportation to the interior was the only remaining option.

This presented a problem of its own: where would the deportees go, and what would they do once they got there? Eisenhower's idea was vintage New Deal: he imagined the Nikkei moving from the West Coast to "reception centers" in the mountain states, where they could pour their energies into various works projects, into agriculture, and into supporting local farming and industry by working as laborers.[16] Looking for support for his ideas and advice on how to implement them, Eisenhower turned to none other than the JACL and its energetic national secretary, Mike Masaoka. Masaoka and the JACL were eager to help, understanding that this invitation to do business with the WRA was both an opportunity for the organization to showcase the exemplary loyalty of the Nisei and a precious chance for members of the Japanese American community to exert some influence over their own removal and internment. Eisenhower asked Masaoka and other JACL leaders to form an advisory council to represent the internees, and they quickly agreed. Thus was launched a long relationship of cooperation between the WRA and the JACL, one that would last through the entire wartime period.[17]

In order to accomplish the mass deportation, though, Eisenhower needed the cooperation of more than just the internees (or, more precisely, the organization that purported to speak for them). He also needed the cooperation of the states he hoped would host the reception centers that the WRA planned to build. He therefore called a conference on the topic for Salt Lake City on April 7, 1942, and invited the governors and attorneys general of Nevada, Utah, Colorado, Wyoming, Montana, and Idaho to attend.

The WRA director opened the conference with a speech that emphasized the need to maximize the deportees' productivity: "We are taking hold of the problem with this idea, that . . . having these people engaged in productive work is just as much of a military necessity as is evacuating."[18] Eisenhower described at some length his hope that the deportees might be welcomed in the assembled governors' states at reception centers, where they would have an opportunity to harness their fabled Japanese industriousness in the service of the state, the region, the nation, and the war effort. Although he assured the governors that he did not imagine the deportees freely leaving the reception centers except on furloughs to work in local farming and industry, he certainly did not contemplate that the reception centers would look anything like concentration camps.

This was not an acceptable plan to the western governors. Among the bluntest in saying so was Governor Chase A. Clark of Idaho, a man who, ironically, would later sit in judgment of the Nisei draft resisters from the Minidoka Relocation Center. Before expressing his grave concern about Eisenhower's plan, Governor Clark first admitted to a debilitating prejudice against the Nikkei: "I want to admit right on the start," he announced, "that I am so prejudiced that my reasoning might be a little off, because I don't trust any of them. I don't know which ones to trust and so therefore I don't trust any of them." His reasoning led him to conclude that the West Coast states' Japanese population would be welcome in Idaho only under certain conditions. First, they must arrive and travel in Idaho only under military supervision. Second, they should be forbidden from buying land in Idaho and forced to return to the West Coast at war's end. He was astonished that the federal government could not promise these things: "If the Army has the right to bring the Japs into Idaho," he insisted, "then certainly it has the right to take them out." Finally, and most pointedly, Clark urged that any "Japanese who may be sent [to Idaho] be placed under guard and confined in concentration camps for the safety of our people, our State, and the Japanese themselves." Only with these assurances, said the governor, would he be able to rest assured that subsequent generations of Idahoans would not "hold [him] responsible . . . for having led Idaho full of Japanese during [his] administration."[19]

A sober Milton Eisenhower closed the Salt Lake City conference, noting that "[w]e asked for frankness and we got it."[20] He understood that his progressive vision of a network of agricultural and industrial works projects was dead, and resigned himself to the fact that his task would be to run concentration camps. Two months later, depressed and disgusted with his job, he himself resigned the directorship of the War Relocation Authority. Before leaving, he contacted Dillon S. Myer, a former colleague from the Department of Agriculture, to see whether he would be interested in taking over at the WRA. Myer asked Eisenhower whether Eisenhower really thought he should take the job. "Yes, if you can do the job and sleep at night," responded Eisenhower. Myer, "sure that [he] could sleep," took the job. He slept fine.[21]

Almost immediately, the government began building the ten camps that would soon open as WRA "Relocation Centers"—Tule Lake and Manzanar in eastern California, Minidoka in south central Idaho, Heart Mountain in northwestern Wyoming, Granada (also called Amache) in southeastern Colorado, Topaz in south central Utah, Poston and Gila River in southern Arizona, and Rohwer and Jerome in eastern Arkansas. They were built like prison camps, just as Chase Clark and the other western governors wanted them, mostly in vast, arid plains that were hostile to farming. The camps were surrounded by barbed wire fences that were patrolled by armed military policemen. Staggered around each camp's boundary were tall wooden guard towers equipped with searchlights. Internees were forbidden to leave camp without a pass issued by the top WRA official in camp, the project director. Army guards were under instruction to shoot anyone trying to leave without a pass or refusing to halt when ordered to do so, and were also authorized to come into the camps to quell disturbances on several occasions. The guards exercised these powers with deadly results at several of the camps.[22]

The internees were shipped from the assembly centers to the ten relocation centers in the late summer and fall of 1942. They were told their destinations—"Heart Mountain in Wyoming," "Minidoka in Idaho," and the like—but to most internees, these were just names on a map. They had no idea what actually awaited them. Yosh Kuromiya remembers the train trip from the Santa Anita racetrack to Heart Mountain as an anxious time. There were "rumors . . . that they were sending us to some place in Wyoming, wherever that was. And we didn't know why." Yet few complained. Most forced their minds onto the details of the moment, rather than dwelling on the larger significance of what was being done to them. As Kuromiya recalls, "[I]t was just a matter of getting in the right line, and . . . trying to keep the family together. You know, wondering where we were supposed to be eating, . . . [w]ondering if we were going to get fed on the train."

The train trips seemed to take forever. George Nozawa and his family spent four days and three nights on the train to Heart Mountain; Amy Uno Ishii's train took ten days and nights to reach the same destination because it first traveled to four or five other relocation centers as far east as Arkansas before doubling back to Wyoming.[23] Nights on board the train were especially difficult. Everyone had to try to sleep sitting up and grew very uncomfortable from the hard seats and the lack of sleep. Even more stressful was the fact that the army demanded that all of the train's window shades be pulled down whenever the train passed through any population center or military zone. Yosh Kuromiya caught his first glimpse of the bright lights of Las Vegas when he nervously pulled back the shade to sneak a peak in the middle of the night. For those who did not dare to cheat, though, the drawn shades only heightened their sense of dislocation and alarm.

For some of the internees, especially the younger Nisei, the trip to the inland camps was something of an adventure. As Yosh Kuromiya's train left the arid Nevada desert and began its climb into the Rocky Mountains, Kuromiya "thought it a beautiful place." On steep inclines, the tracks would wind around long curves, giving Kuromiya a view of "both ends of the train and the tops of the trees down below." He "hadn't seen anything quite like that before, except in movies. It was kind of exciting."

For a brief time, the train's mountain transit kindled optimism in Kuromiya. "They said we were going to 'camp,'" he recalls, and he found himself thinking, "Oh, vacation! Pine trees and log cabins, and all that good stuff." But "then we started coming down" out of the mountains into the high desert terrain of northwestern Wyoming, and "things began to look pretty bleak." As the train pulled into the small depot at Heart Mountain, Kuromiya found himself in "a godawful place"—not the mountain hideaway he had allowed himself to imagine. "Do we have to stop here?" he remembers asking himself. "Can't we go a little further? It's got to get better than this."

Like Kuromiya, most of the internees, accustomed to the green farmlands and busy urban areas of the West Coast, were stunned by the vastness of the landscape that greeted them at their destinations. Amy Uno Ishii, who arrived at Heart Mountain on September 12, 1942, has said that she "knew that America was huge, but . . . didn't know it was this huge, to have so much barren, open space the way they had up there. For miles and miles around, you could look as far as your eye could see and you couldn't see the first tree. No trees, nothing green, it was all brown and there was this mountain just sitting behind us."[24]

The climate was as disorienting to the newly arrived Nikkei as the landscape. The internees, most of whom had grown up in the generally mild and often damp weather of the coast, were utterly unprepared for the extremes of temperature they encountered in the high desert—the searing heat of the summer days and the frigid cold of the winter mornings that would turn wet hair to icicles. Snow would often seem to fall sideways in the howling Wyoming wind. Pipes often froze in the ground and shut down the latrines.

Neither were the internees prepared for the enormous dust storms that were churned up by the wind. One such storm greeted Yosh Kuromiya as he and his family got off the train at Heart Mountain, and he soon discovered that there was no shelter from the dust: it would make its way into their living quarters, no matter how tightly they stuffed their towels into the cracks around their windows and doors. It even made the food gritty in the mess halls. Amy Uno Ishii has described the dust storm that greeted her as being so powerful that "you couldn't open your mouth because all the dust would come in. . . . Inside your ears, up your nostrils, you could just feel the grit and grime, and when you rubbed your teeth together, you could feel all this sand. You could just barely see, and the only way to keep your eyes clean was just to cry and let the tears wash your eyes out."[25]

The internees were lodged in tarpaper barracks, much like the ones they had been occupying at the West Coast assembly centers. Each long barrack structure was about twenty feet wide and one hundred feet long, and was divided into four to six simple box-shaped rooms that ranged from twenty by sixteen feet to twenty by twenty-five feet. Couples without children got small rooms, and families—even very big ones—got large ones. Furnishings were sparse: army cots with army blankets, perhaps a pillow, a bare light bulb, a pot-bellied stove. Floor and wall boards quickly warped and exposed internees to the elements from outside and the vermin from below.

Yosh Kuromiya moved into a single large room along with his mother, his father, his two sisters, his brother, and his sister-in-law—seven people in a twenty-by-twenty-five-foot unit. After several weeks, his brother and sister-in-law were able to move to their own small unit—undoubtedly a relief for the newlyweds—and left five behind in the Kuromiya family barrack. To create at least a modicum of privacy, the family strung up blankets that divided the entire room roughly in half, and one of those halves into thirds. On the subdivided side of the central divider, Yosh Kuromiya took one tiny subsection for his cot, his two sisters shared the slightly larger middle subsection, and his parents slept in the third. The other, more open half of the room, where the pot-bellied stove sat, was the family's living area. Kuromiya recalls that some of the more talented internees managed to make chairs and tables from the scrap lumber to which they were given access. "But my dad wasn't that talented," admits Kuromiya, "and I really didn't care" about the décor of the unit, so the Kuromiya family made do with discarded produce crates as living room chairs. Orange crates, remembers George Nozawa, were downright "priceless" because they had a partition down their middle. Stood on end, they became shelving units.

The barracks were situated in groups or "blocks" of twelve to fourteen, separated by dirt roads and alleys that turned to seas of mud in the rain and to sheets of ice in the cold. Each block had a communal latrine, a laundry facility, a recreation hall, and a mess hall. The mess halls quickly became the center of Nikkei community life, in part because they were spacious and in part because internees could get permission to use the halls from their relatively sympathetic internee managers without first obtaining clearance from less friendly white administrators. In addition, nearly every family had at least one member on the kitchen crew, so it became, in Yosh Kuromiya's words, "an unofficial secondary communications center via the grapevine," secondary to, and at times more trustworthy than, the camp newspaper, the *Heart Mountain Sentinel,* which "was known to be heavily pro-administration."[26] Internees quickly grew accustomed to standing in line for everything—the toilet, the shower, the laundry, and especially meals. To many, the lines for meals hardly seemed worth the trouble; the food was generally bad at the outset and improved only slightly once the internees took over the cooking operations. Early on, the cooks even managed to ruin rice—the staple of the Issei diet. "It took them a little while to catch on to how to cook it," Kuromiya recalls, "especially in a big tub and at higher elevations. For a while there, it was terrible—you could hardly eat the stuff." For the Nisei, the menu was often no more satisfying. They were the generation of the drive-in, and the bland meals served up in the mess halls could not compare to the burgers and shakes they craved.

Of course, in the context of the entire internment experience, going without burgers and shakes was a small sacrifice. Perhaps the greatest sacrifices were borne by the Issei, who were forced to give up their property, their livelihoods, and in some cases even their sons to the demands of the U.S. government. But the Issei also paid a spiritual price. Torn by conflicting loyalties to bellicose Japan and the America that was so badly mistreating them and their citizen children, the interned

Issei entered a period of enforced idleness that took a huge toll on their physical and emotional well-being. Family life was transformed overnight. There was no privacy, either within a family unit or between a family and its neighbors. Quarters were so cramped that the younger generation typically spent most of the day outside the family home. As the Nisei spent more time with each other and less with their parents, the Japanese tradition of strong parental control began to falter. Issei fathers, accustomed to unquestioned authority as family breadwinners, won no bread and began to lose their authority. Mealtimes, the anchor of family life, were no longer private matters, but communal affairs that often scattered family members across a mess hall by gender and generation, rather than by family unit. Once children reached their teenage years, George Nozawa recalls, they would "just go to meals when they felt like it." "Who," he asks rhetorically, "would choose to eat with Mom and Dad" with so many friends around? These conditions strained family unity and discipline to the breaking point, and often beyond it.

For many Nisei, of course, particularly those in their late teens and early twenties, these changes in family life were not necessarily so unwelcome. Indeed, especially at the outset, the internment was not predominately a time of tears for most of the Nisei. Many of them, including many of those who went on to resist the draft, managed to greet their time in the high desert camps as an adventure, a change of pace, and a bundle of new experiences. "Some people said that it was bleak," recalls Heart Mountain draft resister Takashi Hoshizaki, "but . . . I guess I was more attuned to that type of thing because I was in the Boy Scouts and I was used to going camping." The Nisei found pleasure in each other's company and were only too happy to spend the ample time socializing with their peers. Many found jobs in the camps and replaced their fathers as breadwinners, even on the rather paltry WRA salaries of between twelve and nineteen dollars per month.

This is not even remotely to say that the Nisei experience of the internment was joyful and painless. As their incarceration wore on over months and then years, and their government made increasingly difficult demands on them, even the most resilient of the Nisei experienced more than their share of boredom, stress, sorrow, hopelessness, and pain. But, young people that they were, the Nisei managed, more often than not, to find at least some good in their bad situation. In the words of one young Nisei woman,

> Camp wasn't a dreadful place, it wasn't a wretched place, but I think the most significant thing for me was our loss of freedom. I did have some good times in camp. As I said, I met a lot of kids and learned how to interact with my peer group. but the overriding feeling that I had, without even being conscious of it at that time, was the deprivation of freedom, and that is a very traumatic thing. You don't appreciate it until you don't have it.[27]

As the tumultuous year 1942 drew to a close, then, this was the situation: more than 110,000 Nikkei from the West Coast were spread from Arkansas to California in ten closely guarded prison camps, unsure of when they might be released, whether they would ever be permitted to return to their homes, and whether they would even have homes to return to. Over 60,000 of the internees were U.S. citizens. They were there because the military had deemed their loyalty to this country "unknown or doubtful" and had concluded that it could never successfully determine the actual loyalty of each individual Nisei because of the "undiluted racial strains" in their blood and the impenetrable psychology of the Japanese.[28]

In truth, Nisei loyalties in late 1942 undoubtedly were something of a continuum. At one end of the spectrum was the JACL, an organization that was, in the words of Mike Masaoka, its national secretary, "on a crusade . . . to sell Japanese Americans to the government and the public at large as good Americans worthy of their heritage."[29] In the name of advancing the cause of Nisei loyalty, it had counseled compliance with the deportation program and forged an alliance with the WRA to help that agency administer the internment and relocation programs.

At the other end of the continuum was a small number of militants, many of them Kibei, with at least some pro-Japanese sympathies. These young internees, perhaps more highly sensitive than the typical Nisei to their mistreatment at the hands of the American government due to their stronger attachments to Japan, were angrily milling about the camps and looking for a fight. By mid-November of 1942, this group had staged a strike with strong pro-Japanese overtones at the Poston Relocation Center in Arizona; a few weeks later a similar group would stage a somewhat more violent outburst at the Manzanar Relocation Center in California. Not surprisingly, the most common targets of the pro-Japan fringe were internees affiliated with the JACL, whom the militants saw as collaborators in their mistreatment.

In the middle of this spectrum was the vast majority of Nisei, deeply distressed but not utterly dejected by their circumstances, loyal but resentful. On the one hand, they saw the Norman Rockwell–inspired patina that the JACL wished to place over the ugliness of their internment. Many Nisei were not interested in living this lie. On the other, they had even less interest in the pro-Japanese slogans of a handful of militants; they were American citizens and still hoped for a bright American future. As the year 1943 approached, they were content to sit in their barracks and wait to see what the government's next move would be.

FOUR INSULT TO INJURY

The next move came on February 1, 1943, when President Franklin Roosevelt announced that the War Department would organize a segregated combat team for Nisei who wished to volunteer. In a letter to Henry L. Stimson, his secretary of war, Roosevelt said that "the principle on which this country was founded and by which it has always been governed is that Americanism is a matter of the mind and heart; Americanism is not, and never was, a matter of race or ancestry." "No loyal citizen of the United States," he argued, "should be denied the democratic right to exercise the responsibilities of his citizenship, regardless of his ancestry." Roosevelt noted that the new combat team of Nisei volunteers would "add to the nearly five thousand loyal Americans of Japanese ancestry who are already serving in the armed forces of our country" and would be "a natural and logical step toward the reinstitution of the Selective Service procedures which were temporarily disrupted by the evacuation from the West Coast."[1]

The "temporary disruption" to which Roosevelt referred had occurred on January 5, 1942, at the height of anti-Japanese sentiment in the wake of Pearl Harbor, when the government changed the classification of all Nisei Selective Service registrants to IV-C, the category for "aliens not acceptable to the armed forces, or any group of persons not acceptable." Most Nisei had been understandably offended by this change in their draft status. The government had not made clear whether it saw the Nisei—American citizens all—as "aliens" or instead as some other "group of persons not acceptable," but it certainly looked to the Nisei as though, in the eyes of the military, they were suddenly less than full citizens.

This is also how matters looked to those Nisei already in the service at the time of the Japanese attack on Pearl Harbor—the "nearly five thousand loyal Americans of Japanese ancestry who are already serving in the armed forces of our country," as Roosevelt described them. Within a month of Pearl Harbor, these soldiers had been reassigned to menial labor; stripped of their weapons, ammunition, and other combat gear; forced to drill with wooden rifles; heaped with verbal and physical abuse; and, in some cases, even discharged. Indeed, when President Roosevelt visited Fort Riley, Kansas, to review the troops shortly after Pearl Harbor, the five hundred Nisei and Kibei soldiers on the base were rounded up and herded into a warehouse for the day with machine guns fixed on them for "security reasons." In short, the military had spent most of 1942 either deeply suspicious of the Nisei or openly hostile to them. Yet in February of 1943, the military was suddenly inviting them to volunteer.[2]

As astonishing as this invitation may seem, it was actually one that the Nisei—or, more precisely, *certain* Nisei—solicited. The JACL, acting in the tradition of Tokie Slocum and his battle for citizenship for the Issei veterans of World War I, had lobbied hard for the right of the Nisei to serve in the military. Just before Thanksgiving in 1942, as the Nikkei of the West Coast were settling in for their first winter behind barbed wire, the JACL held a Special Emergency National Conference in Salt Lake City. Delegates, selected by the JACL rather than through any democratic method of selection by the internees, attended the conference on WRA-granted furloughs from their concentration camps. The agenda for the conference covered life in the camps, cooperation with the War Relocation Authority, and the overall status and financial health of the JACL's programs. But the main purpose, in the view of the JACL's leader, Mike Masaoka, was to get "a ringing, unequivocal resolution demanding restoration of Selective Service responsibilities for the Nisei."[3]

That is what Masaoka called for when he addressed the convention delegates. "We believe that we are entitled to share in the good things of democracy just as much as we should share in the sacrifices and the heartaches of our country," he argued. "[B]eing deprived of the right to serve our country in the armed forces today," he continued, meant that the Nisei were "being deprived of our biggest chance to prove to those who are skeptical that our loyalty is as great as that of any other group." His conclusion was rousing: "Somewhere, on the field of battle, in a baptism of blood, we and our comrades must prove to all who question that we are ready and willing to die for the one country we know and pledge allegiance to."[4]

The delegates undoubtedly received Masaoka's plea for a baptism of blood with some nervousness. After all, they were the ones who would have to return to the camps and preach Masaoka's bloody catechism. Masaoka therefore solicited their reactions, noting that "[s]ome hints have been dropped which indicate that there may be some bitterness in the centers on the part of the fellows to be drafted." The minutes of the conference reflect that most of the delegates spoke out in support of Masaoka's call. Just one delegate, V. Ichisaka from the Topaz Relocation Center in Utah, spoke in opposition. Ichisaka argued that the loyalty of the Nisei and the contribution of the Nisei to the war effort should not be judged solely on the basis of military service. He reminded the delegates that the Nikkei had submitted to their own deportation and internment in the relocation centers. "[T]hat," he argued, echoing JACL President Saboru Kido's words of just six months earlier, "is our contribution to the war effort." Ichisaka believed that the JACL would "seek[ ] justice by asking for a system of volunteering" rather than demanding conscription. When the question was called, however, even Ichisaka backed down. The delegates unanimously passed Masaoka's motion calling for a resolution asking that the Nisei be "reclassif[ied] . . . on the same basis as all other Americans."[5]

The JACL's message fell on receptive ears in at least some government quarters. Dillon Myer, addressing the JACL's conference a few days later, said that he "consider[ed] it important that all citizens have the right to fight for this country." Myer announced that he had been lobbying within the government for Nisei military service for some time and suggested that he had found "a great deal of sympathy" for the idea with "people who are in a position to almost make the decision" in the War Department.[6]

The people to whom Myer referred were undoubtedly Assistant Secretary of War John J. McCloy and his staff. McCloy, a graduate of the Harvard Law School and a combat veteran of World War I, had been a top assistant to Secretary of War Stimson since joining the department in 1940. Both McCloy and his boss were prominent Wall Street lawyers who had stepped out of their conservative and lucrative practices for stints in public service. For McCloy, it would certainly not be his last such stint. He would go on to serve as an informal adviser to every succeeding president until Ronald Reagan and would occupy leadership positions in many of the country's most important banks, foundations, and corporations. His biographer accurately describes him as "the ultimate power broker, virtually chief counsel to the American century."[7] In 1942, however, he was the War Department's jack-of-all-trades, a young, energetic, and trusted counsel to his seventy-two-year-old boss, Henry Stimson.

McCloy had gotten to know Mike Masaoka and several other JACL leaders early in 1942, at the time when the government was removing the Nikkei from the West Coast. McCloy had been pleased by the JACL's stance of cooperation and had struck up a strong friendship with Masaoka. Like Myer and Masaoka, McCloy believed that military service would be crucial to what his office termed the "rehabilitation" of the Nisei.[8] On the question of military service, the JACL, the WRA, and the Office of the Assistant Secretary of War were in agreement by the end of 1942.

All three, however, faced powerful opposition to the idea of military service for the Nisei. The JACL's opposition came from within the Japanese American community itself. The organization's leaders were, of course, expecting some opposition. At the end of the emergency Salt Lake City conference, JACL President Saboru Kido warned the delegates that some would have to go back [to camp] to a pretty bad situation. But it is our duty," said the president, "to go back and face the music." The leaders could not have imagined how bad the music would be. No sooner had the JACL delegates returned to their relocation center barracks than they began receiving threats from fellow internees. On December 5, 1942, a delegate was accosted in his Manzanar barrack and beaten so badly that he had to be hospitalized. Two JACL leaders suffered the same fate at the Jerome Relocation Center in Arkansas. Late in January of 1943, Saboru Kido himself was clubbed viciously in his barrack at the Poston Relocation Center. This was a baptism of blood, to be sure, but undoubtedly not the one that Mike Masaoka had in mind.

Other Nisei reacted to the JACL's military gambit with words rather than clubs. On January 6, 1943, sixty-three men from the Poston Relocation Center in southern Arizona sent a letter to President Roosevelt decrying the JACL's demand for resumption of the draft. "This resolution . . . should not apply to the people of Poston Relocation Center, for the reason that Mr. Saboru Kido did not represent the people of Poston, Arizona." The letter made clear that its signatories were loyal American citizens who "would not hesitate to sacrifice [their] flesh and blood to [their] nation." But, it continued,

> unfortunately, we the Americans of Japanese Ancestry are not treated like that [*sic*] of any other Americans. We believe it utterly undemocratic to segregate any people or group of people on account of race, creed, or any other reason whatsoever; on account of the compulsory mass evacuation of Americans of Japanese ancestry together with all Japanese people, all of us sacrificed our rights granted by the Constitution of the United States as free man [*sic*] and great many of the people lost properties which they worked for many year [*sic*].

The letter concluded: "We are all willing to support the resolution of the J.A.C.L. protesting the reclassification to 4-C provided our government will recognize all our constitutional, and civil rights of American citizenship by granting privilege to citizen and alien families returning to their original places prior to evacuation and United States Government will reinburse [*sic*] us for all the properties and losses incurred by both citizen and alien on account of evacuation."[9] The signatories to the Poston letter turned the JACL's position on its head: recognize us as citizens, they said, and we will gladly serve in the army; but we will not serve in the army to persuade you to recognize us as citizens.

Dillon Myer and John McCloy also faced opposition to the idea of Nisei military service, primarily from branches of the military that viewed the concept of "Nisei loyalty" as an oxymoron. Early in 1942, General John L. DeWitt had ordered the West Coast Nisei from their homes and into detention on the theory that their loyalty to the United States was deeply questionable and probably impossible to ascertain. That was what had them behind barbed wire. How, then, less than a year later, could the military accept these seemingly disloyal people into the military, issue them weapons, and entrust them with the nation's defense? The career branches of the military at first could not get beyond this concern; a War Department study that was finalized in September of 1942 recommended against Nisei service on the theory that the Nisei were simply not trustworthy enough.[10]

The Office of War Information, however, saw marvelous international propaganda value in a Nisei combat team, a response to Japanese propaganda in the Far East that it was fighting a racial war and defending Asia against the forces of caucasian imperialism. Its director, Elmer Davis, appealed to President Roosevelt to overrule the military's recommendation, urging that "[l]oyal American citizens of Japanese descent should be permitted, after individual test, to enlist in the Army and Navy." Interestingly, Davis did not recommend what the JACL had requested—restoration of the draft. "It would hardly be fair," Davis wrote, "to evacuate people and then impose normal draft procedures." But "voluntary enlistment would help a lot."[11]

Davis's memo, referred for comment to Secretary of War Stimson, gave Assistant Secretary of War McCloy a new chance to make the case for Nisei military service. He pursued the point vigorously with Stimson, knowing that a combat team of Nisei would help persuade not just the Asian nations, but also a domestic audience that Japanese Americans could be loyal Americans. Stimson was persuaded and let his chief of staff, General George C. Marshall, know that he favored the creation of a Nisei combat team: "I don't think you can permanently proscribe a lot of American citizens because of their racial origin," he wrote to Marshall. "We have gone to the full limit in evacuating them. That's enough."[12] On January 1, 1943, Marshall ordered the creation of a segregated combat team for the Nisei.

This decision, of course, created a major conceptual and logistical problem—how to know which of the thousands of presumptively disloyal young men behind barbed wire were loyal enough to serve as American soldiers. The military quickly proposed a procedure called "registration." (Confusingly, this was a wholly separate process from "registering" for the draft—the rite of passage that all American males, regardless of race, reached at their eighteenth birthday.) Teams of four military men would be dispatched to each of the ten relocation centers with a new Selective Service form called a "DSS 304A." It was a four-page questionnaire exploring background and loyalty. The registration teams would see to it that all draft-age Nisei males filled out the registration form and would also encourage them to volunteer. A board of military and law enforcement officials would review each internee's answers to the questions on the DSS 304A and make an individualized determination as to his loyalty. Those certified as loyal would then qualify for release from WRA captivity and either induction into the military or employment in plants and facilities important to the war effort.[13]

The navy was singularly unimpressed by this proposed procedure and declined to have any part in it, refusing to accept any Nisei at all.[14] Within the army, the registration plan faced strong opposition from none other than General DeWitt, who clearly saw the process of gauging the loyalty of the Nisei on a case-by-case basis as undercutting the entire basis for their mass deportation and continued exclusion from the West Coast. In a withering memorandum to the army chief of staff, DeWitt bluntly stated:

> One of the most fundamental questions presented by the subject proposal is this: If the War Department and the Joint Board (representing the Federal establishment) do certify as to the loyalty of certain Nisei . . . , how can the Government continue to justify the prohibition against their re-entry to . . . the evacuated zone of the Western Defense Command[ ]? Perhaps it will not. If the Government will not or cannot justify its position in this regard, critics are certain to force a confession of original mistake in evacuation.

DeWitt reminded the chief of staff that at the time of the wholesale "evacuation" of the Nikkei from the West Coast, "critics . . . questioned the necessity for mass total evacuation and asked why it was not confined to aliens or others known to be disloyal." The military had responded at the time "that it was substantially impossible to determine the loyalty of the Japanese." Now, DeWitt was sure, "[t]hose elements originally critical of mass evacuation will ask: Why was not loyalty determined during the assembly center phase if it can be done now? At that time the evacuee group was under complete military control and security requirements were satisfied—there was time to determine loyalty without expending 50 to 60 millions on relocation centers." This was a tough question indeed, one with no good answer.

DeWitt pressed further and questioned the very feasibility of gauging Nisei loyalty at all. "Is the proposal," he asked, "based on a 'negative' or a 'positive' approach?"

> Are all Nisei presumptively loyal—a presumption to be rebutted only by the development of derogatory evidence? Or is the presumption the converse—to be rebutted only by the development of evidence in affirmation of loyalty?

Either presumption was problematic, DeWitt argued. "If the presumption is favorable to loyalty[,] then the Federal Government would seem to be embarrassing its original position that evacuation was a military necessity. . . . This follows because it was the fundamental premise that Japanese loyalties were unknown or doubtful." If, on the other hand, the presumption was "unfavorable to loyalty[,] then the chances of determining the loyalty of any substantial segment will probably be low" because most Nisei were too young to have any significant records on file. In short, DeWitt's memorandum lampooned the very idea of building an important government program around a quality as elusive as loyalty.[15]

In the end, DeWitt did not win the day. As noted earlier, at the beginning of February, President Roosevelt publicly announced his approval of the new all-Nisei unit, to be called the 442nd Regimental Combat Team. At around that time, an assistant of McCloy's, Colonel William Scobey, called Mike Masaoka to his Pentagon office to let him know that the JACL's dream of military service for the Nisei was about to come true. Masaoka was disappointed, however, to learn that the army's plan was to recruit volunteers rather than extend the draft to all Nisei. Even more disappointing to Masaoka was the decision that the volunteer Nisei would be cordoned off in their own racially segregated combat unit rather than assigned to serve on an equal basis with white soldiers throughout the military. The JACL had been requesting service on an equal basis with all other citizens. How would Masaoka and the JACL manage to drum up support for this discriminatory plan in the camps?[16]

Scobey defended the military's decision as being in the best interests of the Nisei. Because there were millions of Americans in uniform, Scobey argued, a few thousand Nisei scattered among them would be invisible, and their loyalty and bravery would go unnoticed. But nobody would be able to ignore the accomplishments of a regiment-sized outfit of Nisei fighting as a unit. The 442nd, Scobey argued, would be a public relations bonanza for the Nisei, exactly the sort of opportunity to prove Nisei patriotism the JACL had been seeking.

In reality, some of the military's reasons for segregating the Nisei into their own combat team were a good deal less friendly to the Nisei than Scobey admitted. The military was concerned that most American soldiers simply would not tolerate a Nisei in their midst. For example, in a memorandum debating the wisdom of drafting the Nisei, Brigadier General M. G. White, the assistant chief of staff of the War Department's Personnel Division, worried openly about the possibility that a Nisei doctor or dentist might end up treating a wounded white soldier: "The psychological effect upon a wounded white soldier of being treated by a doctor or dentist of Japanese ancestry can well be imagined," he wrote. White therefore opined "that doctors and dentists of Japanese ancestry can render greater service in relocation centers or civilian communities where they can care for people of their own racial origin."[17] Some in the military's top ranks were also concerned about the potentially explosive effect that integrating the Nisei would have on black soldiers, all of whom were in racially segregated units. In a November 1943 memorandum opposing the assignment of Nisei draftees to white units, Provost Marshall General Allen W. Gullion noted that "the readoption of general assignment of Japanese-Americans" would "emphasize" the fact that black troops remained segregated. "In view of the fact that the colored people and their friends have, since the beginning of this war, been increasingly bitter in their protests against segregation of colored people," Gullion argued, "no one short of the Commander-in-Chief should order the general assignment of Japanese-Americans with its resulting emphasis on colored segregation."[18]

Masaoka, however, took Scobey's argument for a segregated battalion at face value. He was persuaded. Not only did he commit the JACL to support the plan, but also he volunteered for the combat team on the spot and became its first member.

The 442nd would, however, need thousands more soldiers, and most of them would have to come from the camps. The military, influenced in part by Masaoka and the JACL's eager assurances of Nisei enthusiasm, hoped for upwards of thirty-six hundred volunteers from the approximately ten thousand eligible internees in the camps. By February 6, 1943, it began sending its hastily convened and poorly trained registration teams to the camps to sift the loyal from the disloyal.

Registration was supposed to produce volunteers, but in reality produced mostly turmoil and strife. It was, in a word, a disaster. Much of the blame for its failure lay with the WRA. Originally, registration was to have been just a military matter. Young men of draft age would be asked to fill out loyalty questionnaires to facilitate recruitment and enlistment. However, once the WRA realized that the military was going to be assessing the loyalty of some of the internees in its camps, it saw an opportunity to advance a program of its own. It called that program "relocation," but a more apt word for it would be "resettlement." By late 1942, the WRA had become a jailer of more than 110,000 people, and it did not wish to keep such a large number under lock and key indefinitely. It therefore began encouraging the internees to look for new jobs and new homes somewhere in the nation's interior, and it set up offices in major inland cities to help the internees find their way. In order to leave the camp, however, an internee needed to apply for what the WRA called "leave clearance"—formal permission to leave camp indefinitely. Of course, the WRA could not release internees to take jobs or attend schools in Chicago or Saint Louis unless it could certify that they were loyal to the United States and posed no security risk. The WRA therefore prevailed upon the military to extend the registration process to *all* internees—Issei and Nisei alike, men and women—rather than just to draft-age male Nisei. Thus, in the month of February 1942, the government undertook the task of interrogating (at least on paper) every person in the ten camps over the age of eighteen about his or her background, interests, and loyalties.

In choosing and phrasing its questions, the government could not have done more to arouse, confuse, and anger the internees. Question 27 asked the male internees, "Are you willing to serve in the armed forces of the United States on combat duty, wherever ordered?" The even more provocative question 28 asked, "Will you swear unqualified allegiance to the United States of America and faithfully defend the United States from any or all attack by foreign or domestic forces, and forswear any form of allegiance or obedience to the Japanese emperor, or any other foreign government, power, or organization?" These two questions instantly plunged the internees into a sea of anxieties.

In the first place, these questions appeared on a form that the WRA had foolishly labeled "Application for Leave Clearance." Most Issei, having already lost their careers and their possessions when they were evicted from the West Coast, had little interest in striking off for parts unknown in the American interior. They did not wish to apply for permission to leave the camps. Yet the title of the form led the Issei to believe that they were applying for leave simply by filling out the form, opening themselves up to being forcibly relocated yet again. That was not the WRA's intent; it wanted merely to gather information about all of the internees to use in the event that any internee later decided to resettle and seek leave clearance.[19] But to the Issei, it looked as though the WRA was forcing or tricking them into resettling against their will.

For male Nisei, question 27 also seemed to be something of a trap. How could a person answer "yes" to question 27 without simultaneously (even if unintentionally) volunteering into the army? A Nisei might be willing to serve in the armed forces of the United States if he was drafted and had no choice, but have no interest at all in volunteering. Indeed, this was probably the most common sentiment among the draft-age Nisei. Would a "yes" answer to question 27 reflect that position? Or would it instead be understood as a choice to volunteer into the military, which was, after all, what the registration teams had been sent to the camps for in the first place?

Question 28 was even worse. It asked the Nisei to "forswear" an allegiance to Japan that they had never sworn in the first place. The question dripped with the racist suspicion that had placed the Nisei behind barbed wire, and most Nisei resented it bitterly. For the Issei, question 28 was essentially unanswerable. They were all Japanese citizens, forbidden by racist American law from ever applying for naturalization as United States citizens. Yet here the government was asking them to forswear their allegiance to the emperor or any other foreign government. It was, in effect, asking them to make themselves stateless. Undoubtedly, many Issei felt considerable loyalty to Japan and would have been unlikely to renounce that loyalty in any event. But now the government was asking them to renounce their Japanese citizenship without any hope of American citizenship to replace it. On top of the countless losses and indignities of their removal from their West Coast homes and the mistreatment of their American citizen children, this was simply too much for most Issei to bear.

In short, Nisei and Issei alike were stunned by the government's questions. Yosh Kuromiya simply could not believe that the government was serious. "We were warned," he remembers, "that there could be implications and if you answered a certain way that you were either volunteering for the army or you are going to be regarded as disloyal. How can they make that kind of determination on one stupid question that's not even written clearly?" The government was, however, serious. Its registration teams, schooled in the military's and the WRA's view that military service and resettlement were what the Nikkei most desired, arrived in the camps in early February with the charge, and the expectation, of running a quick and orderly program. The War Department's plan called for the teams to complete the registration process in ten days.[20]

At a few of the camps, the internees' negative reactions remained deeply buried, and registration did in fact proceed smoothly. Perhaps the smoothest, and most surprising, of the registration efforts was at the Poston Relocation Center in Arizona. Poston had been the scene of a general strike and incidents of anti-JACL violence late in 1942 and had produced the petition of sixty-three dissidents disavowing the JACL's demand for Nisei military service. When the army's registration team arrived in February of 1943, however, Poston rolled out the red carpet. The members of the registration team and the young volunteers they had recruited were feted at a gala dinner sponsored by the camp administration in a mess hall decorated in red, white, and blue. Guests were treated to patriotic speeches, a floor show, an orchestra concert, and a humorous skit, and ended the night dancing.[21]

Registration went swimmingly at Minidoka as well. From the moment of its opening, Minidoka had enjoyed the reputation of the WRA's "model camp"—an outpost that had avoided the open protest and confrontation that had plagued many other centers. In responding to registration, Minidoka's residents did nothing to tarnish that reputation. Part of the reason for the success of registration at Minidoka was the skill of its administrators. For a week leading up to the recruitment effort, a popular camp administrator met with Issei and Nisei leaders and made the case to them that "the future of the Japanese in the United States depended upon the response evacuees showed to the program."[22] By the time the registration team arrived at Minidoka, the internees were aware of the program and its significance and had had an opportunity to ask questions and reflect on their responses.

An additional, and more troubling, part of the explanation for the success of registration at Minidoka was an important misstatement of the nature of the recruitment effort that went uncorrected. In the first couple of days of registration, the army team discovered that a generational dispute among the internees was hindering the process. In the words of the commander of the recruitment team, "The [Issei] parents, for financial reasons (and some for general bitterness) do not want the sons to volunteer. On the other hand, nearly all of the young ones want to go."[23] What resulted was a compromise: many Nisei were telling the recruitment team that they would simply wait for the reinstatement of the draft rather than anger their parents by volunteering. When President Roosevelt announced the volunteer program, he had described the creation of the all-Nisei volunteer unit as "a natural and logical step toward the reinstitution of the Selective Service procedures which were temporarily disrupted by the evacuation from the West Coast."[24] The Minidoka Nisei took him at his word and expressed their preference to wait for this "natural and logical" next step.

The registration team responded by telling the Minidoka Nisei that, notwithstanding President Roosevelt's assurance that the draft was coming, there would be no eventual draft of the Nisei unless a healthy crop of internees first showed their enthusiasm for military service by volunteering. This message broke the logjam, and young men began to volunteer.

A week later, with registration proceeding smoothly and large numbers of Minidokans volunteering, the registration team learned from the War Department that its earlier advice had been mistaken. In reality, the military was prepared to resort to the draft to fill the ranks of the 442nd even if—perhaps especially if—an unimpressive number volunteered. However, because things were going so well at Minidoka after the earlier false announcement, the registration team decided not to provide the internees with this correction, "as it was so directly contrary to our previous statements, and would definitely hinder, rather than help, our present volunteer program."[25] In other words, because falsehood was generating more volunteers than the truth had, it was better to keep the internees in the dark.

In the enthusiasm of its response to recruitment and registration, Minidoka topped all of the other internment camps. Not only was the process speediest at Minidoka, but also the Minidoka recruitment team returned to Washington with the longest list of volunteers: three hundred Minidoka Nisei signed up to serve with the 442nd. These three hundred men amounted to a full 25 percent of all Army internee volunteers—an extraordinary number for a camp that was home to less than 7 percent of the eligible Nisei internees. Still more impressive, while 28 percent of the eligible Nisei from all camps answered in the negative when asked to forswear allegiance to the Japanese emperor—a number that revealed the depth of the disillusionment and anger of the Nisei over their treatment—only 9 percent of the Minidokans gave "no" answers.[26]

At Heart Mountain, by contrast, registration produced more vitriol than volunteers. After a day or two, the registration team reported hopefully to headquarters that "[e]verything is going along very fine. There is a lot of enthusiasm."[27] But if it ever really existed at all, that enthusiasm vanished once the internees had a chance to hear the registration team's informational speeches and to examine the registration forms. The night before registration was to begin, a call went out from a small number of Nisei for the formation of a body to debate the merits of the registration program. The next morning, as registration was to begin, a group of about five hundred internees descended upon the registration site "in an orderly fashion . . . , insisting that the registering not start until they had had time to think it over and clear up some questions."[28] They threatened to kick the team's table over if the team tried to begin registering internees. The team relented, wishing to avoid a clash, and decided simply to hold further "educational" gatherings for a time.

That night an ad hoc group calling itself the "Congress of American Citizens" gathered in one of the mess halls to try to coordinate a response to registration. A self-appointed representative from each of the camp's residential blocks was present. Fairly quickly, the congress proposed and approved a number of resolutions, all of which centered around the idea that the Nisei would refuse to register unless the government first "clarified" their citizenship rights.[29] The delegates did not make clear precisely what sort of clarification they wanted, but their complaints focused on their incarceration, their disqualification from work in the civil service and the defense industries, and the racial segregation of the combat unit for which they were being asked to volunteer.

With a high-profile and at least moderately organized group publicly resisting the government's efforts, the registration process barely got off the ground. By February 18, a full week after registration began, the registration team had processed registration forms from only 107 of the nearly 7,600 Heart Mountaineers eligible to register and had managed to recruit only 3 volunteers.[30]

The government responded to this crisis with a mix of pleas and threats. On February 17, Colonel Scobey from Assistant Secretary of War McCloy's office sent a telegram to the head of the registration team counseling him that

> [a]lthough the present program is voluntary the combat team will be raised if necessary by [the] draft. However, you should make every effort to obtain your quota of volunteers since the advantage of the voluntary program to the Japanese Americans cannot be overemphasized. They must realize that a voluntary combat team constitutes a symbol of their loyalty which can be displayed to the American public and to those who oppose the Japanese Americans. Involuntary induction by means of the draft greatly detracts from that symbol.[31]

Of course, a year later the government would characterize the draft very differently when it instituted that method of turning internees into soldiers; at that later date, the government would argue that the *draft* would show the Nisei in their best light. But what McCloy's office wanted in February of 1943 was volunteers, and so the draft became a matter of shame, not pride.

These entreaties were quickly followed by threats. On February 17, Guy Robertson, Heart Mountain's project director, had a meeting with the Heart Mountain community council and block leaders, who (unlike the self-appointed delegates to the Congress of American Citizens) were elected representatives of the internees. Robertson "read [them] the Riot Act, . . . quietly telling them that this was not a matter to be controlled by majority vote by anyone . . . and that if anyone interfered . . . they'd be going counter to the Espionage Act and that action would be taken accordingly."[32] Robertson was resorting to big guns here; the Espionage Act made it a felony punishable by up to twenty years' imprisonment and a $10,000 fine to "willfully obstruct the recruiting or enlistment service of the United States."[33] About two weeks later, with registration still lagging and few volunteers stepping forward, Robertson added to his threat of prosecution a prediction of community shaming. In a memorandum to the camp's block leaders, Robertson preached that it was "definitely the obligation of the community leaders to see that Heart Mountain maintain at least a comparable position with the other centers." Preying on the Japanese cultural concern for saving face and preserving reputation, Robertson predicted to the Issei "that life-long stigma w[ould] be borne by their children who fail to assume their responsibility in a democratic government."[34]

All of these ploys were in vain, even counterproductive. By the time registration concluded at Heart Mountain in mid-March of 1943—weeks later than the military had expected it would conclude—only 42 out of more than 1,700 eligible men had volunteered into the service. Almost one in four of the draft-eligible men answered "no" to question 28, the question probing their loyalty to the United States. Even more tellingly, 329 Nisei filed requests for "expatriation"—requests to abandon their American citizenship and to be transported to Japan. One hundred fifty-one Issei filed similar requests for "repatriation" to Japan. When the registration team left Heart Mountain, it left a very different camp from the one it had found on its arrival five weeks earlier, a camp that had nearly overflowed with resentment and bitterness and that was beginning to experiment with organized resistance.[35]

The resentment and bitterness at Heart Mountain, however, were dwarfed by the rage that engulfed the registration team at Tule Lake. At the outset, the reaction at Tule Lake was similar to that at Heart Mountain. Few registered and fewer still volunteered, while many of the internees met in block meetings to debate the merits of registration and to vent their concerns and their anger over questions 27 and 28. Eventually, these block meetings produced a dizzying list of nearly 150 questions about the registration process that internee leaders presented to the registration team. The questions ranged from the general ("Why the sudden enlisting of Nisei boys after putting them behind fences at this camp?"), to the specific ("Why are we not eligible to serve in the marine, navy, and air corp [*sic*]?"), to the devastatingly blunt

("What will happen if everybody refuses to register?"). The hastily assembled and poorly trained registration team was caught off guard by the sheer volume of the internees' questions and concerns and had no way to answer them all.[36]

Opposition to registration then took even firmer root than at Heart Mountain. Entire blocks began vowing not to register. One block voted to sign up en masse for repatriation (in the case of Issei) or expatriation (in the case of Nisei) to Japan. Requests for repatriation and expatriation began to flow in to the registration team at a far faster pace than registration and enlistment forms.[37] In some blocks, the few who dared to register were harassed, taunted, and mocked as *inu*—Japanese for "dogs," or collaborators with the administration. The registration process ground to a virtual standstill.

Faced with recalcitrance, the project director decided to try to break the opposition by threatening the internees with prosecution under the Espionage Act. When this strategy did not produce more registrants, the project director began ordering the internees, block by block, to register by specific dates. One block in particular, Block 42, dug in its heels. Thirty-five Nisei from Block 42 appeared at the camp administration building with a petition announcing that they would refuse to register, but would happily sign applications for expatriation to Japan. The administration responded by ordering these thirty-five men to register the next day. When they refused to register, the project director called in twenty-four armed military policemen from the camp's perimeter to arrest them. The soldiers surrounded Block 42 and apprehended the thirty-five Nisei at bayonet point. As a huge and angry crowd looked on, American soldiers placed American citizens under arrest at gunpoint for refusing to fill out Selective Service paperwork and then trucked them off to a nearby county jail.

This strong-arm tactic did little to quell the opposition at Tule Lake; indeed, it may have emboldened it. Registration—a process that had been expected to last a couple of weeks—ended up taking more than two months. By the time it was over, the authorities had arrested well over one hundred Issei and Nisei. Forty-nine percent of the eligible Nisei and 42 percent of the eligible Issei at Tule Lake either refused to comply with registration entirely or answered "no" to the loyalty question. A militant, pro-Japanese mix of Kibei and Issei had a large segment of the camp in its thrall, and much of the rest living in fear.[38]

In the final analysis, registration at the ten WRA centers was a failure for everyone concerned—the military, the WRA, and the internees. The military got barely one-third of the volunteers it was expecting from the camps; it would end up staffing the 442nd Regimental Combat Team primarily with Nisei from Hawaii who had never been deported and interned and who therefore eagerly volunteered by the thousands. The WRA was left with a fractured and restive internee population, of whom one in seven had either refused to register entirely or answered "no" to the loyalty question. And the internees themselves were in turmoil, with the lines of division in their community laid bare for all to see.

Naturally, these lines of division were visible not just to the internees, but also to the outside world. The national press closely covered the registration debacle, emphasizing the large number of "disloyal Japs" who were being accommodated in supposed luxury at government expense. Hearings and investigations by the U.S. Senate and House of Representatives quickly followed. From these hearings, a proposal emerged to separate or "segregate" the disloyal from the loyal internees. This was an idea that the JACL had been pressing on the WRA for some time,[39] but that Dillon Myer had opposed. Myer believed it far better to reopen the states that made up the Western Defense Command to loyal internees and allow as many of them as possible to return to at least the vicinity of their former homes. This, Myer believed, would speed up the resettlement process and largely empty the camps of everyone but those who posed an excessive security risk. The War Department, however, took the position that the solution was not to readmit the Nikkei to the West Coast, but instead to cordon the disloyal off even more tightly by segregating them in a single camp. At a meeting in late May of 1943, the project directors of the ten relocation centers unanimously agreed that the time had come for segregation.

Tule Lake was the obvious choice for conversion to a segregation center. A large percentage of the approximately eighteen thousand residents of Tule Lake had already answered "no" to the key questions on the registration forms, and many there had gone so far as to attempt to renounce their American citizenship and request expatriation or repatriation to Japan. It would make little sense to ship such a large group off to some other camp; better, the WRA reasoned, to transport those of questionable loyalty from the other camps to Tule Lake and to transfer Tule Lake's "loyal" population to other camps. Thus, in the fall of 1943, just a year after it had forced the internees into their relocation center homes, the government undertook a massive program of reshuffling them by the thousands. In all, nearly 19,000 people were hauled to or from Tule Lake.

Most of those who moved to Tule Lake fell into three categories. One was the group of internees who had applied for expatriation or repatriation to Japan, either before or during the registration controversy. The second group was the "no-nos"—those who had answered "no" to questions 27 and 28 on the registration forms or who had refused to answer the questions at all. The final category consisted of family members of individuals in the other two categories. This was by far the hardest and most controversial grouping because many who fell into this category really had no choice but to go to Tule Lake. In the words of the late Michi Weglyn, an early chronicler of the internment experience, they were "those who could not be left behind"—"grandparents, close relatives, the old, the young, [and] the enfeebled."[40]

The WRA did leave a choice about segregation to certain family members—those who were seventeen years old or older. Thus, the eighteen-year-old son or daughter of Issei parents who had requested repatriation or answered "no-no" to registration could, at least in theory, decide not to follow his or her "disloyal" parents to Tule Lake. In practice, however, few Nisei in their late teens and early twenties were willing to break their families apart in this way. For example, Tom Noda, eventually a draft resister at Tule Lake, ended up moving there from Heart Mountain out of deference and obedience to his father's choice. Noda recalls that his "dad said he had his mind made up to go back to Japan, because there's nothing to live for over here." Noda's Issei father had "worked fifty years of his life and ended up in the camp, after all those years he busted his butt over here. So he said, 'I'll just go back to Japan. I got property back in Japan, so I might as well leave.'" The younger Noda's decision was therefore made for him. "That's the reason I didn't have any choice," he explains. "If he felt that way I had to follow his steps to take care of him because he wasn't a young man anymore." Thus, regardless of their own feelings and preferences, most chose to follow their parents to segregation at Tule Lake in the name of keeping the family together. Whatever disruption the family structure had suffered in the camps, this basic allegiance to one's elders remained largely intact.

With the fiasco of registration behind it, the military turned to the task of outfitting and training the newly formed Nisei combat team. Settling in at Fort Shelby in Mississippi in May of 1943, the Nisei volunteers trained with gusto and quickly began impressing the caucasian officers who had been assigned to lead them. A month into their training they were joined by an outfit of volunteers from Hawaii, the 100th Infantry Battalion. The 100th, a segregated Nisei unit formed in mid-1942 from the ranks of the Hawaiian Territorial Guard and the National Guard of Hawaii, had been in training for a year and was nearly ready for combat. In August of 1943, the 100th Infantry Battalion was sent to North Africa for combat and saw its first action late in September in Italy. By all accounts, the men of the 100th fought admirably in those early months of combat, accomplishing the objectives assigned them and suffering many casualties.[41]

Against this developing backdrop of impressive service by the Nisei volunteers, Assistant Secretary of War McCloy took up the question of the draft with others in the Pentagon. For McCloy, this was a necessary follow-up to the recruitment of volunteers. When President Roosevelt announced the program of recruiting volunteers for the 442nd in early February of 1943, he had described the program as a "natural and logical step" toward the reinstatement of the draft. McCloy and Dillon Myer both still supported the idea of drafting the Nisei, and the JACL continued to press for it as well.[42] For McCloy, the draft was inevitable, and in the late spring of 1943, he explicitly asked the War Department's Personnel Division, G-1, to set the process in motion.

G-1, however, was not impressed with the idea. Noting that the 100th and 442nd battalions were at that time still untested and reminding McCloy of the embarrassingly poor results of registration, G-1 took the position that the military had satisfied President Roosevelt's directive by allowing the Nisei the opportunity to volunteer. To McCloy's office, however, G-1's response was inadequate, "a lot of foot-shuffling [that] doesn't mean anything." McCloy pressed further, reminding G-1 that "the suggestion of the President has been partly carried out, but the President also suggested reinstitution of Selective Service procedures." "To bring the matter to a head," McCloy demanded "the judgment of G-1 on the desirability or practicability of reinstituting Selective Service. . . ." In the face of McCloy's pressure, G-1 relented, but with an important caveat. In a memorandum to McCloy, G-1's assistant chief of staff wrote on April 26, 1943, that he no longer objected to the draft for the Nisei, "[p]rovided arrangements can be made to make the existing loyalty test a part of the screening process, and provided also that the number to be inducted can be controlled and assignments limited to existing combat units presently designated to be composed of personnel of Japanese ancestry." In other words, G-1 would assent to the draft for the Nisei so long as the soldiers were loyal and would remain segregated, serving as replacements for those killed or wounded in action with the 100th and the 442nd.[43]

This presented a new problem for McCloy, one that he never managed to overcome. During registration, McCloy and his staff learned that most internees had been angered by the War Department's decision to segregate the Nisei into their own unit rather than making them available for "general assignment" across all branches of the military. As one of McCloy's assistants explained at the time, there had been "an immediate and violent reaction by the evacuees in the relocation centers against the formation of a separate unit. There were cries of discrimination, segregation, and cannon fodder." Many internees had been mollified by the War Department's assurances that the segregation of the 442nd was in the best interests of the Nisei—an arrangement that one of McCloy's assistants said would "shock the country into realizing what the true situation was with respect to Japanese American loyalty."[44] But McCloy and his staff doubted that the internees would swallow this explanation a second time, in connection with a racially discriminatory draft. In his debate with G-1, McCloy therefore began pressing for general assignment of the drafted Nisei. "I question the desirability of going through the motions of reinstituting Selective Service," McCloy argued, "merely to fill out the requirements of the recently established combat team. . . . Reinstitution of Selective Service means placing loyal persons of Japanese ancestry on the same basis as all others subject to the draft. The number to be taken, and their assignment," he concluded, "should not be restricted, but the same standards applied as for all others."[45]

On this point, however, the Personnel Division would not budge. G-1 simply did not believe that the army was ready for soldiers with

Japanese faces spread among its ranks. "Until the psychology of other personnel of the Army is altered by the impact of events or demonstrations of self-sacrificing loyalty by soldiers of Japanese ancestry," G-1 maintained, "segregation of such personnel in [all-Nisei] units seems eminently desirable."[46] G-1's position was that the soldiers of the 100th and the 442nd, already committed to risking their lives so that American society might someday accept the Nisei as true Americans, would also have to spill their blood so that Nisei draftees could serve in the army alongside white soldiers.

Through the fall of 1943, the War Department continued to debate whether to draft the interned Nisei and whether to assign them on a segregated or an integrated basis. Most of the debate centered on G-1's concern that the army was not psychologically prepared for general assignment of the Nisei and on the logistical objection that it would be difficult to remove a handful of Nisei soldiers from units that might suddenly be called to duty in the Pacific theater. During the discussions, however, an additional issue emerged: how could the army possibly integrate the Nisei while simultaneously segregating black soldiers? In a memorandum on the advisability of drafting the Nisei and assigning them generally throughout the army, Provost Marshall General Allen W. Gullion made his observation, quoted earlier, that general assignment of the Nisei would inevitably draw attention to the continued segregation of blacks in the army. Gullion made clear that integrating the Nisei was a political can of worms that only Franklin Roosevelt could open. Facing what it saw as an overwhelming array of logistical, political, and morale-related problems, the War Department determined in December of 1943 to reinstitute the draft for the Nisei, but to assign the Nisei draftees only to segregated combat units.[47]

All that remained was to publicize the decision. McCloy and those in his office appreciated the risk that the announcement would anger many internees in the camps. Indeed, they made clear that they "believed that the success of th[e] program of induction [would] depend largely upon the type of publicity which is given it and the method in which this publicity is handled."[48]

They had practical reasons for worry: not only was the atmosphere still tense in many camps as a result of the registration fiasco and of segregation, but also the internees were beginning to absorb the devastating news of the many casualties that the Hawaiian Nisei of the 100th

Battalion were suffering on the front lines in Italy. The atmosphere was so tense that one of McCloy's top assistants spoke of the "probability that the reinstitution of the induction of loyal Japanese Americans" would lead many Nisei to "the interpretation that the reinstitution of selective service was designed as an 'exterminating measure' for Japanese Americans."[49] Thus, in the space of a year—1943—the draft had transformed itself from something that the JACL had predicted the Nisei would welcome to something that the War Department feared the Nisei might see as a program of extermination. Still, the War Department complied with the JACL's request for confidential advance notice of the reopening of the draft so that the organization could break the story in its newspaper.[50] "The [JACL]," explained an assistant of McCloy's to the Pentagon's publicity office, "has been a good influence. It has pursued a policy of full cooperation with the War Department and other federal agencies."[51]

McCloy and his staff were not the only ones in Washington who were worried about how the inmates in the camps would receive the news of the reopening of the draft. Dillon Myer at the WRA learned about the change in policy late in the month of December, after the decision had been made. Like McCloy and the JACL, Myer had long supported the reinstatement of the draft, and like them, he had always argued for general rather than segregated assignment of the Nisei troops. He shared their disappointment at the decision to continue with segregation rather than to permit the drafted Nisei to serve across the military. But unlike McCloy and the JACL, Myer had a unique practical problem: he had the relocation camps to run. "It is my judgment," he wrote in a December 22, 1943, letter of protest to the assistant secretary of war, "that institution of the program as laid out will lead to many complications and administrative problems within the War Relocation Authority that have not been foreseen by those in the Army who have given consideration to this program."[52] The year 1943 had itself been a year of enormous "complications and administrative problems" for the WRA, the military, and the internees. And Myer was right: the draft would create new ones in 1944. They would, however, turn quickly from administrative problems to legal ones.

FIVE REACTION

The War Department formally announced its new policy of drafting the interned Nisei on January 20, 1944. Citing "the excellent showing which the [442nd Regimental] Combat Team has made in training, and the outstanding record achieved by the 100th Battalion . . . now fighting in Italy," the War Department announced that "Japanese-Americans considered acceptable for military service w[ould] be reclassified by their Selective Service boards on the same basis as other citizens, and called for induction if physically qualified and not deferred."[1] And so it was official: the policy of conscription for which the JACL, Dillon Myer, and John McCloy had been pressing was finally law. Young Nisei men from the camps were now to be not merely invited to join the army, but compelled to do so by force of law.

News of the new policy reached the camps quickly, by radio reports and in the camps' newspapers. At first, there was little reaction. According to the community analyst at Heart Mountain, the announcement of the reopening of the draft "seem[ed] to have been taken largely as a statement of intent. It was something that lay in the future, something not quite concrete or real."[2] It became very real, however, in early February, when the first orders to report for preinduction physical examination began arriving in the mail. As with registration, the internees again were put to a choice: Should they follow government orders and leave their families under army guard in the camps so that they could themselves join the army? Or should they resist?

This new dilemma was, however, different from the registration controversy in two basic ways. First, the stakes were higher. To comply with registration was to go on record about one's loyalties and risk some sort of internal WRA sanction for answers the government might deem dangerous. To comply with the draft was to risk one's life. Second, the draft cast a much narrower net than registration. Because registration affected everyone, the entire population of each camp had a common interest in debating how to respond. Even at the camps where registration was peaceful, internees gathered to discuss the process and to try to make sense of what was being asked of them. The draft, by contrast, did not affect everyone; it directly touched only a segment of each camp's male citizens. And it did not even touch all of them at once because they received their draft notices at different times. As a result, the dilemma facing the drafted Nisei was at once more serious and more solitary than the dilemma of registration.

Silent Protest: Tule Lake

At most of the camps, there was comparatively little public discussion of the draft, and most of the Nisei made up their minds on their own about how to respond to their government's orders. Curiously, this was especially true at the WRA's most troublesome camp, Tule Lake. Late in 1943, Tule Lake had been paralyzed by a second round of riots and strikes (the first had been triggered by registration), and the military police had again been brought in to restore order.[3] The camp remained under military control until January 14, 1944, just days before the announcement of the reopening of the draft. Thus, when draft notices began arriving at Tule Lake, the camp was in a state of edgy stillness. Most internees were staying indoors, partly because of the cold and partly just to keep out of harm's way.

When the time came for young men to report for their physicals, those who decided to comply with their orders were spirited out of camp at night in order to avoid triggering unrest or endangering their families. Those who decided not to comply simply refused to leave camp. Jimi Yamaichi was one who made this decision. Yamaichi was a young man from San Jose who had been segregated from Heart Mountain to Tule Lake at his father's insistence. A carpenter, Yamaichi had spent his time at Heart Mountain and Tule Lake doing construction work—something of an opportunity for a man who had been barred before the war from joining the carpenters' union because he was Japanese American. When his draft notice came, Yamaichi simply said to himself, "I'm not going to do it. Too much trouble." By that time, Yamaichi had spent nearly two years in various concentration camps. He had seen his brother, an American soldier at the time of Pearl Harbor, placed under military guard and issued a wooden gun. He had seen his cousin barred from leaving camp to visit his dying father. The indignities and injustices of the deportation and internment were just too much for the young man.

Tom Noda, another of the Tule Lake resisters, had a similar reaction to Yamaichi's. The young man had been expecting to spend the fall of 1942 as a college freshman, but instead ended up in a tarpaper barrack at Heart Mountain. In deference to his father's wishes, Noda had moved to segregation behind the barbed wire of Tule Lake and was awaiting expatriation to Japan along with his parents and his sisters. For him, it was not at all a hard decision to leave camp for an uncertain fate at the hands of the legal system. "The way I figured," he recalls, "it couldn't be no worse than it was anyway. We were in prison to begin with. Going to a state [*sic*] prison wouldn't have been too much different; even the food might have been better. That's the thought I had." For a person who had already spent time in three jails (Santa Anita, Heart Mountain, and Tule Lake), the threat of time in another was not much of a deterrent.

On an assigned day and time, the twenty-seven Tule Lake resisters were directed to assemble near the camp's gate, told only that they should bring with them a change of clothes. There they were met by several U.S. marshals, placed in cars in groups of five, and driven 250 miles to the small coastal town of Eureka, where a judge from the U.S. District Court for the Northern District of California in San Francisco was soon expected to arrive to hear a week's worth of cases. The marshals trusted their captives, leaving their weapons out on the front seat of the car as they drove the young men across the state. Others trusted them less; when they stopped at a roadside café for lunch, a waitress told the marshals in no uncertain terms that the restaurant "did not serve Japs." The marshals threatened to shut the restaurant down unless they served the boys from Tule Lake, and the waitress relented. When they arrived in Eureka, they were placed by twos into cells at the Humboldt County Jail to await the arrival of the federal judge from San Francisco.

Hushed Protest: Minidoka

At Minidoka, internees responded to the reopening of the draft with at least somewhat more public comment than at Tule Lake. In part, this more open dissent was a reflection of changing times at the camp. In the year since registration, the camp's administration had grown more callous in its dealings with the internees, the camp had been the site of significant labor strife, and it had absorbed some transferees from Tule Lake who arrived with a more combative attitude than Minidokans were accustomed to.

Word of the restoration of the draft reached Minidoka's Nisei through the *Irrigator,* the camp's internee-run, generally proadministration newspaper. "Selective Service Open to Nisei," screamed the banner atop the paper's January 22 edition.[4] Quoting the War Department's statement in full, the lead article praised the government for "[g]ranting the full restoration of rights as American citizens to the Nisei." It is hard to see how the restoration of rights to the Nisei was "full": even though draftable, the interned Nisei remained behind barbed wire and under army guard and were still forbidden from returning to the West Coast. Still, the paper's editorial page optimistically opined that the War Department's announcement had "erased forever the stigma of doubt and disloyalty on American citizens of Japanese descent in the United States by restoring the privileges and responsibilities of their citizenship through the restoration of selective service." "We are now really Americans in every sense of the word," the editorial glowed. "Let us not be found wanting."[5]

Many of Minidoka's residents did not share the newspaper's enthusiasm. At secret block meetings held throughout the project, Issei and Nisei alike conferred in hushed tones about the injustice of the government's demand and the sacrifice it would entail. The Minidokans, however, stayed true to their peaceful reputation and, at least initially, kept their dissatisfactions to themselves. Camp remained calm.

Part of the reason for the early acquiescence at Minidoka was undoubtedly the government's saber-rattling about the consequences of defiance. By late February, it began to grow clear to the government that potentially large numbers of Nisei were contemplating noncompliance with the draft. The government responded by emphasizing to the Nisei that resisting the draft was serious business. In a late February memorandum, Dillon Myer, the director of the War Relocation Authority, announced to the internees that "[a]ny evacuee in a relocation center who refuses to report for induction, when called, is guilty of violation of the selective service act, and is subject to criminal penalties." "No real or fancied grievances," said Myer, would "be allowed to interfere with its operation." To squelch any growing sentiment for resistance, Myer counseled community pressure. "The wiser heads among the evacuees," he suggested, "may want to talk to . . . young men [contemplating draft resistance], to their parents, and help them realize the serious consequences to the young man . . . and to the whole group"[6] of Americans of Japanese ancestry.

Myers's words resonated with at least the most administration friendly of the Nisei, who began to echo them. In a February 26 editorial in the *Irrigator,* editor Kimi Tambara implored her fellow Minidokans to "present a united front" on the draft—a united front supporting military service. Tambara conceded that "[t]he reinstitution of the draft ha[d] brought back into [*sic*] life many skeletons that were hitherto carefully locked up in the closets," "[g]rievances concerning the evacuation, restrictions placed on us concerning the places we may go, questions concerning our loyalty to the United States." She also noted that "there [were] certain weak points in the reopening of the draft to the nisei," most notably the racial segregation of all Nisei soldiers in the 442nd. Yet she argued that American society was actually opening itself to the Nisei much more quickly than it had to other groups, especially black Americans, and that "little by little" the Nisei were gaining acceptance. "We cannot let petty things stand in our way," Tambara contended. Referring obliquely to those in camp who were complaining about the draft, she asserted that "[w]hen we bring up situations for which no person has a pat answer at this moment, we are being selfish." And looking at things unselfishly, rising above "our own narrow world," Tambara concluded, the Nisei would "realize that the reinstitution of the draft, no matter its limitations, is beginning to open the door for further privileges for us and the rest of the minority groups."[7]

The prodraft effort at Minidoka got a very public boost from its best-known resident, an Oregon-born Nisei attorney named Min Yasui. In the spring of 1942, Yasui had dared Portland police to arrest him for violating the dusk-to-dawn curfew that General DeWitt imposed on Japanese Americans. When the police finally charged him, Yasui took his case challenging the legality of the curfew all the way to the United States Supreme Court.[8] In so doing, Yasui incurred the wrath of the JACL, which, having declared itself "unalterably opposed to test cases to determine the constitutionality of military regulations," publicly mocked Yasui as a "self-styled martyr" and questioned his loyalty to the United States. Yasui lost his constitutional challenge in the High Court, spent nine months in solitary confinement in a Portland jail, and upon his release was shipped to Minidoka.[9]

His battle with the government made him something of a folk hero among the Nisei, especially those most inclined to protest. Yet Yasui came out solidly for the draft, perhaps because he was himself a reserve officer in the U.S. Army and perhaps because he was looking for a way to return to the JACL fold. In an open letter to all Nisei, Yasui responded to the "confused people in the centers who are trying to bargain with the government . . . and others who are trying to evade the draft," telling them that they should "welcome the draft of the Nisei as an opportunity to get into the fight." Yasui conceded, as had Tambara in her earlier editorial, that the Nisei had legitimate grievances. But he urged that the "Nisei must demonstrate our willingness to assume fully and patriotically the obligations of citizenship before we are in any position to petition for a redress of our grievances." He optimistically predicted that if the Nisei proved their American loyalty on the battlefield, "no one can and no one will want to deny equal citizenship rights to equal Americans." Looking to the future, Yasui predicted that "[o]ur quiet and yet patriotic acceptance of the draft shall be one criterion by which we shall be judged." "In this," he urged, "we cannot fail."[10]

Yasui made his case not just to his fellow Minidokans. He also circulated and then submitted to President Roosevelt, Secretary of War Stimson, and General Delos Emmons (who had replaced John L. DeWitt as commander of the Western Defense Command) a petition pledging Nisei support for the draft, but asking for freedom to return to the West Coast and the opportunity for the Nisei to serve in all units and branches of the military. Yasui's petition on behalf of Minidoka's Nisei made clear at the start that those "awaiting call into the United States Army under the Selective Service [were] highly gratified by the recognition by the federal authorities of [their] rightful place in America, and . . . proud of being given the opportunity to serve [their] country in its hour of need." The Nisei, "willing to offer our lives for our country, if need be," and "eager to fulfill conscientiously and patriotically every obligation of American citizenship," asked in return that the government recognize their freedom of movement (especially into the Western Defense Command), their right to own property on the same basis as others, their right to "equal choice of service in the armed forces" and to participation in special military training programs, their right to an equal chance at advancement and promotion within the armed forces, and their right to equal employment in industry. Yasui's petition, however, did not demand these rights as a condition of military service; it committed the Nisei to serve and pleaded for equal treatment in return. In the petition's own words, "We feel that the cheerful and willing assumption of our obligations as American citizens reciprocally calls for the unequivocal restoration of our full citizenship rights."[11]

For a while, these sorts of exhortations had their intended effect at Minidoka. On February 23 and 24, 1944, the first preinduction physical examinations for internees were held at Boise. One hundred twenty Nisei draftees showed up for their physicals. Only two young men, Jack Uno and George Murakami, refused to report. Of these two, one was reported to be " 'cocky' in his attitude," while the other was "sincere in his belief that his rights as an American citizen were jeopardized as a result of the evacuation" and preferred to "serve a term in jail rather than . . . serve in the army." Both were arrested on March 4, 1944, charged with violating the Selective Service Act, and taken to the Ada County Jail in Boise when they could not make the $2,000 bail set by the United States commissioner.[12]

For six weeks, into mid-April, the two men sat in the Ada County Jail. They sat there alone; none of the many Minidokans called to report for their physicals during March and early April chose to follow in Uno's and Murakami's defiant footsteps. Eventually, however, the two resisters came under strong pressure from other internees to give up their fight. Their families disagreed strongly with their stand "and the . . . sister of one made two week-end trips to see her brother before she finally persuaded him to accept army service." By April 24, 1944, both men had relented and "agreed to immediate induction into the army," and had therefore been released from the county jail.[13] As the month of April ended, and the numbers of draft resisters at other camps were rising, Minidoka's rate of compliance was 100 percent.

But that was soon to change. Resentment over the draft, which had silently smoldered since late January, finally began to flare up late in April. On Thursday, April 26, fifty-seven Nisei were called for induction, but six of them—just over 10 percent—did not show up. One of the six was Gene Akutsu. The younger Akutsu brother had endured quite a bit by the time he received his draft notice. His father, Kiyonosuke, had been among the Issei men seized within hours of the Japanese attack on Pearl Harbor. Gene, his brother, and his mother did not see him for two years. Finally, on a cold Idaho day in December of 1943, a gaunt, old-looking man appeared at Block 5 of the Minidoka Relocation Center. Bundled up against the wind and with a hat pulled down over his head, the man approached Gene and asked him where the Akutsu residence was. "I'll take you up there," the eighteen-year-old said. He showed the man to unit F of barrack 4, a small room at the end of the wood-and-tarpaper structure. The man stepped inside, took off his hat, and said, simply, "I'm dad." Father and son had not even recognized one another. Kiyonosuke had dropped from one hundred thirty-five to about ninety-five pounds during his two years away, and Gene's adolescent frame had filled out to an adult's.

The Akutsus enjoyed a happy family reunion, something Gene remembers as a "warming" of their chilled Minidoka quarters. Nao Akutsu, Gene's mother, had weathered the storm of the family's eviction from Seattle, detention in an assembly center, and transfer to Minidoka alone, with only her two sons for support. The pressure on her had been enormous and had taken a toll on her. "Finally," Gene recalls, his mother was "together again with the one she loved."

This brief moment of family happiness, however, did nothing to salve the anger that Gene felt toward the land of his birth. So disillusioned had he grown that a few weeks after the reopening of the draft, on February 10, 1944, Akutsu filed a petition for "repatriation" to Japan. "Repatriation" was a somewhat odd request for a young American citizen who had never "patriated" Japan in the first place. Many other frustrated Nisei in Akutsu's position filed petitions for "expatriation" to Japan, which, as a matter of semantics, made more sense. But Akutsu denominated his petition as a request for repatriation for a specific reason: his treatment at the hands of his government had "proven to him that he is a Japanese, no longer an American citizen."[14] The government had not acted on his petition, except to announce that it would treat all such petitions filed after January 20, 1944, the day of the reopening of the draft, as efforts at draft avoidance rather than good-faith requests for transport to Japan.[15]

Akutsu was feeling no more affection for America in April, when he received his draft notice, than he had in February. He simply felt that the government "had been kicking us around a lot," and he was "not going to stand for that" any longer. Thus, Akutsu recalls, when "the day finally came for [me] to go for induction[,] I didn't go." He told a few of his friends of his decision and triggered "a big argument" that, in a way, has not yet ended: one of his old friends from camp still will not talk to him, fifty-five years later. When Akutsu told his parents, his mother, Nao, was not pleased. She had just been reunited with her husband after two years apart, and now she faced the loss of her younger son. She worried aloud that "we don't know what is going to happen to you, . . . [or] whether we'll ever see you again." Sadly, she asked Gene to give her a clipping of his hair and his fingernails so that "if anything should happen that we should never see you again, at least we['ll] have something to have at your funeral."

Just after lunch on April 29, 1944, a deputy U.S. marshal appeared at the door of the Akutsu family's barrack with a warrant for Gene's arrest on the charge of failing to report for induction in the armed service of the United States, in violation of Section 311 of Title 50 of the United States Code. Gene surrendered peacefully—there was "no use trying to run around," he recalls—and got into the deputy marshal's car for the three-hour drive to Boise. As he climbed in, he was surprised to see another Nisei, Smith Yoshito Hayami, already under arrest and in the backseat. Akutsu had no idea that anyone else at Minidoka had decided to resist the draft. As the deputy marshal drove Akutsu and Hayami to Boise, he tried to persuade them to give up their fight and submit to the draft, warning them that "you guys are going to be put behind bars and you're going to lose all your privileges that you've got," but suggesting that "if you volunteer and go into the service, we'll forget all about this and you can have your liberty." The young men, however, remained silent in the face of this pressure. Once in Boise, the deputy marshal took them to city hall, where the local United States commissioner set bail for each at $1,000.[16] This was, of course, a sum that neither of the young Nisei had any hope of producing. The deputy marshal therefore packed them back in the car and drove them to the Ada County Jail, where they would sit for more than four months awaiting their September trial date.

With two of its residents in the Ada County Jail, four more charged and subject to arrest, and hundreds of restless young men awaiting their induction notices, Minidoka suddenly had a protest on its hands, and it stood to sully Minidoka's reputation as a model camp. The camp administration was no doubt relieved that the arrests of these first draft resisters coincided with what they expected would be a public relations bonanza for the cause of Nisei military service. On May 2, 1944, Technical Sergeant Ben Kuroki arrived at Minidoka for a highly publicized five-day visit. Kuroki, a Nisei, was a Nebraska farm boy who had managed to buck the army's anti-Japanese prejudices and serve heroically on an air corps bomber for thirty perilous missions in the European theater.[17] Kuroki had agreed to go on a publicity tour through several of the camps in the spring of 1944, as it became clear to the government and the JACL that the interned Nisei were not reacting as enthusiastically to the reopening of the draft as its proponents had hoped. A visit by a Nisei celebrity and war hero such as Kuroki would undoubtedly boost the internees' spirits—or so thought the planners of the visit. Instead, Kuroki's mission to Minidoka did little more than lay bare the internees' growing disenchantment with the idea of compulsory military service.[18]

Despite the blitz of publicity announcing Kuroki's arrival on May 2, 1944, the crowd that gathered to welcome the war hero at the gate was embarrassingly small and subdued. Only about one hundred fifty of the camp's many thousands of residents showed up, and the majority were Nisei girls. As Kuroki was welcomed by the camp's administrators and the internees' community council, "most of the people only stared at him, dumbly."[19] Kuroki was placed in an army jeep and driven at the head of a ragtag parade through the camp, with Minidoka's Boy Scout bugle corps providing music and various camp administrators trailing behind. By coincidence, Kuroki's arrival precisely coincided with the arrival of the very first group of Minidoka draft inductees, back from Fort Douglas, Utah, as reservists awaiting training and assignment. They fell in at the tail end of the parade for a time, only enhancing the resentful speculation of many internees that Kuroki's visit was nothing but a government ploy to drum up more Nisei bodies for the front lines.

For the next five days, Kuroki was whisked from block to block, giving speeches, playing pickup baseball games, attending dances, and even crowning the high school's May Day Queen. The rather self-effacing technical sergeant gamely played the role of celebrity, even though his discomfort, tiredness, and embarrassment were often apparent. At nearly every event, his reception was cooler, and the turnout lower, than the planners of his visit had expected. At least twice Kuroki's public remarks drew a few boos amidst the tepid applause. One evening the sergeant was bluntly refused admission to a dining hall at dinnertime because he was not a block resident and had to eat his meal in an internee's living quarters. Only one of his addresses was a rousing success, garnering him a five-minute standing ovation from an enthusiastic audience. But, tellingly, this was a speech to the camp's caucasian appointive staff, who were far more receptive than most of the Nikkei to Kuroki's expression of gratitude "that the red blood shed by the Japanese-Americans in Europe and the Pacific areas would be allowed to mingle with the red in the American flag, and thus guarantee to their brothers and sisters the chance to be accepted as real Americans."[20]

Kuroki's mission to Minidoka ultimately did little but expose the rifts that were deepening at the War Relocation Authority's "model camp." For those who thought that the visit was, as one internee put it, "just a pure propaganda exhibition to try and get some of the boys to pull away from the family and join the army," nothing happened to change that impression. To the extent that camp morale improved at all, it did so mostly among Nisei youngsters—schoolchildren and teenage girls. As for the sergeant's most crucial audience, the young men of draft age, the effect of Kuroki's visit was difficult to gauge. Minidoka's community analyst, however, expressed the tentative impression that "they seem to have taken on, at least for the time being, a more positive point of view."

If this impression was accurate, it was unquestionably short-lived. The next month 11 out of 108 inductees—again, just over 10 percent—refused to appear for induction. On other occasions throughout the summer of 1944, more Nisei joined the ranks of those refusing to appear for induction, always at a rate of at least 15 percent of the total number of inductees called. By the end of the summer, a total of thirty-eight Minidokans had opted for resistance. The War Relocation Authority's "model camp" had gone from being its most compliant camp to one of its least.[21]

Minidoka's administrators knew that their camp was faring poorly in the overall effort to produce draftees and took steps—unavailing ones, as it turned out—to contain the virus of noncompliance that was infecting the camp. One strategy was to lobby the local Selective Service board to call suspected antidraft agitators for induction as quickly as possible so that they could be arrested, removed from camp, and thereby silenced. Jim Akutsu, for example, who the camp's administrators were persuaded was urging others to resist the draft, came into possession of a copy of an embarrassing letter written by Minidoka's project location officer in May to the local draft board. The letter "recited, among other things, that the Draft Board had accommodated WRA before in calling troublesome '1A's,'" and asked "that Jimmie Akutsu be called at once."[22] As requested, Jim Akutsu was called at once, charged and arrested when he failed to report in July, and then whisked away to join his brother in the county jail in Boise. A mere six months after Kiyonosuke and Nao Akutsu were reunited, they were suddenly childless.

Another strategy that the administrators urged for stemming the tide of resistance was to prevail upon Idaho's federal prosecutor to arrest the resisters in a troubling and unnecessary way. A federal criminal case is typically initiated by the filing of a complaint, a sworn document alleging the commission of a federal crime. If the alleged crime is a felony, however, the Fifth Amendment to the U.S. Constitution requires the prosecutor to replace the complaint with a formal indictment from a grand jury. It was the prevailing practice in 1944 to arrest a criminal defendant after the grand jury indicted him, rather than when the complaint was filed, unless there was reason to worry that the defendant might flee the jurisdiction before the grand jury could complete its work.[23]

Those who refused to show up for induction at Minidoka did so in the late spring and summer. The grand jury, however, was not scheduled to meet until early September. As a result, those who resisted the draft were charged by complaint when they refused to appear for induction, but were then left free to go about their business in camp. This posed a problem for Minidoka's administrators, who were trying to ensure maximum compliance with the draft laws and were not pleased to have resisters circulating among the general population, dramatizing to others that draft resistance seemed to have no consequences. Minidoka's project director and project attorney grew "concerned over the leaving of the 'evaders' free to go about the Center" and wanted "to prevent possible bad influence of these men upon others."[24] The administrators therefore prevailed upon the local United States attorney to arrest and detain all of the men when their complaints were filed rather than waiting until September. This was a distortion of policy, of course, because it is hard to imagine a criminal defendant who poses a smaller risk of flight than a Japanese American internee living under armed guard and behind barbed wire in a concentration camp. Still, the camp management had its way, and as a result, the Minidoka draft resisters spent much of the summer of 1944 in county jail cells rather than together with their families in their camp quarters.

The Ada County Jail in Boise was certainly a change of scenery for the Minidoka resisters, but it was no vacation. His first night in jail Gene Akutsu saw what he thought were watermelon seeds on his thin mattress. In the morning when he awoke, he was covered with bites. He lifted the mattress and saw that the underside was covered with bed bugs. Killing the bugs, he recalls, took "weeks and weeks." Akutsu's sleep was not helped by the barred windows that the jail left open day and night; daytime was pleasantly warm, but the nights got colder than the single thin blanket he was issued could handle. And the food, Akutsu remembers, was dreadful: "mush and toast, pork and beans," served two times a day. The food got a bit better only when a resister arrived who had been a cook back at Minidoka; he tasted the jail's offerings and volunteered to do the cooking for the Nisei from that point on. The Minidoka resisters' lives droned on in this dreary way through the rest of the summer of 1944, as they awaited the September session of the grand jury.

Noisy Protest: Heart Mountain

Unlike Tule Lake and Minidoka, where the reaction to the reopening of the draft was at least relatively subdued, Heart Mountain quickly gave birth to the best-organized and most articulate resistance movement that ever took shape on any issue at any of the ten WRA camps. An organization called the Fair Play Committee (FPC) sprang into being and quickly captured the camp's attention and sympathies. The WRA and the Justice Department eventually crushed the movement, but not before it succeeded in encouraging eighty-five young men to resist the draft.

The FPC came into being a few weeks before the January 20 announcement of the reopening of the draft. It was founded by Kiyoshi Okamoto, an outspoken and somewhat eccentric Nisei who had been a thorn in the camp administration's side virtually since the camp opened. Okamoto was a slight, bespectacled man in his midfifties who, according to some who knew him, faintly resembled Mahatma Gandhi. He had been openly critical of Heart Mountain's administration on a number of occasions and had vocally opposed registration as a delegate to the rump Congress of American Citizens that had formed itself a year earlier.

Okamoto and several younger Nisei men had begun meeting in December of 1943 to grouse about camp conditions and to try to stimulate discussion among Heart Mountain's citizen internees about the lawfulness of their internment. The younger men were drawn to Okamoto, seeing him as a visionary and a constitutional scholar. Okamoto had no legal training and developed his rather elaborate and sometimes idiosyncratic views on the Bill of Rights and the Constitution entirely from his own study. For this reason, his detractors tended to see him as an "intellectual hobo" and a "latrine lawyer," a man who was "over-radical, unreasonable, irresponsible, and verbose."[25] These labels are, of course, a matter of opinion, but the charge of verbosity was unquestionably well taken. In his rambling writings, Okamoto would never say in a single sentence what he could say in three. Yet for all of their grandiosity, their ersatz erudition, and their verbiage, Okamoto's writings from camp also showed great passion, creativity, and a willingness to speak bluntly that was rare among the Nisei. It was these latter characteristics that, in the eyes of the younger men of the FPC, made him an inspiring figure, an unusual man who was willing to speak his mind publicly and fearlessly, even if it meant angering the powers that be. These were characteristics that were, in the eyes of resister Yosh Kuromiya, utterly "atypical of the quiet, contained Japanese image."

The announcement of the draft presented the fledgling FPC with an extraordinary opportunity, and the organization pounced on it. On Friday, February 8, 1944, just four days after the first orders to report for preinduction physicals arrived in the mail, the FPC held its first public meeting. About sixty Nisei attended and heard speeches from Okamoto and another FPC leader, Paul Nakadate, about the unconstitutionality of the internment and the unfairness of applying the draft to the interned Nisei.[26] The following night the FPC held another public meeting in another block's mess hall, and the numbers in attendance swelled into the hundreds. So, too, did the FPC's membership, which was offered to the camp's Nisei for a payment of $2 in dues. The FPC's leaders were, however, careful to restrict membership to those who professed loyalty to the United States and willingness to serve in the military once their civil rights were restored. They knew that some resisters at other camps had grown so disillusioned with the United States, and perhaps so convinced that their future lay with or in Japan, that they were asking for expatriation and categorically refusing American military service under any conditions. The FPC wished to blunt any suggestion that its members were against the draft out of either fear or pro- Japan feeling; it wanted rather to be seen as a truly loyal opposition.

Through the rest of February and into early March, the FPC held similarly well-attended meetings nearly every night in mess halls all over the camp, at first with the administration's permission and then, once the project director recognized what he saw as the organization's subversive purpose, without it. These meetings were lengthy and sometimes boisterous affairs, typically announced at the last minute by mimeographed circulars that would appear throughout the camp's mess halls. George Nozawa, just barely of draft age and somewhat dazzled by the FPC's show of confidence, remembers these public meetings as being "as lively as pre-rodeo dance halls. The speeches by [the FPC leaders], and then the rebuttals and questions from the audience would go on for hours." The young man was deeply impressed by Okamoto, Nakadate, Frank Emi, and the other older Nisei in the FPC leadership. "For every doubt and apprehension brought up," he recalls, "the [leaders] had an undeniably sound and power-laden reply. The term 'without due process of law' would precede or follow statement after statement." Nozawa was just "totally impressed by the knowledgeable leaders."[27]

Yosh Kuromiya, a contemporary of Nozawa's, also attended a number of FPC meetings. Kuromiya, though, remembers that he was a bit doubtful about the FPC when he first attended. Entering the mess hall, he looked for a familiar face, but saw nobody he knew and sat in the back of the hall between two strangers on a hard wooden bench. From that vantage point, "and with all the smoke in the room, I couldn't see very well, but . . . I was here primarily to hear, not see." Besides, "close access to the rear door was reassuring" to Kuromiya because it allowed him an easy escape "in case I didn't like what I was to hear."

He did like what he heard, at least once Kiyoshi Okamoto stood and began to hold forth. "His language was brutally crude, sprinkled generously with four-letter expletives," Kuromiya recalls, but the young man found the content of Okamoto's speech to be "essentially an articulation of my own deeper thoughts, values, and feelings." Not only that, but Okamoto struck Kuromiya as having "an impressive knowledge of the constitutional law, indispensable in any civil rights forum." That evening Yosh Kuromiya paid his $2 and began attending FPC meetings more regularly, each time sitting "a little closer to the front table." What especially impressed him was the fact that the FPC's leaders were taking risks they did not need to take: "Most were too old for the draft, or had dependents, which would get them easy deferments." One—Guntaro Kubota—was "not even a U.S. citizen, but was concerned with the plight of those who were." Kuromiya knew that these men were courting danger by speaking out against a law that would never apply to them, and he respected them for it.[28]

During this period, the leaders tried to keep the tone informational, knowing that they were risking prosecution if they openly urged noncompliance with the draft. They summed up their message well in a question-and-answer bulletin they mimeographed and distributed throughout the camp on March 1, 1944:

> Q. What's this Fair Play Committee about?
>
> A. The Fair Play Committee (FPC) is organized to inject justice in all the problems pertaining to our evacuation, concentration, detention and pauperization without hearing or due process of law, and oppose all unfair practices within our center, State, or Union.
>
> Q. How do you think it can do just that?

A. By educational process; the use of the press; thru the courts; or if the FPC cannot do it itself, it will work jointly thru outside organizations.
Q. Who can join this organization?
A. Citizens only. . . .
Q. What does the FPC think is the right thing for any loyal American citizen to do in our present status?
A. The FPC believes that the first duty as loyal American citizens is to protect and uphold the Constitution of the United States. THE CORNERSTONE OF THIS INSTRUMENT OF OUR GOVERNMENT IS JUSTICE, LIBERTY, FREEDOM, AND THE PROTECTION OF HUMAN RIGHTS, AND THE DESCRATION [*sic*] OF ANYONE [*sic*] OF THESE IS A DIRECT ATTACK UPON THE FUNDAMENTALS THAT MOULDED [*sic*] OUR DEMOCRATIC INSTITUTION. . . .
Q. What does the FPC think about this present draft program?
A. The FPC believes we have a right to ask that the discriminatory features in regards to this selective service be abolished, our status be clarified, and a full restoration of our rights before being drafted. THIS ABSENCE OF A CLARIFICATION OF OUR STATUS, AND THE LIFTING OF DISCRIMINATORY RESTRICTION [*sic*] IS THE KEYSTONE OF OUR ATTITUDE TOWARDS THE PRESENT PROGRAM OF DRAFTING US FROM THIS CONCENTRATION CAMP. . . .
Q. Do you think that the FPC can succeed in its aims?
A. No guarantee can be made. But, this is the crucial test. If we are successful, it would have been worth every sacrifice we would have made for the right of Niseis and all minorities to enjoy the right [*sic*] and privileges accorded to them in the principles and ideals of the Constitution. To those of you whose heart, whose interests, and whose ideals are with us in these critical times, please lend us your support, morally and materially as this is the only way we can succeed in achieving our aims.[29]

This was vintage Okamoto—a bit vague, long on rhetoric, short on legal precision, and infused with a potent mix of quiet outrage and self-assurance. The document shied away from openly counseling draft resistance, and it also avoided explaining in any detail how opposing the draft would, as a legal matter, call into question the lawfulness of the Nisei's "evacuation, concentration, detention and pauperization without hearing or due process of law." It did, however, shatter the tense silence that hung over the camp on the draft issue and bravely initiated a new kind of public discourse about the lawfulness of the internment. It was very effective pleading in the tense and resentful atmosphere at Heart Mountain. Attendance at the FPC's mess hall meetings continued to grow.

Not everyone at Heart Mountain was taken with the FPC's advocacy. Late in February, the FPC's leaders made an appearance before the Heart Mountain Community Council, the rather stodgy representative body for the internees that had official recognition from the WRA. The council was populated largely by people with JACL attachments or sympathies who knew that the FPC had little regard for the JACL's position supporting the draft.[30] The FPC leaders urged the council to take an aggressive posture against the draft and to endorse the FPC. The council, however, declined the invitation, saying that it had its own committee studying the question. The council eventually put together a rather tepid petition to President Roosevelt that was reminiscent of Min Yasui's at Minidoka; it pledged full support for the draft and politely asked for a reciprocal restoration of rights from the government.[31] But when the council made the petition available for internees to sign at the very end of February, almost nobody did. By that point, the FPC's more assertive stance had largely captured the camp's mood and imagination.

Equally unimpressed by the FPC was Heart Mountain's internee newspaper, the *Heart Mountain Sentinel.* The *Sentinel* was a weekly eight-page newspaper that ran stories of national interest to the internees, stories of goings-on in camp, box scores of camp ballgames, a social column, and the like. It was, at least in theory, independent of the camp administration, but it rarely tested that independence with a story or editorial that seriously challenged WRA policy on an issue of importance, and it was seen by many internees as a mouthpiece for the

WRA and the JACL.[32] Early in March, its editor took the FPC to task in a front-page editorial for daring to oppose the draft. "The American public," wrote the editor, "has the right to know that the majority of nisei and their parents believe wholeheartedly in selective service" and "[t]hat we, as a new race in this nation, cannot and must not be judged by a small, disgruntled group" such as the FPC. Deriding the FPC as an organization "conceived in the mind of one of the center's most persistent and clever trouble-makers" and the young draft resisters as "deluded youths," the *Sentinel* editor expressed his hope that the FPC would "soon be broken and dispersed on the solid rocks of reason and law" and that the Federal Bureau of Investigation (FBI) and the United States attorney would quickly take the resisters into custody.[33]

As the draft controversy moved into the month of March, the *Sentinel* editor's hope showed no signs of being fulfilled. Rumors circulated that the FPC was under investigation, but the group continued to meet in public without hindrance and to post and distribute its circulars and bulletins all over camp. The group also picked up the strong editorial support of the *Sentinel*'s rival publication, a Denver newspaper for the Japanese American community called the *Rocky Shimpo*. The *Shimpo* was the most widely read newspaper at Heart Mountain. Late in February, the leadership of the FPC had begun sending news of the organization's activities and copies of its writings to the *Shimpo*'s English language editor, Jimmie Omura. (The *Shimpo* published in both English and Japanese.) Omura had been at the helm of the *Shimpo* for only a short time, but had written and worked for years in the Japanese American press and was known as one of the JACL's fiercest and most vocal critics. Omura began running editorials that questioned the lawfulness and propriety of applying the draft to the interned Nisei, as well as news items that reported favorably on the FPC's activities at Heart Mountain. These pieces not only bolstered the credibility of the FPC in the eyes of many camp residents, but also boosted the *Shimpo*'s popularity and increased its camp circulation by 20 percent.[34]

With favorable reports in the press and a burgeoning membership list, the FPC reached the peak of its prestige in the first two weeks of March 1944. Emboldened by the seeming indifference of the camp's administration, the FPC's leaders decided to abandon any pretense that they were merely educating the Nisei about broad principles of law and justice, and instead to state clearly that they planned to defy the draft. In a March 4 circular, the FPC made its case for resistance in forceful terms, set out underneath a banner quoting the Fifth Amendment's Due Process and Takings Clauses and the Thirteenth Amendment's prohibition on involuntary servitude:

> We, the Nisei have been complacent and too inarticulate to the unconstitutional acts that we were subjected to. If ever there was a time or cause for decisive action, IT IS NOW!
>
> We, the members of the FPC are not afraid to go to war—we are not afraid to risk our lives for our country. We would gladly sacrifice our lives to protect and uphold the principles and ideals of our country as set forth in the Constitution and the Bill of Rights, for on its inviolability depends the freedom, liberty, justice, and protection of all people including Japanese-Americans and all other minority groups. But have we been given such freedom, such liberty, such justice, such protection? NO!! Without any hearings, without due process of law as guaranteed by the Constitution and Bill of Rights, without any charges filed against us, without any evidence of wrongdoing on our part, one hundred and ten thousand innocent people were kicked out of their homes, literally uprooted from where they have lived for the greater part of their life, and herded like dangerous criminals into concentration camps with barb [*sic*] wire fence and military police guarding it, AND THEN, WITHOUT RECTIFICATION OF THE INJUSTICES COMMITTED AGAINST US NOR WITHOUT [*sic*] RESTORATION OF OUR RIGHTS AS GUARANTEED BY THE CONSTITUTION, WE ARE ORDERED TO JOIN THE ARMY THRU *DISCRIMINATORY PROCEDURES* INTO A *SEGREGATED COMBAT UNIT!*

"Is that the American way?" the circular asked rhetorically. Then, having described the injustices the Nisei had suffered in such powerful terms, the circular went on to urge defiance of the draft laws:

> The FPC believes that unless such actions are opposed *NOW*, and steps taken to remedy such injustices and discrimina-

> tions *IMMEDIATELY*, the future of all minorities and the future of this democratic nation is in danger.
>
> Thus, the members of the FPC unanimously decided at their last open meeting that until we are restored all our rights, all discriminatory features of the Selective Service abolished, and measures retaken to remedy the past injustices thru Judicial pronouncement or Congressional act, we feel that the present program of drafting us from this concentration camp is unjust, unconstitutional, and against all principles of civilized usage, therefore, WE, MEMBERS OF THE FAIR PLAY COMMITTEE *HEREBY REFUSE TO GO TO THE PHYSICAL EXAMINATION OR TO THE INDUCTION* IF OR WHEN WE ARE CALLED IN ORDER TO *CONTEST THE ISSUE.*[35]

And so there it was: for the first time, the FPC was openly and plainly stating that it planned to violate the draft laws and at least implying that others should do the same.

The FPC's new and more forceful message quickly took root. On Monday, March 6, 1944, two young men refused to get on the bus to Cheyenne, Wyoming, for their preinduction physicals. The next day three more refused. And to the glee of the FPC, the camp administration did nothing to censure these five men. They were briefly questioned and then released to return to their barracks. On Tuesday evening, the five seemingly victorious resisters took center stage at a standing-room-only public meeting of the FPC. They told the crowd that they had been questioned and released, and it was clear to everyone in attendance that these young men were still at liberty—or at least the comparative liberty of the barbed wire enclosure at Heart Mountain. The effect of this display was to enhance the FPC's stature: many Nisei left the meeting saying, "See? Nothing really happens if you don't report. The Fair Play Committee will take care of you."[36] The next day, Wednesday, seven more men refused to board the bus, bringing the week's total of resisters to twelve.

Yosh Kuromiya received his notice to report for a preinduction physical on March 16, 1944. He regarded the notice "as yet another insult." "How could I continue to go along with this morally corrupt charade?" he asked himself. Kuromiya felt that he was "being asked, not to serve in defense of my country, but in a war of aggression in foreign lands, ostensibly for principles I was denied here at home," and all of this was "presented as an opportunity to 'prove my loyalty.'" Kuromiya could not abide what was being demanded of him.

Kuromiya thought about cheating. "Should I take *shoyu* (soy sauce)?" he asked himself. Rumors were circulating through camp that "some of the fellows were flunking their medical exams by taking heavy doses of *shoyu* just before their exams." Kuromiya knew that he could pull this off easily; his father worked in the block's mess hall, and "they probably wouldn't miss a few bottles anyway." But Kuromiya did not know how to ask him. More important, even if his father agreed to slip him the soy, Kuromiya did not know if he "would . . . ever be able to look him in the face again."

The next FPC meeting Kuromiya attended was mobbed. The crowd "was well over the fire restriction capacity for the building, perhaps by as much as 50 percent." In keeping with its new, more brazen image, the FPC's leaders "called for a show of hands of those who [had] received their pre-induction notices since the last meeting." Kuromiya, by now sitting at the very front of the room, put up his hand and turned to notice that perhaps a dozen others also had their hands raised. A leader then asked the young man, "perhaps because I was at the closest table, what I intended to do about it." Kuromiya "stood up and explained [that] I was instructed to be on the bus to Powell on the morning of the 23rd [of March]." Feeling the pressure of "a million eyes" on him, he then declared, "I will *not* be on that bus." The crowd greeted Kuromiya's announcement with "a sudden cheer that rattled the windows." Kuromiya, overwhelmed by the moment, felt his knees buckle and thumped back down onto the bench beneath him. Kuromiya knew that he "had passed the point of no return" and that "there would be no turning back."[37]

Around the time that Kuromiya was making his mess hall declaration, the *Rocky Shimpo* for March 10 arrived by mail at Heart Mountain, bearing the banner headline "WYOMING DRAFT RESISTANCE HAS AUTHORITIES STUMPED." The article reported that "[f]ederal [a]uthorities and W.R.A. administrative staff members were said to be facing a baffling problem . . . arising from the refusal this week of five members of the Fair Play Committee to appear for pre-induction physical examination." Penned by Omura on the basis of a "special exclusive dispatch to the paper" that could have come only from the leadership of the Fair Play Committee, the article recounted the story of the first five resisters' questioning and release by camp officials. "[F]ederal authorities and camp officials are said to be obviously stumped as to how to proceed in the matter," the article maintained. "The replies offered by the five draft protestors seemingly have created a baffling problem and a delicate one."[38] And, indeed, that was just how the situation must have appeared to the FPC and its leaders in those heady days of early March. To all appearances, the draft resistance movement at Heart Mountain was bringing the Selective Service System to a standstill and the WRA to its knees.

Those appearances were deeply deceiving. In reality, as the FPC's influence and Jimmie Omura's readership grew, the War Relocation Authority and the Department of Justice—with help from the JACL—were gearing up to use WRA regulations and the federal criminal process to crush Heart Mountain's draft resistance movement and to silence Jimmie Omura and the FPC. By the end of March, dozens of young men from Heart Mountain would be behind bars in jails across Wyoming. By mid-April, Omura would be out of his job at the *Rocky Shimpo,* and by early May, the leadership of the FPC and Jimmie Omura would all be under federal indictment in Cheyenne, Wyoming, charged with conspiring to counsel draft evasion.

Although the camp administration kept a low profile throughout the month of February 1944 and did not try to forbid the FPC from meeting until mid-March, Project Director Guy Robertson and his staff were deeply concerned about how events were unfolding virtually from the start. On February 19, as the camp began to turn its attention to the FPC's early efforts at educating the Nisei about the wrongs of the internment and the unfairness of the draft, Robertson instructed his staff to undertake an educational counteroffensive. The schools were to have lessons on the Selective Service laws; camp administrators were to try "to have Selective Service discussed in church groups"; community meetings were to be scheduled to offer the internees information on the draft.[39] A few days later, just moments after the FPC leaders made their appeal for support to the community council, the camp's assistant project director appeared before the council, "express[ing a] desire to suppress any infavorable movement in this center concerning re-institution of the draft status for nisei, which might create further enemies, destroy[ ] friends, and alienat[e] feeling among [the] general public to the evacuees and subject [them] to acute criticism." He warned the council that Heart Mountain's residents had "a serious responsibility" to think carefully about the implications of resisting the draft and to try "to reach [the] right solution" and keep "this matter of the draft" from "go[ing] too far."[40] Of course, the administration-friendly council needed no such warning; it was prepared to endorse the draft. The assistant project director was really trying to speak through the council to the thousands of Heart Mountain residents who were beginning to pay more careful attention to the antidraft message of the FPC than to the prodraft sentiments of the camp administration, the JACL, and the *Heart Mountain Sentinel.*

As time passed and the FPC grew in stature, the camp administration grew more alarmed and began raising the specter of criminal prosecution. At a March 11 meeting of the camp's top administrative staff, the assistant project director explained that the government had a procedure in place for investigating and prosecuting those who failed to show up for their preinduction physicals. Under that procedure, any man failing to report for his physical was immediately reported to the FBI. The FBI would contact the delinquent's draft board to make sure that there were no pending appeals of his draft status and that all of his paperwork was in order. If everything in the delinquent's file was in order and there were no unresolved appeals, the draft board would issue an immediate call for the delinquent's induction. If he then defied the call for induction, his case would be presented to a federal grand jury, and if he was indicted, he would be prosecuted for evading the draft.[41] The assistant project director made clear that this procedure had already been set in motion for the twelve men who had thus far failed to appear for their physicals. He also indicated that he would explain the mechanics of criminal prosecution to the internees' community council so that council members could publicize it to the internees generally. When he did so later that day, his presentation was prominently featured in the *Heart Mountain Sentinel.* The administration wanted the FPC's members to get the message that they were risking disaster by flirting with noncompliance.

As it turned out, within days of the staff meeting at which the prosecution plan was presented, the project director began urging the Department of Justice to change it. The plan did not envision prosecuting delinquents merely for failing to show up for their physicals; it required the local draft board to take an additional step and issue a formal call for induction into the military. Only when the draftee refused that later call would he be prosecuted. The reason for this two-step process was strategic: as the assistant project director explained at the March 11 staff meeting, if the delinquent refused to report for induction, "the Army w[ould] have a stronger case than apprehending the boy when he [was] just called for a pre-induction physical."[42] Between the missed physical and the defied call for induction, weeks would pass—weeks in which the resister would remain in camp, circulating among his fellow internees as a living symbol of the government's apparent inaction and lack of resolve.

Indeed, that was precisely what had occurred on Tuesday, March 7, when the first five resisters were showcased at an FPC meeting. Their appearance had emboldened the FPC and spurred seven more men to resist the very next day. Project Director Robertson recognized that if the government did not move against the resisters immediately and wrest control of the draft issue from the FPC, he might well lose control of the camp entirely. He therefore contacted Carl Sackett, the United States Attorney for the District of Wyoming, and asked that the resisters be arrested right away for failing to report for their preinduction physicals.

Carl Sackett would end up prosecuting the Heart Mountain draft resisters and the leadership of the FPC and would make clear in those trials that he had no sympathy whatsoever for them and saw them as traitors. He did, however, object to Robertson's request that the resisters be arrested and jailed immediately. Sackett explained to Robertson that the next federal grand jury for the District of Wyoming would not meet in Cheyenne until the first week of May. Even if his office were to charge the delinquents immediately by complaint, Department of Justice policy would not call for their arrest until after the grand jury indicted them unless there was a risk that they might flee the jurisdiction before indictment. Plainly, the Heart Mountain draft resisters presented no risk of flight; they were behind barbed wire and under U.S. Army guard. Sackett said he would not have the resisters arrested until May.

This was not a satisfactory response for Robertson; he had a relocation center to run and needed the troublemakers out immediately. He therefore complained to Dillon Myer at the WRA in Washington, asking the WRA to intercede with the Justice Department. Myer recognized the risks that the resisters posed to the draft program and to the orderly administration of the Heart Mountain Relocation Center and had the WRA's solicitor (its chief legal counsel), Philip Glick, contact the Justice Department to do Robertson's bidding. Glick was able to persuade an assistant attorney general of the need for prompt action, and as a result, Carl Sackett was ordered by his superiors in Washington to file complaints against the resisters and have them arrested as soon as they defied their orders to report for their physicals rather than waiting either for the grand jury to return indictments or for the resisters to receive and defy an actual call for induction into the armed forces. This directive worried Sackett; he saw no good reason to deviate from department policy and would have preferred to wait and move against the resisters for disobeying eventual calls for induction. But Sackett's concerns did not win the day.[43] In the contest between sound prosecutorial policy and the WRA's quest for order in camp, the WRA's interests prevailed.

On Saturday, March 18, 1944, while still pressing for early arrests, the project director decided to take his fight directly to the FPC in camp by forbidding the organization to schedule any further public meetings. This shot across the FPC's bow triggered an angry response from the organization. Its leaders sent a bitter letter of complaint to Robertson, accusing him of arbitrary and dictatorial action that violated the Constitution, and also sent a letter to the secretary of the interior in Washington, demanding Robertson's removal. This letter, which Jimmie Omura reported in the *Rocky Shimpo,* caused something of a stir in camp. So, too, did the FPC's open defiance of Robertson's ban on public meetings; the organization continued to meet in the mess halls despite Robertson's prohibition, and the administration did nothing to stop it. Again, for a time it appeared that the FPC had the upper hand.

All of that changed for good, however, during the week that began on Saturday, March 25, 1944. On that day, late in the afternoon, agents from the U.S. Marshals Service descended upon Heart Mountain to arrest the first group of twelve young men who, two weeks earlier, had refused to show up for their physicals. Pulling up to the resisters' barracks in huge black automobiles, the marshals took the Nisei into custody without incident. Issei parents choked back tears of anger, indignation, and shame as they watched their sons carted off to jail.

Even though the delinquents themselves had been alerted that they would be arrested, Heart Mountain's community analyst recorded that the arrests "seemed to come as a shock" to the rest of the camp. "People appeared to be sort of stunned," he wrote. "There was tenseness but no great excitement. Nor was there much discussion one way or the other." There was mostly just that shock that "*it*"—the arrest of some resisters—"had happened."[44]

The arrests did not dampen the spirits of the FPC, however. Over the next several days, twenty-five more young men refused to report for their physical examinations. In addition, Sam Horino, Frank Emi, and Min Tamesa, three of the FPC's leaders, tried to walk out of the camp's front gate without a pass in order to prove that they were not free citizens. They were arrested by military police, and Emi and Tamesa were held in military custody for several days.[45]

The project director met these additional acts of resistance with punishing blows of his own. He quickly arranged to have Kiyoshi Okamoto and Sam Horino brought before him for what he euphemistically called "leave clearance hearings," but were in fact full-blown interrogations about the activities of the FPC. These hearings were utter shams; neither Okamoto nor Horino had applied for any sort of leave from Heart Mountain. Project Director Robertson nonetheless denied them the leave clearance for which they had not applied and ordered them shipped off for indefinite segregation with the "disloyals" at Tule Lake. Within hours, they were gone, victims of the camp director's manipulation of the WRA's leave regulations.

Robertson's abuse of the leave clearance process was egregious enough to draw the attention of the American Civil Liberties Union (ACLU). Up to this point, the ACLU had kept itself at a careful and rather disdainful distance from the resisters. It had refused Okamoto's request to represent the FPC, publicly—and embarrassingly—announcing that the resisters had "a strong moral case, but no legal case at all." But Robertson's mistreatment of Okamoto and Horino spurred Roger Baldwin, the ACLU's national director, to write to Robertson in early April of 1944, inquiring about the summary transfers to Tule Lake. In response, Robertson explained to Baldwin that Okamoto's case was "a peculiar one." Okamoto, said Robertson, was "a shrewd person, very much embittered because of the evacuation and what he considers loss of rights and, consequently, . . . his own worst enemy." Robertson noted that Okamoto had helped "interfere" with the registration program a year earlier, was "very voluble and bitter in his denunciation of the United States government for carrying out the evacuation," and claimed not to care whether Japan or the United States won the war. "Action was taken on [Okamoto's] case," Robertson summarized, because he "would certainly be a poor representative of the evacuees on the outside and might generally interfere with the relocation program." The project director concluded with a gratuitous word of reassurance: "We do not," he said, "deny leave clearance and send people to Tule Lake merely for disciplinary reasons."[46]

This defense was evidently enough for Baldwin; the ACLU did not pursue the matter further. But the defense was also phony. In an April 25 letter to J. Edgar Hoover, WRA Director Dillon Myer thanked the FBI director for the FBI's help in investigating the "difficulties which [had] developed [at Heart Mountain] during the last month or so incident to the re-institution of Selective Service for American citizens of Japanese ancestry." The FBI's investigation, Myer explained, "ha[d] uncovered a considerable amount of information which should be useful to the War Relocation Authority in maintaining discipline at the Center and in determining what persons should be transferred to the Segregation Center at Tule Lake." Myer asked Hoover for a copy of the FBI's final report on the FPC, expressing confidence that "the privilege of using the report . . . would assist us materially in maintaining order in the [Heart Mountain Relocation] Center."[47]

"Maintaining order" was the true explanation for Robertson's bogus denial of "leave clearance" to Kiyoshi Okamoto, who had been an irritant at Heart Mountain for over a year. At the time Robertson ordered Okamoto to Tule Lake, the project director had already been trying to break the draft resistance movement by securing the early arrest of the young resisters themselves, even if the Justice Department had to set aside sound procedure and strategy to do so. He could not get Okamoto out of camp on draft evasion charges; Okamoto was far too old for the draft. The leave clearance process was thus Robertson's only method to rid himself of Okamoto and restore order in camp, and that is the one he used.

By the end of March 1944, forty-one young Nisei were in county jails across Wyoming awaiting trial on draft evasion charges. Two of the FPC's leaders were in isolation at Tule Lake, and two others had spent several days under military arrest at Heart Mountain. Anti-FPC editorials and news items continued to appear in the *Heart Mountain Sentinel,* and the camp administration began arranging patriotic send-off ceremonies for the Nisei who had complied with the draft and were leaving for induction. Finally, with the help of the JACL, the WRA arranged for a five-day publicity visit to Heart Mountain by Nisei war hero Ben Kuroki.[48] Thus, even though the number of Heart Mountain resisters would eventually rise to eighty-five, the ascendancy of the FPC was at an end. Through propaganda, bogus denials of leave clearance, and speeded-up arrests of the resisters, the WRA and the Department of Justice managed to squelch the draft resistance movement at Heart Mountain.

The efforts of the WRA and the Department of Justice did not stop at the perimeter of the Heart Mountain Relocation Center, however. Jimmie Omura, the Denver newspaperman who had covered the FPC story, remained at the editor's desk of the *Rocky Shimpo.* Even though he had never visited Heart Mountain, had never met any of the members of the FPC, and enjoyed the First Amendment's protection of the freedom of the press, the government went after him as well.

The *Rocky Shimpo* and Jimmie Omura had come to the government's attention well before the draft controversy erupted in the early spring of 1944. As early as mid-1942, the *Rocky Shimpo* (under an earlier name, the *Rocky Nippon,* and under Issei ownership) had come under surveillance by a number of government agencies, including the Special War Policies Unit of the Department of Justice's War Division, the FBI, and the Post Office Department. "An examination of numerous past issues," wrote a Department of Justice attorney in September of 1942, "indicate[d] a seditious tendency on the part of the editors."[49] Scrutiny of the paper mounted throughout 1942 and into the summer of 1943, when the government decided to place the newspaper under the supervision of the Office of the Alien Property Custodian, the government office responsible for managing all enemy-owned property.[50] The government wanted to keep a close eye on the paper, to make sure that it published nothing seditious.

Jimmie Omura first emerged as a person of government concern early in 1943, long before he actually had a job with the *Rocky Shimpo,* when he began writing columns for the *Rocky Nippon.* Many of those early columns were openly antagonistic to the JACL and its stance of cooperation with the removal and internment of the West Coast Nikkei. This was what first brought Omura to the government's attention; in a handwritten note penned in late February of 1943, a Justice Department lawyer reacted to Omura's criticisms of the JACL by formally urging that "analysts should watch" the paper's objections to the JACL's activities.[51]

When the government announced the reopening of the draft to the Nisei, Omura quickly found himself in a very public war of words with two publications that supported the government's policy—the *Heart Mountain Sentinel* and the JACL's newspaper, the *Pacific Citizen.* In a March 19 editorial, Omura castigated the *Sentinel* for its stance against the FPC, which he phrased a "malicious attack[ ]."[52] The *Sentinel* responded in kind, laying the blame for the FPC's successes at Omura's feet and expressing its wish that Omura would be indicted for sedition. A few days later Omura blasted the president of the JACL, Saboru Kido, for a prodraft column Kido had published in the *Pacific Citizen,* in which Kido had taken Omura to task for publishing what Kido deemed a "misleading" story about the FPC and its legal position. Omura took offense at the "inference of sedition made in Mr. Kido's article" and speculated that the JACL president "would enjoy nothing better than to silence *The Rocky Shimpo* on such a charge."[53]

This sounds like faintly paranoid speculation, but it was not. In a mid-April letter to WRA Director Dillon Myer, an officer in the WRA's Denver office explained to his boss that "the JACL . . . was working hand and [*sic*] glove with the FBI to hang Omura if they possibly can." The writer also offered Myer his assessment that "[i]t would certainly appear desirable for the benefit of all of the War Relocation Authority centers and the persons of Japanese ancestry, whether in centers or out of centers, to do all that we can to have the Alien Property Custodian either close the *Shimpo* down entirely, or change its editorial writers."[54]

This is precisely what the government set about to do. Early in April, another Denver WRA officer opened discussions with the *Rocky Shimpo*'s attorney, identifying several of Omura's pieces as arguably seditious. The paper's attorney, quickly sensing that the WRA wished Omura out as the English language editor, volunteered that "the editorial policy of the paper would improve if a new editor were installed."

The WRA officer responded that "it would, since the troublesome articles did not appear in the *Shimpo* until Jimmie Omura became editor."[55] Shortly after this discussion, the alien property custodian ordered the *Rocky Shimpo* to have Omura alter his stance on the draft to one of support. Omura, sensing that his job was on the line, urgently contacted the leaders of the FPC and asked them publicly to exonerate him of any connection with, or responsibility for, the FPC's antidraft activities. The FPC complied, but it was too late. At the end of March, a representative of the alien property custodian appeared at the *Rocky Shimpo*'s offices and threatened to close the newspaper down if Omura was not immediately removed as English language editor.[56] Recognizing that he had no choice, Omura resigned. He was promptly replaced in the English language section by a Nisei editor who had been screened by the WRA for his "attitude toward the United States government."[57] Thus, the government not only silenced one of its few vocal Nisei critics, but also managed to install in his place a much friendlier editor who was prepared to throw the support of the ostensibly independent *Rocky Shimpo* behind the draft and the relocation program.[58]

But the government was not finished with Jimmie Omura, and neither was the JACL. On May 10, 1944, a federal grand jury in Cheyenne, Wyoming, returned a sealed indictment charging Omura and seven of the FPC's leaders with conspiring to counsel, aid, and abet young men at Heart Mountain to evade the draft. As to the FPC's leaders, the theory of the conspiracy indictment was that Okamoto, Horino, Nakadate, Emi, and several others had illegally counseled draft evasion through the meetings they sponsored and the circulars they distributed at Heart Mountain. As to Omura, the charge of conspiracy hung entirely on Omura's publication of news stories about the draft resistance movement at Heart Mountain and editorials supporting the FPC's position that the Nisei deserved restoration of their civil rights before complying with the draft. The only alleged links between the FPC leaders and their supposed co-conspirator Jimmie Omura were the news items, circulars, and letters that they sent to him at the *Rocky Shimpo.* There was no suggestion that Omura had ever met, or even spoken to, any of the Heart Mountain men. Neither was there any indication that the young men who resisted the draft at Heart Mountain had ever even read Omura's writings, let alone considered them when deciding whether to comply with the draft. For these reasons, Carl Sackett, the United States attorney for the District of Wyoming and the man who had drafted the indictment, was quite worried about the strength of his case, especially against Omura.[59]

He got some help, however, from the Japanese American Citizens League. On April 28, 1944, two JACL leaders from Denver, Joe Masaoka and Min Yasui (who had been released from Minidoka and had thrown himself firmly behind the JACL's cause), presented themselves at Carl Sackett's office, asking for permission to visit and interview the Heart Mountain draft resisters in the county jail awaiting trial. In the report they later prepared—ostensibly just for the JACL's national office—on their meetings with Sackett and the resisters, the two JACL men explained that "[b]y interviewing the boys in the Cheyenne County Jail," they hoped to gain "some indication of the processes of thinking and the manner of organization behind the draft resistance . . . , so as to be able to work the best procedures and the most practical programs to counteract such influences in the relocation centers."[60] Of course, Masaoka and Yasui knew that only the War Relocation Authority had the ability to arrange and authorize such programs and procedures and were careful to include in their report a number of recommended steps for the WRA to take. And promptly upon completing the report, they mailed a copy off to the War Relocation Authority. Thus, when Yasui and Masaoka asked for permission to interrogate the Heart Mountain resisters, they were certainly operating with the WRA's interests in mind and were quite possibly functioning as informal agents of the WRA.

During their meeting with Sackett, however, they offered the prosecutor some help as well. Yasui and Masaoka began the meeting by suggesting that "the action of these boys was not a deliberate and intentional act of disloyalty, but rather an . . . ill-advised protest against the injustices and suspension of certain civil rights for the past two years suffered by those of Japanese ancestry." Sackett made clear to them that he did not care what their motives were and thought them all disloyal. He minced no words. "These boys," he told Masaoka and Yasui, "are a detriment to the war effort and are sabotaging this country in the present war." He said that he "had more respect for the man who would declare his loyalty to another country openly." Sackett believed that these boys "were merely exploiting the matter of this 'protest refusal' as a cover, pretext, and excuse" and that "when they were given an opportunity to demonstrate their loyalty" to the United States, "they had come out into the open regarding their real loyalties."

Sackett undoubtedly felt quite secure in his self-appointed role as judge of the American loyalties of the Heart Mountain resisters. Sackett himself came from the oldest American stock.[61] He traced his lineage, along one paternal line, to "the same blood as George Washington" and, along another, to brothers named John and Simon Sackett, who had "crossed the ocean in the good ship Lyon, in company with Roger Williams and bride Mary, and 26 Puritan colonists, about ten years after the Pilgrim Fathers landed at Plymouth, Mass." According to information that Carl Sackett kept in his office files, his forebear Simon both "laid the foundation of Cambridge, . . . Mass. in 1631" and sired "the first white child born in Cambridge . . . in 1632." The Wyoming prosecutor liked to boast that his ancestors had fought in the Revolutionary War, the French and Indian Wars, what he called "The Battle of the Frontier" (by which he meant the nation's enduring hostilities with the various Indian tribes who stood in the way of its Manifest Destiny), and every other major war in American history.

Sackett's life had been the stuff of American fable. According to a family history that the prosecutor wrote, his father and mother had struck out from their home in Illinois in 1872 for the West, "to the open range country where the buffalo were grazing and moving in vast numbers from Texas to the [C]anadian border." Sackett's father roamed the Black Hills of South Dakota as a buffalo hunter, while his wife tended a small frontier home in western Nebraska. Carl was born in February of 1876 "with no doctor available in a sod house by the last main buffalo trail at Driftwood in southwestern Nebraska." At the age of four, his parents again set off westward in wagons to find better quarters and settled on a tract of land along a branch of the Hanna Creek in north central Wyoming in the place that would become the town of Big Horn. There they spent the winter in a rough-hewn log cabin, with snow piling up outside "as high as a small boy's arms." Soon they moved into a larger home and took up farming and ranching. Young Carl started school in 1881 at the age of five in a converted trapper's cabin with a dirt floor, a low chimney that filled the cabin with smoke when the wind blew, several split log benches, a few slates for writing, and the handful of books that the settlers had brought with them. Even in these meager surroundings, however, the boy excelled, and by the age of twenty-six, he graduated with his LL.B. from the Ohio State University. He returned to Wyoming to practice law in 1902, just a few miles from his boyhood ranch in the growing town of Sheridan. He served two terms as Sheridan's city attorney, was elected to the Wyoming House of Representatives in 1919, served as first vice president of the Sheridan Trust & Savings Bank, and was appointed Wyoming's United States Attorney by the newly elected President Franklin Delano Roosevelt in 1933.

Carl Sackett very much looked the part of the frontier lawman. Thin and a bit hawklike, he proudly wore the hat and boots of his ranch upbringing. To the two Nisei from the JACL who met with him on that late April day, Sackett was an emblem of egalitarian justice, the keeper of what they described as the tradition of "the old West, where a man's worth and conduct, rather than his antecedents, counted in the estimation of men." This was undoubtedly an attractive image to Masaoka and Yasui, two men trying hard to step out of what they saw as the shadow cast by their own "antecedents." Yet their assessment of Sackett was probably mistaken. Sackett was quick to peg a man by his national origin. For example, when the U.S. Supreme Court reversed the espionage conviction of a pro-Nazi agitator by a five-to-four vote, Sackett derided the Court's majority opinion as "the decision of one Irishman" because Justice Frank Murphy had written it.[62] A man's antecedents mattered a great deal to Carl Sackett.

The JACL men, however, admired Sackett, and once they had heard the prosecutor's assessment of the Heart Mountain resisters as traitors, they saw an opportunity to strike at the FPC's leaders and at their old nemesis Jimmie Omura. Coyly, they suggested to the prosecutor that "the boys were victims of misinformation and incorrect advice."[63] Sackett evidently understood the gist of their suggestion; he "declared that there might be grounds for a possible conspiracy charge against the malefactors." Masaoka and Yasui then asked for permission to question the jailed resisters. Sackett responded by noting that others had applied to him for permission to visit the boys in jail and that he had denied every other request. But he told Masaoka and Yasui that he would make an exception for the two of them and let them in to question the boys. Thus, while their report does not say so explicitly, it suggests that the JACL men and Sackett reached an understanding that day: the JACL men would do some intelligence gathering for the prosecutor to help him build his conspiracy case against Omura and the leadership of the FPC.

Masaoka and Yasui's conduct of the actual interviews tended to confirm this understanding. To be sure, they spent much of their time doing the information gathering for the WRA that they described as their main purpose, "probing into the basic attitudes of the boys" on the draft, their internment experience, and their sources of moral and financial support. At a certain point in each interview, however, Masaoka and Yasui turned the questioning to the FPC leaders and to Jimmie Omura, asking whether the resisters had been influenced by the FPC leaders and whether they had read and relied upon Omura's articles and editorials in the *Rocky Shimpo.* Masaoka and Yasui ultimately made little headway in this area, later reporting that "[a]ll, without exception, emphatically reiterated that his decision to refuse to report for the pre-induction physical was his own personal decision, influenced by no other persons. Each seemed to be aware that any other admission would implicate some other person." Even this admission, however, reflects on Masaoka and Yasui's purpose in posing the questions in the first place: they were unquestionably seeking incriminatory information against the FPC and Omura.

It is not known whether the JACL men sent a copy of their report to the United States attorney or the FBI, as they did to the WRA.[64] It is, however, exceedingly likely that they did because they included in their report a number of recommendations that could have been only for the prosecutor's eyes. The most chilling of these was a recommendation by the JACL leaders that each of the young resisters be held alone in his own cell rather than together with his fellow Nisei. "It seems," they wrote, "that the incarceration of these boys in one group bolsters and inspirits each other [*sic*]. . . . Those who might want to change their minds, convinced of the error of their ways, would probably not be tolerated" by the others. "For these reasons," Masaoka and Yasui advised, "separate and individual cells would allow considerable introspection and self-analysis. It would supplant individual decision for group pressure." This was plainly a recommendation that the named recipient of the report, the JACL's national office, was in no position to do anything about. Only the prosecutor could arrange for this sort of psychological pressure. Thus, it seems clear that Joe Masaoka and Min

Yasui of the JACL lent a helping hand to the government not just in fighting the spread of draft resistance in the internment camps, but also in jailing the resisters, their leaders, and a newspaperman who had dared to criticize their organization. When a WRA official reported that "[t]he JACL, Joe Masaoka particularly, is working hand and [*sic*] glove with the FBI to hang Omura if they possibly can," he was undoubtedly referring to these sorts of hidden efforts.[65]

By June of 1944, then, a total of sixty-three young men from the Heart Mountain Relocation Center were in jails across Wyoming, awaiting a joint trial on charges of evading the draft for insisting upon the restoration of their civil rights as a precondition to military service. The leadership of the FPC and Jimmie Omura of the *Rocky Shimpo* were under a sealed indictment for conspiracy to counsel draft evasion, and the government was hard at work building its case against them. The battle over the drafting of the interned Nisei had come to an end within the barbed wire confines of the Heart Mountain Relocation Center, just as it had come to an end at Minidoka and Tule Lake. But it was about to begin again, this time in federal district courtrooms across the West.

SIX JAILS WITHIN JAILS

On October 14, 1944, an item in an internal Department of Justice newsletter caught the eye of Attorney General Francis Biddle. The item reported that Judge T. Blake Kennedy of the U.S. District Court for the District of Wyoming had recently sentenced the sixty-three Heart Mountain draft resisters to three-year terms in federal prison. Biddle was concerned enough by Judge Kennedy's action to write a brief memorandum to Herbert Wechsler, his assistant attorney general in charge of the Justice Department's War Division. "Does not this" case, he asked of his assistant, "involve the constitutionality of the whole program" of detaining Japanese Americans in concentration camps? This was a touchy subject for Biddle. Not only had the "constitutionality of the whole program" been argued before the U.S. Supreme Court just a few days earlier,[1] but also Biddle had opposed the mass deportation and internment of the Nikkei from the start. Biddle did not mask his displeasure with the outcome of the Wyoming draft cases. "It seems to me," he wrote to Wechsler, "that the sentences were pretty stiff."[2]

Wechsler, who would go on to become one of the leading constitutional scholars of his generation, responded to the attorney general in a memorandum two weeks later.[3] He argued that the attorney general's concern for the length of the resisters' sentences was misplaced. The three-year sentences they had received, he pointed out, were no stiffer than average for conscientious objectors—missing entirely the fact that the Nisei resisters were not in fact conscientious objectors. On the larger question of the lawfulness of drafting internees, though, Wechsler agreed with his boss. He noted that "many of these individuals refused to serve in the armed forces on the ground that they had been denied their rights as American citizens and therefore had no obligation to serve if the covenant of citizenship was first broken by the Government." But, he said, "the [Justice Department's] Criminal Division [was] prepared to argue on . . . appeal that the validity of detention in a relocation center is irrelevant and is no excuse for failure to report for preinduction physical examination." "On this theory," he concluded, "the validity of the detention program will not be directly involved, though the legal issue seems to me quite as difficult as you suggest."[4]

This exchange of memoranda reveals that the Nisei draft resisters found some sympathy somewhere in the Justice Department. But, ironically, they found it only at the Department's very highest levels—in the attorney general himself and in one of his brightest assistants—and only after the resisters were already in prison. Through the summer and fall of 1944, federal prosecutors in a number of western states openly scoffed at the notion that drafting the interned Nisei might implicate what their boss in Washington called "the constitutionality of the whole program." And, with a single exception in California, judges and juries joined them in the scoffing, sometimes, as in Wyoming, after more-or-less fair trials and sometimes, as in Idaho, after sham ones.

The Heart Mountain Draft Resisters in the District of Wyoming

The Trial of the Resisters

At the end of March 1944, with many of the Heart Mountain resisters under arrest and their trial pending, the Honorable T. Blake Kennedy sat down to write a letter to an old friend. Kennedy, nearly seventy years old, was Wyoming's lone federal district judge, and had been for more than twenty years. Kennedy wrote to his friend about his frustrations with his judicial calendar. He complained of having spent an inordinate amount of time sitting by special assignment in Salt Lake City, Utah, for the trial of some Mormon polygamists. Then, he wrote, "[i]n addition to all this trouble I have . . . coming up at the next term . . . the prospect of several Japanese objectors which ought to keep me busy far beyond the opening of the golf season."[5]

The "Japanese objectors" who were hindering Judge Kennedy's golf game were, of course, the draft resisters from the Heart Mountain

Relocation Center. By late spring, however, Judge Kennedy had more than just "several" on his docket. A total of sixty-three Nisei from Heart Mountain sat in county jails around Wyoming, awaiting trial on charges of evading the draft. They were scattered around the state not to keep them apart, but simply because Wyoming did not have a facility large enough to house them all. For their trial, however, they all had to be in Cheyenne. And so the government packed all sixty-three of them into the Laramie County Jail in Cheyenne—a jail built to accommodate no more than half that number.

Yosh Kuromiya, who spent more than two months there, recalls that the jail was a "dirty, smelly, and depressing" place. A long row of barred cells stretched along a narrow corridor. Each six-foot-by-five-foot cell was designed for two men, with bunk beds, a toilet, and a sink. With so many more inmates than there was space, though, it quickly became "so darn congested that they [could] not even stretch their legs."[6] Mattresses covered the floor of the corridor so densely that "you had to watch where you walked when you wanted to get down the corridor to the shower." Opposite the cells and across the corridor was a long barred wall that made a cage of the entire unit. Twice a day the guards would shove "barely edible" meals through the bars for the young men to eat off of steel shelves in the corridor. "Most of the stuff that they fed us," though, "went down the toilet," says Kuromiya, "although in those conditions nothing would've tasted good." Bare light bulbs hung from the ceiling on the guards' side of the barred wall and provided the only light supplementing the faint natural light that came through small, grimy windows in the guards' area.

Kuromiya remembers that the resisters were confined to these quarters twenty-four hours a day. They were not even allowed out to exercise. They spent their days "stretched out on their bunks, playing cards, reading, and just joking around," trying to keep their minds occupied and their spirits up. Naturally, they had no visitors; anyone who might have wished to see them was behind barbed wire at Heart Mountain. The only break in the monotony, Kuromiya recalls, came on Sunday mornings, when "a Christian minister would come to preach to us and make us feel guilty." Most in the congregation were, of course, Buddhists.

Despite the conditions, most of the Heart Mountain resisters were feeling at least cautiously optimistic when they were brought to Judge

Kennedy's courtroom on June 12, 1944. The leadership of the FPC had retained Samuel Menin, a firebrand of a lawyer from Denver, to represent them, and they had confidence that Menin would mount an aggressive defense.[7] Menin was one of Denver's most prominent civil rights lawyers, an old-school liberal with a penchant for unpopular causes and clients. In his more-than-fifty-year career, he made his reputation by representing alleged communists, by challenging the distribution of Bibles to Denver public school students, and by advocating for African American and Mexican American victims of civil rights abuses. The reputation he made was not untarnished; he was a burly and aggressive man who had gotten himself into more than one fistfight with opposing counsel in the well of the courtroom.[8] The resisters, however, were pleased to have a fighter on their side.

One of Menin's first decisions was to waive the resisters' Sixth Amendment right to a jury trial. This was a sensible decision. Menin undoubtedly feared the judgment of twelve white laymen plucked from the streets of Cheyenne during wartime. By waiving a jury, Menin placed his clients' fates entirely in the hands of Judge Kennedy, who would sit as both judge and jury. This also seemed a sound decision. Kennedy's life was a classic American success story. Born and raised in modest circumstances on a farm in Ohio, Kennedy graduated from law school in 1897 and tried to make a go of private practice in Syracuse, New York. Frustrated with the large number of lawyers and the resulting lack of opportunity there, Kennedy decided to uproot himself and head west in search of opportunity. He wrote letters to dozens of mayors of western towns and cities, inquiring whether young lawyers might be welcome and needed. When the mayor of Cheyenne responded encouragingly, he decided to try his fortunes in the Wyoming capital. Cheyenne was still a rough-and-tumble frontier town when Kennedy arrived, full of opportunity for an energetic young lawyer, and he quickly rose to the top of the tiny legal community there. He also joined the state's Republican Party and immersed himself in local politics, and when Warren G. Harding was elected to the presidency and Wyoming's district judgeship became vacant in 1921, Kennedy was chosen to fill it.

By the time *United States v. Shigeru Fujii et al.*, the case of the Heart Mountain draft resisters, came before him, Judge Kennedy had earned a reputation as an efficient and hardworking judge. He was well regarded by other federal judges and was often invited to hear cases in other jurisdictions, most frequently New York, when the need arose. Early in his judicial career, Kennedy had made himself known nationally by handling one of the most high-profile and closely watched cases of his day—*United States v. Mammoth Oil Company,* also known as the Teapot Dome Case. This was one of the central pieces of litigation that grew out of the political scandal involving bribery and fraud in the leasing of federal oilfields that rocked the Harding administration in the mid-1920s. Although Judge Kennedy's decision upholding the leases was overturned on appeal,[9] the case established the judge as a capable, if somewhat stern, jurist who kept close and careful control over the proceedings in his courtroom.

The resisters may have been optimistic about their chances before Judge Kennedy, but their first disillusionment came early. On the first day of the proceedings, the judge turned to the sixty-three U.S. citizens on trial before him and addressed them in open court as "you Jap boys." Jack Tono, one of the resisters, recalls being stunned that a federal judge would say such a thing. By the time he and his sixty-two codefendants returned to their cramped quarters in the Laramie County Jail that evening, Tono had lost his optimism: "[W]hen we went back to the county jail I told the guys, I said, 'This son of a bitch, he's got it in for us. Don't have high hopes. This guy, he's going to give it to us.'"[10]

Tono could not have known how right he was about T. Blake Kennedy. The judge's surviving writings reveal him as a racist, an anti-Semite, and a xenophobe. Late in his life, Kennedy compiled nearly one thousand pages of memoirs, and they are studded with sneering references to Jews and blacks. For example, Kennedy tells of a trip through upstate New York during which his wife found a beautiful diamond brooch near the entrance to a hotel. The judge thought it best to report the find to the hotel so that the piece could be "restored to its rightful owner." Before long, the owner of the brooch made a claim for it, and Kennedy notes in his memoirs that the owner "was a very corpulent Jewish lady, traveling in style with her husband, dressed in fashion as though she were about to attend a social function at the Metropolitan Opera House." Recognizing that she would have to return the item to a fat, well-dressed Jewish woman, he recalls, "did not put [his] wife in a very sympathetic frame of mind."[11]

Judge Kennedy also recalls that he himself was briefly in an unhappy frame of mind during one of his trips to New York City as a visiting judge. An old friend of the judge's approached him one day in early October and suggested that the two go down to Philadelphia the next day to see a World Series game between the St. Louis Cardinals and the Philadelphia Athletics. His friend said he had "seats for the game as well as transportation and would assure [the judge] of a good lunch in Philadelphia." Kennedy reluctantly demurred, explaining that he "was then engaged in the trial of an important case." But, "upon more mature reflection," Judge Kennedy considered the fact that "adjournments were frequently made in New York for all kinds of occasions, including all Jewish holidays." (By this, Judge Kennedy undoubtedly meant the Jewish High Holidays of Rosh Hashana and Yom Kippur, which had just concluded when the judge received his baseball invitation.) Concluding that the baseball game was "fully as important to [him] as Jewish Holidays were to the members of that religious sect," Kennedy decided to go to the game.[12]

Kennedy was no kinder to blacks than to Jews in his writings. Before becoming a judge, Kennedy delivered an address to the Young Men's Literary Club in Cheyenne on the subject of "The Race Problem in America."[13] Kennedy devoted all of his attention to the "problem" of blacks. He began by acknowledging, with a tinge of regret, that the idea of "returning" all blacks to Africa "ha[d] been met with such stalwart opposition of impracticability and impossibility that it is probably no longer seriously urged." This, then, presented him with the question he wished to treat in his address: "The negro is among us, a part of our commonwealth, a part of our citizenship, enjoying our property rights and governmental protection; and in the language of the small boy, 'What are you going to do about it?'"

What Kennedy was prepared to do about it was stunning. First, he endorsed the then-recent legislative innovation of imposing stiff educational requirements for voting—requirements that, as a practical matter, prevented blacks from exercising their right to vote. "These new laws," Kennedy explained, "practically place so high an educational qualification upon the voter that the rank and file of the negros [*sic*] are thereby disfranchised." Although this might seem harsh, he said, this "new factor in southern politics is by no means a bad one.

With it, the thinking men of the south vote according to principle and for the best man without fear that he will be overcome and dominated by the ignorant and illiterate black."

Kennedy had more to say to his audience about "the ignorant and illiterate black" he was demonizing. He argued that black Americans were unable "to keep step with the great onward march of civilization in America" for four reasons. First, "his emotional proclivities are too well defined to make him reliable as a race." Second, Kennedy contended, the black man's "natural laziness [was] too pre-eminent to ensure thrift." Third, "his love of fine clothes and luxury [was] too well developed to allow his mind to grasp the more material things of life." And, finally, "his want of mechanical idea [was] too pronounced." All of these defects, Judge Kennedy emphasized, could be cured through a "slow and . . . practical" education. But in educating the black, the white teacher must "relentlessly thunder[ ] in his ear that the chief ambition . . . must not be to avoid . . . honest, earnest and faithful labor." This message had to be "thundered" because "[s]o many of the misguided colored people get the idea that education is expressly fitting them for a life of ease and sloth."

In his address, Kennedy ventured an additional suggestion for solving America's race problem: the banning of "intermarriage between the white and colored people," a prohibition that "would be a blessing not only to the white but to the colored as well." "Many a heartache," Kennedy explained, "has been caused by the discrimination against a child so nearly white that only the close observer could discover the traces of foreign blood." The solution for Judge Kennedy was to enforce laws that kept the "foreign blood" from mixing with the white.

In other addresses, Judge Kennedy had more to say about "foreign blood"—of the nondomestic variety. In the mid-1920s, several years after becoming a federal district judge, Kennedy spoke publicly in Cheyenne on the turbulent topic of the nation's immigration policy. That policy was undergoing a great deal of change at that time; Congress was debating the Japanese Exclusion Act, which completely closed America's doors to Japanese immigrants, and entertaining proposals for other reductions in immigration. In describing the proposals, Judge Kennedy noted that they tended to favor immigrants from northern Europe at the expense of those from southern Europe and the Orient—"a . . . rule which ought to bring in more foreigners of those regarded as the better classes, or at least from experience shown to be more easily assimilated."[14]

Kennedy elaborated on these views in another talk he delivered after the 1924 changes in immigration law had taken effect. He praised Congress for fixing quotas that favored northern European caucasians over all other immigrants because "the peoples of Northern Europe much more readily assimilate with the American people than do those of any other portion of the globe." These immigrants from the North, he continued, "seemed to more quickly catch the American perspective and the American ideal"—either "due to the true Caucasian color or their more fully grounded system of education, or better standards and more stabilized conditions of life at home."[15]

And what was, for Judge Kennedy, the "American perspective and the American ideal"? The best surviving clue is in the speeches Judge Kennedy delivered to the brand-new American citizens he swore in at naturalization ceremonies. On July 3, 1944, just days after sentencing the Heart Mountain draft resisters to three years in federal prison, Judge Kennedy said to a courtroom full of new citizens that "love for and devotion to one's Country" and "an everlasting faith in the ultimate accomplishment of good government in the country of our birth or adoption" are the hallmarks of good citizenship. And these entailed a commitment to obedience: "If discouraging problems arise in our government or other institutions which at times threaten to shatter our faith, we must work within ourselves to accomplish needed reforms, instead of adhering to the enemy and becoming disloyal."[16] Judge Kennedy said more about this theme a year later in his naturalization remarks to new citizens in July of 1945: "Allegiance," he explained, "signifies fidelity and obedience to our country and its government. The term government itself indicates that its people are to be governed and controlled." For Kennedy, this was an especially pertinent thought "just at this time when we as a nation are caught in the pinch of a double war, making it necessary to undergo substantial sacrifices in the interest of achieving a victorious outcome of the struggle." At such a time, Kennedy warned those he had just sworn in as Americans, "[w]hatever restrictions in our daily lives may in the wisdom of our selected representatives in government seem necessary to accomplish this great undertaking, should be complied with and adhered to." "Let us," he intoned, "fully bear true faith and allegiance to our beloved United States by adhering to all wartime regulations."[17]

This was the judge before whom the Nisei draft resisters from Heart Mountain brought their case of noncompliance with wartime regulations. The six-day trial opened on Monday, June 12, 1944. Prosecutor Carl Sackett's strategy, at least initially, was to keep the trial narrowly focused: to prove that the defendants received notices to report for preinduction physical examinations and willfully failed to report for them. He hoped to steer clear of the resisters' motives for refusing to report. In his opening statement, Sackett said simply that "he would show that all 63 of the defendants were delinquent with their local draft board at Powell[, Wyoming,] through failure to submit to a preinduction physical."[18] And, indeed, that is what he set out to do, calling as his witnesses the clerk of the local draft board, who identified all of the paperwork that proved the defendants' refusals to report for their physicals, and the FBI agents who interviewed the defendants and took statements from them. Sackett wished to present an open-and-shut case of technical noncompliance with draft board orders.

Defense counsel Menin, however, sought over and over again to undermine the prosecutor's strategy by broadening the issues to include the resisters' professed loyalty to the United States, their lack of freedom inside the relocation center, their outrage over their eviction from the West Coast and their incarceration in camp, and their willingness to serve in the military after their civil rights were restored. Menin was able to elicit testimony from the FBI agents to the effect that each and every one of the sixty-three defendants had been courteous, had treated the agents well, had neither said nor done anything "against the United States [n]or indicate[d] any disloyal attitude," had expressed no desire to go to Japan, and had "indicated a desire to fight for this country if he were restored to his rights as a citizen."[19]

The defense lawyer also made much of the statements—confessions, really—that the defendants had made to the agents upon their arrests. Yosh Kuromiya's was typical. As the agent recalled it at trial, Kuromiya told the agent who interviewed him that he "believed it was not fair to be drafted on the same basis as other people after the way he had been treated." Kuromiya also felt that "the way he [had] been treated" was "not constitutional." Kuromiya told the agent of his firm belief that "if he did not protest" his treatment, he "would be just as responsible as those who made the decision" to intern him. With remarkable articulateness, especially for an eighteen-year-old, Kuromiya

Kiyonosuke Akutsu (left) and Nao Akutsu (right) of Seattle in a 1938 family photograph. *Photograph courtesy Gene Akutsu.*

Gene Akutsu, one of the Minidoka draft resisters, shortly after his release from McNeil Island in the late 1940s. *Photograph courtesy Gene Akutsu.*

Tom Noda, one of the Tule Lake draft resisters, in a photo taken shortly before the war. *Photograph courtesy Tom Noda.*

Yosh Kuromiya, one of the Heart Mountain draft resisters, pictured on the steps of the Heart Mountain poster shop in 1943. *Photograph courtesy Yosh Kuromiya.*

George Nozawa *(right)*, one of the Heart Mountain draft resisters, and Frank Emi *(left)*, one of the leaders of the Fair Play Committee, outside a barrack at Heart Mountain in the summer of 1944. *Photograph courtesy George Nozawa.*

The Heart Mountain Relocation Center. *Photograph courtesy Bancroft Library, University of California, Berkeley.*

A thoroughfare at the Minidoka Relocation Center in springtime. *Photograph courtesy Bancroft Library, University of California, Berkeley.*

A member of an army registration team explains the loyalty questionnaires to a group of Nisei internees, February 1943. *Photograph courtesy Bancroft Library, University of California, Berkeley.*

The sixty-three resisters from the Heart Mountain Relocation Center on the first day of their trial in federal district court in Cheyenne, Wyoming, 12 June 1944. *Photograph courtesy George Nozawa.*

T. Blake Kennedy, United States District Judge for the District of Wyoming. *Photograph courtesy Wyoming Division of Cultural Resources.*

Chase A. Clark, United States District Judge for the District of Idaho. *Photograph courtesy Idaho State Historical Society.*

Louis E. Goodman, United States District Judge for the Northern District of California. *Photograph courtesy Eleanor Jackson Piel.*

An aerial view of McNeil Island, 1941. The large building at the center of the photograph is the Big House. *Photograph courtesy U.S. Bureau of Prisons.*

A cell block in the Big House at McNeil Island. *Photograph courtesy U.S. Bureau of Prisons.*

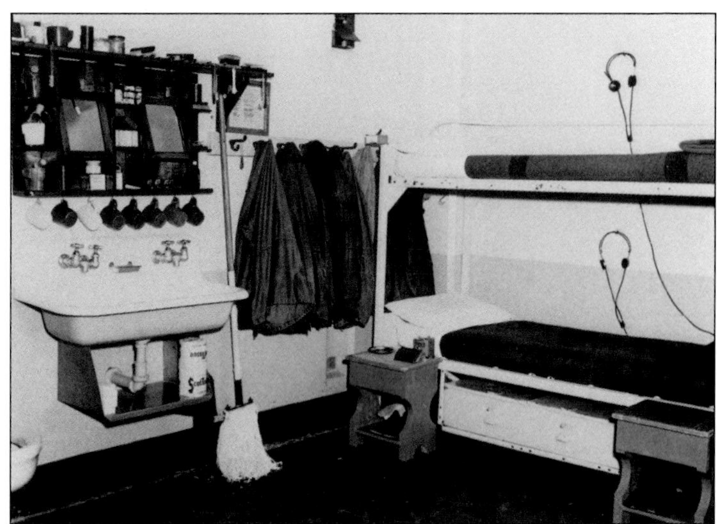

The back corner of a ten-man cell in the Big House at McNeil Island. *Photograph courtesy U.S. Bureau of Prisons.*

Heart Mountain resisters pose in prison-issued suits on 14 July 1946, the day of their release from McNeil Island. Yosh Kuromiya stands in the back row, second from the left. *Photograph courtesy Yosh Kuromiya.*

explained to the agent that "a citizen who will accept bad government without protest is not a good citizen."[20] Menin tried to turn these ostensibly inculpatory statements to the defense's advantage. He used them to call attention to the conditions that produced the defendants' decisions to resist and to remind the jury of his clients' unambiguous avowals of loyalty.

Menin also tried some silly and theatrical ploys. On the very first day, perhaps trying to capitalize on white America's common view of Asians that "they all look alike," Menin insisted that Judge Kennedy had to dismiss the charges because no government agent could identify any of the defendants by name in open court. Menin had himself made the agents' task a good deal harder by proposing to the defendants that they give themselves crew cuts to make themselves that much harder to identify. Many of the sixty-three did cut their hair, and the agents were indeed stumped. But Menin's gambit was in vain. Judge Kennedy ruled that the defendants had adequately identified themselves at the time of their arrest and booking when they signed their names to their fingerprint cards, and admitted those cards in evidence as proof of the identities of the defendants on trial.

Menin's arguments, antics, and aggressive cross-examination did cause the government's case to fray a bit around the edges. For one thing, government witnesses began defensively sugarcoating the conditions at Heart Mountain, trying to make it look like something other than the imprisonment camp it was. Menin, for example, asked an FBI agent whether it was true that the camp was surrounded by barbed wire. "I know it is surrounded by wire. I don't know whether or not it is barbed wire," fibbed the agent, to hoots of laughter from the sixty-three defendants.[21] Heart Mountain's assistant project director, Douglas Todd—the number two administrator at the camp—was even more embarrassingly equivocal in his answers to Menin's questions:

> Q. Is that project [Heart Mountain] patrolled by military police?
> A. No, I wouldn't say that it was.
> Q. Is it guarded by military police?
> A. There are military police there, yes.
> Q. And they are there for the purpose of guarding the project, are they not?

> A. Their function has to do with the Army, and I am not able to say.

Certain of Todd's answers to Menin were just a mixture of Pollyanna and perjury:

> Q. Now, have any of the persons who are confined at Heart Mountain been sent there for violation of the law?
> A. I don't know.
> Q. Do you know why they were sent there?
> A. No, I do not.
> Q. But you do know that those who are there are restrained of their liberties except within the confines of the area?
> A. I don't think they are restrained of their liberties. . . . They are not restrained of their liberties in any sense.

And others were almost laughably insensitive:

> Q. What would happen to an evacuee if he would attempt to leave the Center without obtaining a permit?
> A. That Relocation Center is a military reservation. . . . *The Government is feeding the people and housing them* and they would naturally be expected to comply with such rules and regulations as were set up. . . .

In other words, if the internees were going to avail themselves of the WRA's hospitality, the least they could do was comply with their host's rules.

Menin's blustery strategies ultimately pushed Carl Sackett from the narrow focus with which he began. In his summation to Judge Kennedy, the defense attorney argued "that placing American citizens in relocation centers was 'something Hitler would do.'" Sackett responded with fury, "bellow[ing] out each word[, s]winging his right arm overhead and pointing his finger at the ceiling":[22]

> The defense counsel has compared the system of relocation to something Hitler would do. I resent that. These men and their families have been housed, clothed, fed and schooled by the

> federal government, perhaps better than the court when he was a young man and, I know, better than I was. When the Jews were kicked out of Germany they were left to shift for themselves, but our government cared for these men and their relatives.[23]

Sackett did not leave it at that; he completely abandoned his strategy of confining the case to the technical draft violations and openly called into question the defendants' loyalty—something not even his own witnesses had done. As one listener recalls the summation, Sackett complained to Judge Kennedy that

> [t]he defendants are using my money, your money, everybody's money by having this trial and saying that they will not fight for this country. They want freedom, they say; do they want freedom so that they can go out and signal the [Japanese] submarines? They all admitted they were loyal American citizens; is that a cloak back of which to hide, or an excuse to get away from . . . the draft?[24]

To a courtroom observer, it did not appear that Sackett was making headway with Judge Kennedy; after this rant, the judge interrupted Sackett and told him to finish up within three minutes.

As it happened, however, Judge Kennedy undoubtedly hurried Sackett along not because he was offended by Sackett's line of argument, but because he had already made up his mind to rule in Sackett's favor. On Monday, June 26, 1944, Judge Kennedy announced his decision convicting the sixty-three Nisei resisters on one count each of draft evasion and sentencing them all to three years in federal prison.[25] His opinion, which he read in its entirety from the bench, made clear that he had little sympathy for the internee resisters or their plight. Summarizing the facts, Kennedy noted that the defendants and others of Japanese ancestry had been removed from the West Coast due to fear of a Japanese invasion and placed in relocation centers such as Heart Mountain, where they "were housed and fed in a satisfactory manner and were permitted to live in families and enjoy the ordinary family relations."

After this whitewashing of the internment experience itself, Kennedy turned his attention to what he saw as the defendants' central claims—namely, that the government had discriminated against them by classifying them with enemy aliens in the 4-C draft category and by removing them from their homes to relocation centers and that because of this discrimination, "they should not be reclassified for service in the war at least until such time as their status of citizenship has been clarified." Kennedy found no legal obstacle to the placing of the Nisei in the 4-C category and suggested (without deciding) that the removal and internment of the West Coast Nikkei were within the government's war powers. Kennedy found, as a matter of fact, that the defendants had acted willfully and intentionally when they refused to obey their orders to report for a preinduction physical examination. And, finally, Kennedy rejected out of hand the defendants' claim that they were owed a clarification of their rights as citizens before they could lawfully be called for the draft. The very clarification the defendants wished, argued Kennedy, came from the Selective Service laws themselves: "When . . . they were placed in 1-A and ordered to report for pre-induction physical examination, their pure American citizenship was established beyond question."

Those rulings resolved the case and should have ended the opinion, but Judge Kennedy could not stop himself from offering a moral lesson to the Heart Mountain resisters. It was a message very much like the admonitions he typically offered to newly naturalized citizens. "Personally," he said, "this Court feels that the defendants have made a serious mistake in arriving at their conclusions which brought about these criminal prosecutions." Their mistake was to believe that loyal citizens might protest, rather than submit to, government orders they saw as unlawful. "If they are truly loyal American citizens," Kennedy concluded, "they should, at least when they have become recognized as such, embrace the opportunity to discharge the duties of citizens by offering themselves in the cause of our National defense."[26] It did not seem to occur to Kennedy that the men he was sentencing, by abandoning their West Coast homes and acceding to years of internal exile in a WRA internment camp, might already have discharged "the duties of citizens by offering themselves in the cause of our National defense."

And so the noose of incarceration tightened around the Heart Mountain resisters one final time. After the curfew, temporary detention at assembly centers, indefinite detention in relocation camps, and months in county jails, the Heart Mountain resisters moved off to federal prisons to serve their three-year terms. The older men were sent to the Federal Correctional Institution at Leavenworth, Kansas, where they served out their terms alongside the hard-boiled inmates of that famous maximum-security prison. The younger men were sent to the federal prison at McNeil Island, Washington—ironically, back into the heart of the Western Defense Command, the very zone from which they had been excluded two and one-half years earlier.

In spite of their defeat in the district court, many of the resisters carried some hope with them to Leavenworth and McNeil Island. They had been told from the start that their best chance for victory might lie with an appellate court. And so they and their parents and friends footed the bill for Samuel Menin to take an appeal of Judge Kennedy's decision to the U.S. Court of Appeals for the Tenth Circuit in Denver. Menin wrote a moving brief, rather short on careful legal argument, but long on rhetorical appeal to basic concerns for fairness and due process. Is it the case, Menin asked, "that the government can do no wrong? That it may subject its people to a loss of civil rights and property without due process of law and at the same time require compliance with the draft act . . . ?" What, the defense attorney demanded to know, would the Nisei draftee be fighting for? "So that his parents, his sisters and brothers may continue to remain behind barbed wire under Military Guard?" Menin concluded his brief powerfully:

> If our government cannot trust American citizens of Japanese ancestry so that we can accept them on an equal basis and accord them equal rights, then how can we ask them to fight, and for what do we ask them to fight? Is it to fight for a continuation of relocation centers with armed guards and barbed wire? How can we ask them to lay down their lives in approval of such unconstitutional treatment?[27]

The Tenth Circuit made quick work of the *Fujii* appeal. It noted that, to the extent that any of the resisters objected to his confinement at Heart Mountain, he could have filed a petition for a writ of habeas corpus challenging that confinement. (The writ of habeas corpus allows a court to entertain an incarcerated person's claim that his continued detention is illegal.) "This," said the court, "would have given him the vindication which he seeks." But, instead, the resisters "chose to disobey a lawful order because [they] claimed [their] rights had been invaded." This was impermissible, said the court, because "[t]wo wrongs never make a right. One may not refuse to heed a lawful call of his government merely because in another way it may have injured him." The defendants were citizens of the United States, according to the Tenth Circuit, and "owed the same military service to [their] country that any other citizen did. Neither the fact that [they were] of Japanese ancestry nor the fact that [their] constitutional rights may have been invaded by sending [them] to a relocation center cancel[s] this debt."[28] With that, the Heart Mountain resisters' attack on the lawfulness of the draft ended.[29] While the attorney general of the United States may have believed that the Heart Mountain case potentially called into question the lawfulness of the entire internment program and presented difficult legal questions, for the Tenth Circuit the case was a snap.

The Trial of the Fair Play Committee

On October 23, 1944, with the sixty-three Heart Mountain resisters in jail, United States Attorney Carl Sackett returned to the federal district courtroom in Cheyenne to try another group of Nisei on draft-related charges. This time the defendants were the men he saw as the more serious troublemakers: the leaders of the Heart Mountain FPC and Jimmie Omura, the former English language editor of the *Rocky Shimpo.* The charge against them was conspiracy to counsel Heart Mountain's draft-age Nisei to evade the draft, in violation of Section 11 of the Selective Training and Service Act of 1940.[30]

This trial would not be a simple rehashing of the earlier trial of the sixty-three Heart Mountain resisters. In the first place, many of the key participants were new. Chief among the new faces was the judge's: because Judge Kennedy was out of town, the task of trying *United States v. Kiyoshi Okamoto et al.* fell to Eugene Rice, a visiting judge from the U.S. District Court for the Eastern District of Oklahoma. Rice, a fifty-three-year-old World War I veteran and graduate of Valparaiso University's law school, had been on the federal district court bench in Oklahoma City since mid-1937. He was known as an efficient and hardworking judge, a "disciplinarian [who] rarely overlooked an opportunity to lecture a member of the Bar who deviated from the prescribed rules of conduct" and who was "upon occasion somewhat abrupt and abrasive in colloquy with counsel."[31] Had the defendants been represented by the flashy and abrasive Samuel Menin, there would surely have been fireworks in the courtroom, but the leaders of the FPC opted for different representation at this trial. They managed to retain A. L. Wirin, a well-known Los Angeles attorney who had handled (and would continue to handle) some of the most prominent civil rights cases of his day as counsel to the Southern California Branch of the American Civil Liberties Union. Wirin was also counsel to the Japanese American Citizens League, but undertook to represent the FPC leaders in his capacity as a private attorney rather than as counsel to the JACL. With a Denver attorney named Sidney Jacobs representing Jimmie Omura, the makeup of the defense team was entirely new.

The issues before the court were somewhat different this time around as well. Unlike the sixty-three resisters who had recently been convicted, these defendants were on trial not so much for what they had done (or, more precisely, refused to do) as for things they had said. Sackett's task was therefore a good deal harder at this trial than it had been at the last. Before Judge Kennedy, Sackett had merely had to prove that the sixty-three defendants, all eligible for the draft and in receipt of orders to report for preinduction physicals, had willfully failed to do so. Before Judge Rice, Sackett had to prove that the leaders of the FPC and Jimmie Omura had illegally agreed with one another to urge Heart Mountain's Nisei to defy the draft. By way of defense, the defendants in the *Okamoto* trial had not just the unfairness and claimed illegality of the internment to rely upon, but also the First Amendment's protection of free expression. And for Jimmie Omura, whose alleged involvement in the conspiracy began and ended with his publication of news stories and editorials about the draft resistance at Heart Mountain, the First Amendment was an especially potent weapon. Not only could the newspaperman rely upon its general protection of freedom of expression, but also he could take support from its more specific protection of the freedom of the press.

The defendants filed several pretrial motions. The most interesting of these was an attack filed by Wirin on the composition of the grand jury that had returned the indictment. In a motion to quash the indictment, defense attorney Wirin argued that the defendants' constitutional rights had been violated because "no American of Japanese descent had served on the Grand Jury."[32] In a sparsely populated and overwhelmingly white state such as Wyoming, this might have seemed a frivolous motion. But with it, Wirin tried to make an important point about the situation of the defendants. Although prewar Wyoming was overwhelmingly white, from 1942 through 1945 its racial composition changed dramatically. For those three years, its third-largest city—with a maximum population of about 12,000—was the Heart Mountain Relocation Center, all of whose residents were Japanese aliens and Japanese American citizens. This was nearly 5 percent of Wyoming's total population. Under these circumstances, a handful of Japanese American grand jurors—or at least a handful of Japanese Americans in the pool from which the grand jury was drawn—would not have been a statistical anomaly. Predictably, however, Judge Rice denied the motion, concluding that

> [t]hese Japanese who have been brought into the State of Wyoming, probably against their will, are probably not qualified to act [as grand jurors]—not residents of the State. At least there is no showing of their residence. They are temporary residents. And prior to that time I don't think there was anything that would require that a Japanese be on the Grand Jury or on the jury panel. There is a lacking in evidence and no substantial showing that there were many Japanese in the State of Wyoming or that there was any system of exclusion of that particular group of jurors from the jury box by reason of their nationality.[33]

If the residents of Heart Mountain, forced from their West Coast homes in 1942 for indefinite detention behind barbed wire in Park County, Wyoming, were not "residents" of Wyoming in the fall of 1944, it is hard to know where their true residence actually lay. They were stateless, in a very real sense of the word, and Wirin's pretrial motion pointed that up quite powerfully—even if unsuccessfully.

Trial of the *Okamoto* case lasted a week. Carl Sackett's strategy was to try the internee defendants—that is, all of the defendants but Jimmie Omura—largely on their own words. Most of his case consisted of these defendants' own statements, offered in evidence through the FBI agents who had interrogated them. In these statements, each of the

FPC defendants frankly avowed his own involvement in the formation and running of the FPC, and most of them acknowledged, to greater or lesser extents, the roles that the others had played as well. These statements made the FPC's position eminently clear: the organization was openly committed to the proposition that the Nisei were due a clarification of their citizenship rights as a precondition to military service. They also left the clear impression that the leaders of the FPC had been cooperative with their FBI interrogators, hiding nothing about the FPC's goals and methods. Typical was the response of defendant Sam Horino to an FBI agent's request for copies of the financial records of the FPC: Horino explained to the agent that there were "accurate records of all the funds which the Fair Play Committee had received from the members, and also there was a record maintained of all the speeches which had been made and that all this material should be available [to the agent] inasmuch as the Fair Play Committee was an open book."[34] This was quite right: for better or for worse, the FPC's openness about its goals and methods left it an open book for the FBI, Carl Sackett, and ultimately the jury to read.

None of this was true, however, as to Jimmie Omura. Omura was not an internee, had never been to Heart Mountain, had never met or spoken to any of the FPC's leaders, had never participated with the FPC leadership in the planning or execution of any of the FPC's activities at the camp, and had never given a statement to the FBI suggesting any collaboration (or even personal familiarity) with his alleged co-conspirators. Sackett therefore had no choice but to try the Denver newspaperman on the basis of his published words in the *Rocky Shimpo* and his sporadic written correspondence with the FPC leaders, in the hope that the jury would infer from them Omura's complicity in an illegal agreement.

Omura's words, however, were not invariably—or even predominately—damning. His news stories reported on the draft-related events at Heart Mountain, sometimes accurately and sometimes with a healthy touch of exaggeration, but never with the faintest hint of foreknowledge. His editorials praised the FPC and blasted the WRA and the official camp newspaper, the *Heart Mountain Sentinel*, but nowhere called upon individual Nisei to resist the draft. And his correspondence with the FPC leaders was often more helpful in presenting the apparent good faith of all of the defendants than it was damaging to any of them. For example, in a letter to Frank Emi that was offered in evidence, Omura wrote that he had been interested to learn, in an earlier letter, of Emi's opposition to the JACL's prodraft policies:

> I see where we see eye to eye on this matter. I, too, was brought up with the idea that "real Americans fight for their rights and beliefs" as you say. This belief has led me into considerable difficulties. I see where it is obviously leading you into similar straits. There is something inevitable about a man's convictions. I have held to mine in the face of many verbal tempests and countless attacks. Whither it will lead me, I do not know. Whither it will lead you, let us hope for the best. It is a hard row to hoe; the easy way is the JACL way.[35]

To be sure, the comment about "eye to eye" vision leant slight support to Sackett's claim that Omura was party to a conspiratorial agreement with the FPC. But the overall tone of the passage was not especially damaging to the defendants and arguably placed them in a somewhat favorable light. At the very least, it tended to confirm that the FPC leaders and Jimmie Omura were opposing the draft out of American principle rather than out of fear or disloyalty.

The tone of Omura's letter also bolstered the in-court testimony of the defendants. Each of the defendants testified in his own defense, and each told nearly the same story about the FPC—that it was publicly committed to seeking a redress of Nisei grievances as a condition of agreeing to military service. A. L. Wirin was careful to elicit from the FPC's leaders that they intended the resistance at Heart Mountain to trigger a judicial "test case" on the lawfulness of the internment and of the application of the draft to the internees. He was also skillful in placing before the trier of fact the essence of the defendants' outrage at their mistreatment. For example, he elicited from defendant Min Tamesa that, before Pearl Harbor, Tamesa had been ordered by his local draft board to report for physical examination. At that time, he had complied. But when another such order reached him behind barbed wire at Heart Mountain, he decided to resist:

> I was born and raised in a typical American community on outskirts [*sic*] of Seattle, Washington. I grew up with some

> nice neighbors. . . . When I was living there I received this draft notice and to protect the security and happiness and freedom of my life there I was willing to serve my country. But later I was evacuated to a concentration camp and while in concentration camp I was put on what they call the stop list. Well, it seemed to me and I simply believed that the selective service did not mean for me to fight to protect security and freedom of a barracks room in a concentration camp; also to go to war and leave my dependents behind me in a concentration camp, so I did not report.[36]

During wartime, and to an all-white Wyoming jury, this may not have been an especially moving plea. It was, however, the nub of the defendants' moral position, and A. L. Wirin made sure that it was prominently before that jury.

Wirin saved his best piece of lawyering for last. Throughout his presentation of the case, Wirin emphasized to the jury that the defendants' goal in spurring debate about the draft and ultimately encouraging young Nisei to resist it was to create a test case in court. This was a bothersome strategy to Judge Rice, who, according to Carl Sackett, "d[idn't] have much patience with the 'test case' defense."[37] Wirin tested that patience when he asked that Judge Rice read to the jury the following proposed jury instruction on his "test case" theory:

> In determining whether the defendants acted in good faith or bad faith, you may take into consideration the sincerity or insincerity of the defendants' belief, that the citizenship status and the rights of American citizens of Japanese descent, evacuated from the Pacific Coast and detained at the Heart Mountain Relocation Center, could be lawfully determined or clarified by the Courts, upon a refusal of such persons to comply with draft board orders, and upon criminal prosecutions therefor. If you find that the defendants sincerely and in good faith entertained such a belief, it is your duty to acquit the defendants or such of them as you may find had such a belief.[38]

Carl Sackett was of the opinion that "in th[is] Japanese conspiracy case the defense of a test case is an absurd face-saving proposition

[that] is entirely without merit."[39] Nonetheless, on instructions from the Justice Department in Washington, Sackett urged Judge Rice at least to mention Wirin's "test case" theory and to instruct the jury that it could consider "all the evidence in the case, including any evidence relative to the test case, which might indicate that the defendants did not in fact knowingly conspire together to counsel evasion."[40] Sackett did not mind the Justice Department's meddling; he "wasn't concerned much about the instructions because I expected to win the case, and I wanted the Judge to make the instructions as favorable as he could for the defendants under the facts."[41]

Judge Rice, however, refused to give either Wirin's requested instruction or Sackett's toned-down alternate version. Instead he instructed the jury that

> [A] desire to have a test case . . . does not excuse failure to comply with the selective training and service act. . . . The selective training and service act provides that it is a violation of the law for anyone to counsel another to disobey the draft law or to assist or abet one to evade the draft law. And I charge you that it is a violation of the law, even though it is contended that the purpose was to create a case for the testing of the constitutionality of the law.[42]

Thus, in no uncertain terms, Judge Rice took the defense's "test case" theory away from the jury. This would turn out to be a fateful ruling.

On November 1, 1944, Judge Rice submitted the case to the jury late in the afternoon. Carl Sackett was confident of the outcome: late in the day, by overnight letter, he predicted to Assistant Attorney General Tom Clark in Washington "that the verdict and judgment in this case w[ould] be obtained against each of the eight defendants."[43] Sackett was seven-eighths correct in his prediction. After deliberating for a short time, the jury returned a verdict convicting all seven of the FPC's leaders of conspiracy, but acquitting Jimmie Omura. Judge Rice wasted no time in imposing sentence on the convicted FPC leaders. The next morning he sentenced those he saw as the most culpable—Kiyoshi Okamoto, Paul Nakadate, Sam Horino, and Frank Emi—to four years' imprisonment. Those he saw as playing more minimal roles—Guntaro Kubota, Ben Wakaye, and Min Tamesa—he sentenced to two-year terms. Wakaye and Tamesa were already serving three-year sentences from Judge Kennedy for failing to report for their preinduction physicals, so Judge Rice directed that their two-year conspiracy sentences run concurrently with their three-year draft evasion terms. All seven were promptly shipped off to the maximum-security federal prison at Leavenworth, Kansas, to serve their time.

Naturally, Carl Sackett was disappointed with the acquittal of Jimmie Omura, who had been a bother to both the government and the JACL for quite some time. Sackett was curious enough about the jurors' reasons for acquitting Omura to speak with them after the verdict. What they told him revealed that they had no special fondness for Omura; they simply felt that "the evidence did not show that there was any agreement between the other defendants and Omura, but that Omura acted independently using the material sent by the members of the Fair Play Committee." Sackett took some comfort from the fact that "[i]f the jury had been trying Omura not for conspiracy but for counselling draft evasion, the jury would have convicted him," and suggested to the Department of Justice that Omura might be prosecuted for that offense in the District of Colorado, where his editorials had allegedly spurred a handful of Nisei from the Amache Relocation Center to resist the draft.[44] That suggestion was never pursued, but to Jimmie Omura, it mattered little. His career in the Japanese American press was all but finished. He struggled to find work. He had a stint at the helm of the *Rocky Shimpo*'s English language section in 1947, but left after six months.[45] Eventually, he wound up as a landscape gardener in the Denver area.[46] For the next forty years, his strong and fiercely anti-JACL voice was silenced.

A. L. Wirin had told his clients from the start that their best chances might lie with an appellate court, and so the FPC leaders, incarcerated at Leavenworth, pinned their hopes on a successful appeal. Wirin prepared a rigorous brief for the Tenth Circuit Court of Appeals that highlighted Judge Rice's refusal to give Wirin's proposed "test case" instruction. Here was where the astuteness of Wirin's trial lawyering became clear. At the time of the *Okamoto* trial, the case of *Keegan v. United States*[47] was under review in the U.S. Supreme Court. *Keegan* was a prosecution of a number of pro-Nazi German Americans under the Selective Training and Service Act of 1940 for counseling draft resistance. The trial judge in that case had instructed the jury, over defense objection, that the defendants' desire to use draft resistance to create a case testing the legality of certain laws discriminating against members of a pro-German organization could not be a defense to draft evasion charges. The U.S. Court of Appeals for the Second Circuit had upheld the instruction a few months earlier,[48] but the case was set for argument in the Supreme Court just days after the FPC leaders were convicted. This was why Wirin had demanded the "test case" instruction: he was hoping that the Supreme Court might reverse the convictions in the *Keegan* case and approve of the "test case" instruction in draft evasion prosecutions. And in June of 1945, several months before the *Okamoto* appeal was argued in the Tenth Circuit, the Supreme Court did just that. In a plurality opinion by Justice Owen Roberts, the Court held that a desire to create a legal test case could amount to an innocent motive for not complying with the Selective Training and Service Act and that it had been error to instruct the *Keegan* jury otherwise.

At oral argument on the *Okamoto* appeal in the Tenth Circuit, Sackett labored mightily to distinguish *Keegan* and left the argument with the "impression . . . that the court will try to find some way to affirm the decision of Judge Rice." But Sackett was wrong. The day after Christmas of 1945, the Tenth Circuit filed its opinion reversing the convictions of all seven of the FPC leaders. While rejecting Wirin's claims that the evidence was insufficient to sustain the convictions and that the convictions violated the defendants' First Amendment rights to freedom of expression and assembly, the Tenth Circuit held that Judge Rice's refusal to instruct the jury on the defense's "test case" theory was reversible error. Quoting *Keegan,* the court noted that while "[o]ne with innocent motives, who honestly believes a law is unconstitutional and, therefore, not obligatory, may well counsel that the law shall not be obeyed" and "that its command shall be resisted until a court shall have held it valid, . . . this is not knowingly counseling, stealthily and by guile, to evade its command." It held that "[i]n respect of the issue as to whether the appellants acted with honesty of purpose and innocence of motive in a good faith effort to bring about a test case to determine their exempt status under the Selective Service Act, the [trial] court should have instructed the jury in substantial harmony with the rule . . . in the *Keegan* case."[49]

Sackett immediately wrote a letter advising the Justice Department of the Tenth Circuit's action in *Okamoto*, wryly observing in a handwritten postscript that he had "got[ten] knocked off the Christmas tree."[50] The next day, however, Sackett began to press the Justice Department to petition the U.S. Supreme Court to review the case.[51] The Justice Department's Criminal Division, however, recommended that the solicitor general seek no further review of the case in the Supreme Court. By that time, all of the relocation centers except Tule Lake had been closed; thus, the Criminal Division reasoned, "there [was] little likelihood that the compliance problem that [the *Okamoto*] case presents will arise again" or that the reversal would lead other Japanese Americans to resist the draft. Moreover, the Criminal Division argued,

> [i]nsofar as the individual defendants are concerned, two are serving concurrent prison sentences for substantive violations of the Act, and the remaining five have been imprisoned for more than a year as a result of their convictions in these cases. In these circumstances there is not presented a situation in which, unless the convictions are sustained, the defendants will have escaped punishment for their defiance of the law.

The government, in other words, had already obtained most of its pound of flesh from the FPC's leaders; it needed no more. Finally, in a nod to the compassion that Attorney General Biddle himself had found for the plight of the Nisei resisters, the Criminal Division stated that "the facts of the cases are such as to be troublesome to the Supreme Court even though as a matter of law the Government's position is sound."[52] On the strength of this recommendation, Solicitor General J. Howard McGrath decided on January 23, 1946, not to seek review in the Supreme Court.

Carl Sackett, however, pressed on, asking for permission at least to retry the FPC leaders. The Criminal Division was not sanguine about this option either.[53] On January 31, 1946, the *Okamoto* case finally came to an end when the attorney general himself decided that the FPC leaders should not be retried.[54] In February of 1946, five of the seven FPC leaders were released from imprisonment at Leavenworth, having served more than a third of their four-year sentences. They left behind two of their colleagues, Ben Wakaye and Min Tamesa. These two younger men's conspiracy convictions had, of course, also been overturned, but they still had time left to serve on the three-year sentences that Judge Kennedy had imposed on them for resisting the draft.

The Minidoka Resisters in the District of Idaho

In March of 1943, the WRA's solicitor, Philip M. Glick, shared some news concerning the Minidoka Relocation Center with WRA Director Dillon Myer. Minidoka's project attorney had alerted Glick that both of the state judges sitting on the Idaho District Court for Twin Falls County (where Minidoka was located) had sons who were prisoners of war held by the Japanese. There was some concern that because of this, the judges might not be fair and impartial in handling any litigation involving Minidoka internees that came before them. Glick told Myer, however, that he thought they would be, and "one reason for this conclusion is the very fact that one of the judges ha[d] expressed an opinion that he did not know whether he could be impartial." If a person has the intellectually honesty to "recognize his possible prejudice," Glick opined, "it is a pretty good indication . . . that he will do his best to be impartial."[55]

This was not a particularly heartening theory of judicial bias. Any internee appearing in court in Twin Falls County might well have preferred that such a judge would recuse himself rather than struggle to banish from his mind the image of his own son in Japanese captivity. For the draft resisters from Minidoka, however, these judges would not pose any problem. Although the resisters spent the summer of 1944 in county jails in and around Boise, they were awaiting trial on federal, not state, charges. They would appear before a judge of the U.S. District Court for the District of Idaho.

They would not, however, find much impartiality in the federal system. The judge to whom their cases were assigned was new to the bench. He had been appointed less than two years earlier, after losing his bid to be reelected to the governorship of Idaho. His name was Chase A. Clark—the very same Chase A. Clark who, as Idaho's governor in the late winter of 1942, had spoken out at the WRA's Salt Lake City conference against the plan to move the West Coast Nikkei into Idaho and the other mountain states. At that meeting, his very first words were a frank avowal of prejudice against the Nikkei: "I am so prejudiced," he said, "that my reasoning might be a little off, because I don't trust any of them. I don't know which ones to trust and so therefore I don't trust any of them." A few months later, at a Lions Club meeting in Grangeville, Idaho, Clark was even blunter about the Japanese in America—people who, he said, "act like rats." For Clark, the solution to what he called the "Jap problem" was to "[s]end them all back to Japan, then sink the island."[56] Had Clark owned up to such prejudice when he took to the bench to try the Minidoka resisters, he might have recused himself, and the defendants might have received fair trials. But he did not recuse himself, and the resisters were tried in a kangaroo court.

As Judge Clark took the bench at the Minidoka resisters' September 6 arraignment, the defendants all stood before him without counsel. Naturally, they could not afford to hire their own lawyers; they and their families had lost nearly everything when they were uprooted from their homes in the Northwest two and one-half years before. Judge Clark's first job was therefore to find lawyers for the several dozen young men whose cases he would be trying. This was no easy task in a city as small as Boise. To solve the problem, Judge Clark did something unprecedented: he ordered every available Boise attorney to appear in court that morning. When they got there, he broke the news to them that they were each being appointed to represent one or two of the Nisei resisters and that, under prevailing federal court practice at the time, they would not be paid for their service.

Needless to say, the Boise bar was not especially happy with this plan. The problem, however, was not the lack of pay. The problem was that many of the attorneys wanted no parts of the Japanese American defendants whose cases they were being asked—or, more accurately, ordered—to handle. Gene Akutsu, for example, was appointed a large, "stern-faced" lawyer named R. R. Breshears. After Akutsu entered his plea of "not guilty," Judge Clark gave Akutsu the opportunity to meet with his attorney to discuss his defense. Breshears told his client in no uncertain terms that he was a "damn fool" and then said, "I'll be damned if I'm going to help you." From that point on, the eighteen-year-old Nisei was essentially on his own. Breshears attended later hearings, Akutsu recalls, but the lawyer said and did almost nothing. This lawyer's performance was, moreover, not atypical; the Boise newspaper reported that another attorney assigned to represent one of the Minidoka resisters told Judge Clark that he did not want even to sit at the same table with his client, whom he called a "traitor to his country" in open court. One might have expected the judge to rebuke the lawyer for such a blatantly unethical outburst and to find the defendant a new attorney. Judge Clark did neither. Instead, he merely made this lawyer promise at least "to advise his client in legal processes and court procedure"[57]—a promise the attorney undoubtedly honored with the same degree of enthusiasm as did R. R. Breshears in his representation of Gene Akutsu.

On September 13, 1944, one week after the arraignments, Judge Clark opened the first of the trials of the Minidoka resisters. The first order of business was a motion by Jim Akutsu to quash the indictment. At the core of the elder Akutsu brother's claim was the raw fact of his incarceration behind barbed wire at Minidoka. That fact, he argued, transformed the government's efforts at drafting him into a violation of both the Constitution and the Selective Service Act. The Constitution was violated because "at the time of the alleged commission of the offence [*sic*] charged in the indictment the defendant was not a free agent, was imprisoned and under the force and duress of the armed forces of the United States," and was therefore deprived of due process of law. As for the Selective Service Act, Akutsu cited the language in the statute that referred to the opportunity of those in a "free society" to "share generally" with others in the "obligations and privileges" of military training. He contended that because he was incarcerated in a concentration camp, he had no such opportunity to "share generally" with others in the "fair and just system of selective compulsory military training and service" contemplated by Section 301(b) of the Selective Service Act of 1940.[58]

This motion should have presented something of a crisis for Judge Clark. It was his insistence, as Idaho's governor, on the incarceration of the Nikkei that had led Milton Eisenhower to abandon his hope for open relocation communities in the interior and to resign himself to the inevitability of concentration camps. Now, just over two years later, and wearing the robes of a federal district judge, Chase Clark was presented with an attack on the constitutionality of the very circumstances of confinement that he himself had demanded. Federal law at the time required the disqualification of any judge who had a "'personal bias or prejudice,' by reason of which the judge [was] unable to impartially exercise his functions in the particular case."[59] Jim Akutsu's attorney did not move for Clark's recusal, but sound judicial practice ought to have prompted Judge Clark to remove himself from the case on his own motion. How, after all, could he possibly adjudicate the constitutionality of what he had himself demanded? Yet Judge Clark did not recuse himself. He heard the motion and denied it without recorded opinion.

Having rejected the constitutional attack on the proceedings, Judge Clark set in motion what can only be described as a production line of federal criminal justice. Over the next eleven days, he opened and concluded thirty-three separate jury trials, sometimes hearing as many as four trials in a single day. Needless to say, the trials were hardly elaborate. In each case, the government called a witness or two to establish that the defendant was classified 1-A for the draft, that he was duly and properly called to report for a preinduction physical examination and in some cases for induction, and that he failed to report as ordered. In some cases, an FBI agent offered in evidence a statement the defendant gave upon his arrest, usually expressing anger at the deportation and internment of the West Coast Nikkei and a desire to abandon American citizenship and expatriate to Japan. At that, the government rested.

The typical defense case was also quite spare. The extant judicial records suggest that in each trial, defense counsel called the defendant as the lone defense witness. The recollections of the surviving Minidoka resisters themselves tend to show that even this minimal involvement by counsel was an exaggeration. Gene Akutsu, for example, remembers struggling to mount his own defense while his attorney stood idly by in the back of the courtroom. Another of the Minidoka resisters, Frank Yamasaki, remembers a five-minute consultation with his attorney in the holding cell just before trial, and no further contact. Alone and uncounseled, the young Nisei struggled to communicate their reasons for resisting the draft. While no transcript exists that captures their exact words in court, it is fair to surmise that most of the resisters said something like what one had written to his local draft board:

> If I were treated like an American I would be more than glad to serve in the armed forces but seeing how things are espe-

> cially since now that I'm put behind barbed wires for no reasons, except that I was born of Japanese parents, I must be a Jap, like the rest of the aliens. In that case I'll stick to Japan and you can have my U.S. citizenship papers, its [*sic*] never done me any good.[60]

Akutsu and Yamasaki both remember that their efforts to explain their reasons for resisting were in vain; Judge Clark instructed the jury to disregard as irrelevant any testimony from them about how they had been treated by the government and why the government's conduct prompted them to resist. The issue, Clark instructed the jurors, was simply whether or not the defendant had willfully failed to report for induction.

Akutsu and Yamasaki both have vivid memories of jury deliberations as well. "Deliberations" might be too grand a word for the work of these juries, none of which caucused for more than a few minutes after each case.[61] Gene Akutsu remembers that he stood as the jurors left the courtroom to deliberate, but barely had a chance to sit down before they returned with their verdict of guilty. They had been out of the courtroom "long enough to go in and turn around and come back out[, to c]ircle around the table and come back out again." Frank Yamasaki remembers that, by the time of his trial—his was the twenty-third—the jury was no longer bothering even to deliberate. The jurors simply walked out into the hallway for a few brief moments, stayed long enough for a few drags on a cigarette, said nothing to one another, and returned with a guilty verdict.

Can it really be that the juries in these cases were so cavalier? Or are these instead just the embittered memories of those whom the jury condemned, distorted by the passage of fifty-five years? There is good reason to believe the former. As it happened, Judge Clark was not the only arbiter in the courtroom who was open to a charge of prejudgment and bias. So, too, were the jurors. For the thirty-three trials that Judge Clark ran between September 13 and September 26, 1944, he called a total of thirty-four Idaho citizens to serve as jurors. For each trial, Judge Clark seated a new and slightly different configuration of twelve of these thirty-four people. This meant that, by the time all of the trials were completed, virtually all of the jurors had served on at least ten separate juries. One juror had the distinction of hearing fifteen separate trials of Minidoka draft resisters, eight of those at a rate of two per day. Another juror who heard a total of fourteen trials sat for two separate trials on five different days. The situation grew so absurd that on September 20, the seventh day of the trials, a lawyer for one of the defendants challenged the entire venire from which he was expected to pick a jury. (The venire is the entire pool of citizens from which individual juries are drawn.) He protested to Judge Clark "that members of the jury panel had all sat on juries trying other Nisei on the same charges and thus may not be free of prejudice."[62] Clark said he would give the matter some thought, but the next morning resumed jury selection from the same pool of jurors.

Thus, when Frank Yamasaki recalls that his jurors "deliberated" by stepping into the hallway for a silent smoke, he may well be remembering correctly. Each of his twelve jurors had already heard at least five trials of Yamasaki's fellow resisters; most had heard eight. For two seasoned veteran jurors, Yamasaki's trial was their *eleventh* draft evasion trial in eight days. At that point, what was left to discuss?

Whatever its flaws, this production line of jury trials was unquestionably efficient. In the space of thirteen days, pausing only on Sundays, the juries convicted thirty-three Nisei of draft evasion at an average pace of three per day. Several others entered guilty pleas and thereby avoided trials. One young man fared better: he was able to demonstrate that he had never actually received his induction notice in the mail and was acquitted on this technicality.[63] But even this victory was short-lived; no sooner did he return to Minidoka than he was properly served with an induction notice. Upon refusing to report, he was tried and convicted of draft evasion at a later term of court.

Late in September and early in October of 1944, the convicted Minidoka draft resisters appeared before Judge Clark for sentencing. Those who had entered guilty pleas and spared the court the (plainly quite minor) inconvenience of a trial received eighteen-month sentences. Most of the rest were sentenced to terms of three years and three months in prison and a $200 fine. Judge Clark chose sentences of this length for what he described as a practical reason: he suspected that if the draft law were in effect when the resisters were eventually released from jail, they would again refuse to comply and run the government the expense of another trial. By sentencing them to terms of three years and three months, Judge Clark wished to make sure that they would remain in jail beyond the expiration of the draft law.[64]

With their sentences fixed and their futures uncertain, the Minidoka draft resisters returned to the Ada County Jail for another brief stay before their transfer to federal prison. Their mood was grim, a mix of anger and resentment muted by dull resignation. *Shikata ganai* and *gaman suru,* the Japanese phrases urging acceptance of the inevitable that their Issei parents so often uttered, were about the only comfort these young men would take with them to prison, other than their forced companionship.

SEVEN

A SHOCK TO THE CONSCIENCE

Once a year, in midsummer when the weather was nice, a judge from the U.S. District Court for the Northern District of California used to leave his San Francisco chambers and travel several hundred miles north to the logging and fishing town of Eureka. There he would hear a week's worth of cases from the district's northern reaches. At one time, this practice of riding circuit may have been a necessity, a way of bringing federal justice to the frontier. By the 1940s, however, the trip was generally understood as more of a pleasure trip for the court personnel from San Francisco, and an excuse for the members of the small Humboldt County bar to throw a party. The clerk of the court would line up a few simple cases for the visiting judge to hear, but relaxation and merriment were the main orders of business. Eleanor Jackson Piel, now a prominent civil rights attorney but then a recent law school graduate, made the trip to Eureka in 1944 as the district judge's law clerk. To her, it seemed "absolutely a boondoggle." "Every year," she explains, "the district court went up for a clambake and in order to justify the trip, they brought out a few people who'd sold alcohol to Indians. That's what the people were used to. They were used to having lots of drinking and lots of partying and absolutely no issues ever being raised."[1]

That is undoubtedly what the Eureka bar expected of the district court's visit in July of 1944. Dinners and dances were planned, the champagne was on ice, and twenty-seven Japanese American draft resisters from the Tule Lake Relocation Center sat in the Humboldt County Jail, awaiting trial and, it must have been assumed, conviction on draft evasion charges. In this last particular, however, things would not go according to plan. Louis E. Goodman, the district judge arriving from San Francisco, would not see the case against the Tule Lake resisters as the open-and-shut matter that his Eureka hosts assumed it to be. Alone among all of the federal judges hearing cases that summer against the Nisei draft resisters,[2] Judge Goodman would find sympathy for the plight of the defendants and angrily dismiss their charges.

Goodman was relatively new to the bench in July of 1944; he had been sworn in as a district judge late in December of 1942 after his appointment earlier that year by President Roosevelt. Because he was a new judge, he had never before made the trip to Eureka. But had those welcoming him in Eureka known a bit about Goodman's background and philosophy, they might have suspected that he would champion, rather than condemn, the jailed Nisei resisters. Like the defendants, Louis E. Goodman was a first-generation American, the son of immigrants.[3] Goodman's parents came to this country from Europe, probably Germany, in the latter part of the nineteenth century. They settled first in New York and then sought better fortunes in the rural setting of Lemoore, California. Goodman's father was the owner of a small country store in Lemoore when Louis was born in 1892. Within a few years of the boy's birth, the family moved to San Francisco, and that is where Louis Goodman grew up. He excelled academically as a child and was admitted to San Francisco's select Lowell High School, where he made a reputation for himself as a top debater. Goodman attended the University of California, graduating as a classmate of Earl Warren's in 1913, and did two years of law study at Hastings. He passed the California bar in 1914.

Goodman's parents were not only immigrants, but also Jews, and they raised their son in the faith. Judaism was an important part of Goodman's life. He taught Sunday School at San Francisco's Temple Emanu-El, where he and his wife were lifelong members. He donated generously to Jewish philanthropic causes and gave speeches to organizations such as the San Francisco Lodge of the B'nai B'rith and the Jewish National Welfare Fund. Goodman's surviving papers leave no indication that he encountered anti-Semitism in his youth or as a young lawyer looking for work in San Francisco. It is reasonable to assume, however, that he was not helped by his religion. Even though he was a brilliant and accomplished student, he was not offered a job with any of San Francisco's elite law firms; instead, he practiced with other Jews—first with a family friend named Brownstone and then with the small firm of Altman & Goldman. And one of Goodman's law clerks recalls that later in his life, after he had become a federal judge, he was refused accommodations at a fancy southern resort hotel because he was Jewish. Louis Goodman undoubtedly had some sense, as both a Jew and a child of immigrants, of what it meant to be an outsider in America.

From that sense, Goodman developed an understanding of what he sometimes called "true Americanism," which worked to efface, rather than emphasize, the line between insiders and outsiders, old and new American pedigrees, the powerful and the powerless. In remarks he delivered at "I Am an American Day" in May of 1946, Judge Goodman emphasized that

> [w]e are a nation of immigrants. Very few can trace their ancestry to the first generation. All that matters is that new citizens unreservedly subscribe to the doctrines that have enriched and will continue to enrich our American way of life. Among these, the most important is that of unity. No man or woman can honestly give the pledge of allegiance if there is a reserved intolerance as to a fellow citizen's origin or color or creed. Any who have or assert such reservations seek only to divide us and are unfit to come or remain under the protection of the stars and the thirteen stripes.[4]

Goodman's focus on American "unity" was especially telling: for him, unity was not the duty of the newcomer to make himself identical to others, but the duty of the newcomer to shed intolerance for others.

Goodman elaborated on this understanding of patriotism, and linked it to a duty to defend the oppressed, in a moving sermon he delivered at San Francisco's Temple Emanu-El on Yom Kippur, the Jewish Day of Atonement, in 1947.[5] The judge used that solemn occasion to urge his fellow worshipers to "scrutinize both [their] Americanism and [their] faith" and assured them that they would find an obligation linking the two: the obligation "to cherish the cause of the oppressed or the disfranchised." Goodman began by warning the congregation to be "most watchful of what may happen if we add labels to the word 'American.'" "In the earlier years of this century," the judge explained, "after immigrants were admitted to American citizenship, . . . they were very commonly referred to as German-Americans, Italian-Americans, French-Americans, and the like." From these designations, "the inference followed that they were something less or different than full-fledged Americans." But, Judge Goodman reported, "now we have done with that sort of thing. We no longer refer to naturalized American citizens as hyphenated citizens." He conceded that "[t]he new citizen may still retain what is most natural, namely a feeling of affection and friendship for his land of birth and perhaps for friends and relatives still residing there." But "affection and friendship" were a far cry from "loyalty and allegiance" for Judge Goodman: "When the oath of citizenship is once taken, the new citizen becomes a plain American citizen, without reservation and without qualification."

Judge Goodman then focused his argument on Jewish Americans in particular. "[B]eing an American Jew," he noted, "does not entail any hyphenation." Neither, he argued, should it present any conflict of loyalties because "[s]teadfast adherence to the creed of Judaism does not in the slightest detract from true Americanism." Indeed, Judge Goodman could "think of no better way of maintaining and bettering the American ideals than to practice . . . the ideals of righteousness which are the cornerstone of Judaism." And those "ideals of righteousness" were ideals of compassion and liberation: "[I]n my opinion to cherish the cause of the oppressed or the disfranchised is in itself a noble achievement. It is no less so abroad than it is at home and it needs no apology." Thus, he stressed, American Jews should not hesitate to speak out on behalf of oppressed Jews in other lands, for fear that some in this country might doubt their Americanism. America, he argued, "has fought to free people from slavery and to free nations from dictatorships and oppression." How, then, Goodman asked, can there be inconsistency "in the espousal by American Jews of the cause of oppressed Jews abroad?" To champion that cause "serves the ideals of our own country. It may be courageously and openly maintained."

Goodman concluded his Yom Kippur sermon with a moving call for introspection and courage. "Gallantry and intrepidity in a just cause," he said, "are the essence of strength. They command respect and admiration. They make for security, never for insecurity." And perhaps most important, he maintained, they are the values that link good Americanism with good Judaism: "If the American Jew looks into himself on this Day of Atonement and finds there that kind of courage, the God of Israel should look with favor upon him."

These were the values that Louis Goodman, the son of Jewish immigrants, brought with him to Eureka in July of 1944, to hear *United States v. Masaaki Kuwabara et al.*, the cases of the twenty-seven sons of immigrants who had defied the draft laws at the Tule Lake Relocation Center. Although he did not know it as he arrived, these were also the values that those cases would call upon him to display. It took courage to come to the aid of the jailed Nisei—the "American born Japs," as the local newspaper called them[6]—during wartime and in a hostile town like Eureka.

Prejudice against Asians in Eureka was intense and had a long and well-remembered history. Eleanor Jackson Piel, Judge Goodman's law clerk, recalls a local attorney's boasting to her that a large group of Chinese railroad workers had been driven from town and set to sea in the late 1800s. The incident to which the attorney referred was real, and it had engendered quite a legacy of intolerance.[7] In February of 1885, an altercation between two Chinese men of rival clans in Eureka's small Chinese neighborhood grew violent. Shots were fired. A stray bullet struck and killed David C. Kendall, a Eureka city councilman, as he crossed the street. Within minutes, an angry white mob of loggers, miners, mill workers, sailors, and drifters gathered at the scene of the shooting. With cries of "Burn Chinatown!" and "Hang all the Chinamen!" the mob demanded action. And action was what they got. Within an hour, a self-appointed committee of the town's elders resolved to give Eureka's Chinese twenty-four hours to leave town. The next day all three hundred and ten of them were placed on two steamers in Eureka's harbor, and the ships pushed off for San Francisco. As the steamers pulled away, a large crowd of Eurekans gathered in front of city hall and overwhelmingly resolved "[t]hat all Chinamen be expelled from the city and that none be allowed to return." Their resolution stood for years: in 1937, just seven years before the prosecution of the Tule Lake resisters, the local paper boasted that "Humboldt County has the unique distinction of being the only community in which there are no oriental colonies." The newspaper explained that

> although 52 years have passed since the Chinese were driven from the county, none have ever returned. On one or two occasions off-shore vessels with Chinamen crews have stopped at this port, but the Chinamen as a rule stayed aboard their vessels, choosing not to take a chance on being ordered out.

> Chinese everywhere have always looked upon this section of the state as "bad medicine" for the Chinaman.

In 1941, as the nation entered the war in the Pacific, Eureka's city ordinances still declared that "[n]o Chinese shall ever be employed, either directly or indirectly, on any work of the city . . . except in punishment for a crime." Naturally, the war against Japan only served further to inflame the anti-Asian passions that had burned in Eureka for so many years. In Eleanor Jackson Piel's words, "[T]he prejudice was intense. The Orientals were not . . . wanted around for any purpose."

The fierce anti-Asian sentiment in Eureka was evident even in the local newspaper's coverage of the Tule Lake resisters and their court case. On Monday, July 17, 1944, the day after the defendants arrived at the Humboldt County Jail, the *Humboldt Standard* ran a front-page story captioned, "Not Enough Food, Japs Complain in Jail Here." Its openly mocking tone makes it worth quoting in full:

> "Not enough ricee."
>
> That wasn't exactly the plaint of the Japanese prisoners in the county jail today; their complaint was "Not enough mealee."
>
> According to the custom of all county jails, only two meals a day are served to prisoners by Sheriff Arthur Ross and his assistants. But each of these has plenty of body and quantity, the sheriff's deputies said.
>
> Some kind of meat, such as stews and often a quarter of beef is served every day, and each meal has plenty of succulence and nutriment, said Sheriff Arthur A. Ross. But this doesn't seem to be enough for those who have been raised on rice in the old country.
>
> They want, "three mealees, so solly, please."[8]

Of course, none of the Tule Lake defendants was "Japanese"; they were all Americans. None of them spoke English with the bogus Japanese accent the story attributed to them. And none of them had been "raised on rice in the old country" unless by "old country" the story meant California. Still, to the town of Eureka, the Nisei draft resisters were strangers of foreign "nationality," the hated enemy. They were Japs.[9]

The federal court session in Eureka opened on Monday morning, July 17, 1944. Six of the Tule Lake resisters were marched up the street past gawking onlookers and into the courtroom for their arraignments on the charge of willfully failing to report for their preinduction physical examinations. The defendants asked for counsel. Judge Goodman appointed two well-regarded local practitioners, Arthur W. Hill Jr. and Chester Monette, to represent them and gave them twenty-four hours to determine what plea they would enter.

That evening, the partying began in earnest. Seventy-five invited guests crowded the town's finest restaurant for the annual banquet thrown on behalf of the visiting federal court by a prominent Eureka lawyer, Lawrence F. Puter. According to newspaper accounts,[10] Puter's guests, including the guest of honor, Judge Goodman, feasted on "two large, broiled, juicy steaks, smothered in mushrooms, . . . with shoestring potatoes and whole kernel corn . . . , crab cocktail to begin with, and green apple pie with a slice of cheese to end with." After the meal came speeches, most of which "centered around the 'visiting' Jap delegation of 27 members now housed in the county jail while awaiting to be charged with refusal to obey the selective service laws."

Judge Goodman must have squirmed uncomfortably in his chair through these speeches. One of the first to take the dais was Arthur W. Hill Jr., the evening's master of ceremonies and one of the two lawyers Goodman had appointed to represent the Nisei. Hill spoke about "being appointed by Judge Goodman to defend the Japs" and then mocked his own clients, concluding his remarks by speaking in a phony Japanese accent. Next to speak was a state senator, Irwin T. Quinn, who as a legislator had "investigated conditions at Tule Lake" and was therefore "a man qualified to speak on the subject." Senator Quinn expressed his concern that the situation at Tule Lake could turn into a serious problem "before this thing is over." He explained that the Nisei draft resisters "are born Americans, subject to our Constitution and laws the same as any others, yet that means nothing to them." "Fortunately," he opined, perhaps casting a glance toward the dinner guests from the federal court, "there are laws to take care of that."

Assistant United States Attorney Emmet Seawell, the federal prosecutor from Sacramento who had come to Eureka to prosecute the Tule Lake resisters, picked up on Senator Quinn's theme in his remarks to the banquet guests. "[I]t is wonderful," said the prosecutor, "that we have a democracy in which 27 Japs can be brought here in safety, given all the protection guaranteed by our Constitution and laws, [and] assured of a fair trial, with prominent and leading attorneys appointed to represent them." Even for the prosecutor, the Americans in the Humboldt County Jail were "Japs" who were magnanimously being offered the protection of "our"—not their—Constitution and laws. "It could not happen in any other country in the world," boasted Seawell.

Finally came Judge Goodman's turn to speak. Goodman's first exposure to the Tule Lake cases had come just that morning, and he undoubtedly did not yet fully understand the defendants' circumstances or appreciate the unfairness of their treatment. Yet he could not have helped but notice the bloodthirstiness of the local community, the racism in the newspaper, and the cocky assurance of all at the banquet—even, it seemed, of the defendants' own lawyer—that the Nisei resisters would be convicted. And so he used his remarks as an occasion to urge moderation and patience. Referring obliquely to the jailed Nisei from Tule Lake, Goodman exhorted the people to be "calm and just in spite of all their war sacrifices" and to "adhere to the principles and doctrines of their forefathers." Goodman seemed to sense that his Eureka hosts were expecting a lynching rather than the calm justice he was prepared to mete out.

His suspicions were born out in court the next morning. Defense attorneys Hill and Monette rose to announce that the first group of twelve of their clients was prepared to enter guilty pleas to the charge in the indictment. Judge Goodman asked for the factual basis for the plea. Monette's characterization of his clients' position was not exactly stirring. He explained that the defendants "had been originally classed in 1-A and while waiting for a call had been put into camps." Monette said that "this hurt their feelings and made them feel that they had been classed as enemies although they are all American citizens. And so they ignored the call to appear for examination when it finally did come."[11] Judge Goodman took the opportunity to ask the defendants a few questions about conditions at Tule Lake. Jimi Yamaichi, one of the Tule Lake resisters, remembers telling the judge that they lived with "machine guns around and barbed wire fences. [N]o chance of escape whatsoever." Judge Goodman accepted the guilty pleas.

Later in the day, however, the injustice of prosecuting the incarcerated Nisei for resisting the draft began to nag at him. He and his law clerk began discussing whether it would be possible to dismiss the charges. They both recognized that "if [the defendants] pleaded guilty then that was the end of the case and there wouldn't be any way . . . the judge would be in a position to say that the whole process was wrong." That evening, the law clerk recalls, after another social gathering, Judge Goodman and his law clerk sat up late in a bar "talking about how horrible [the situation] was" and wondering "how in the world we were going to make this decision, how [we] were going to do this, how we were going to pull this thing off." The task they faced was daunting: not only were they on their own in a remote and rather hostile town without a decent law library, but also the defense attorneys in the case showed absolutely no interest in fighting the charges. Judge Goodman decided that if he was going to try to help the Tule Lake resisters, they would need a new lawyer. He placed a call to an old friend and law school classmate of his, Blaine McGowan, and asked the Eureka lawyer if he would join the defense team. McGowan, something of a flamboyant character who often appeared in court in alligator cowboy boots, must have understood that his friend was thinking of dismissing the charges. Why else would the judge be inviting him into the case after already accepting twelve guilty pleas?

McGowan agreed to join the defense team and showed up in jail the next morning to meet his clients. He made quite an impression on them. Tom Noda, one of the Tule Lake resisters, recalls that "[t]he first words he said, when he came in, was that he ha[d] no love for Japs. But he said he had never lost a case and he didn't intend to lose this one." The Nisei gulped when they heard him call them "Japs"; they "thought, 'we have no chance.'" But Blaine McGowan began to mount a defense for them—something Hill and Monette had not done. Later that day McGowan moved orally to withdraw the guilty pleas that had previously been entered. Not surprisingly, Judge Goodman granted the motion and gave the defense team a day to file additional motions.[12]

The next day, Thursday, July 20, 1944, McGowan filed a document he called a "Motion to Quash Indictment and Terminate Proceedings." The motion presented a mix of constitutional, statutory, and factual objections to charges in the indictment. First, McGowan argued, the defendants "ha[d] been, at all times during all proceedings taken and to be taken herein, under duress, personal restraint, confinement and fear by reason of [their] confinement in a Concentration Center, without due process of law, and contrary to the provisions of Amendment 5 of the Constitution of the United States of America." Second, he claimed that they were unacceptable for military service under several provisions of the Selective Training and Service Act of 1940. Finally, he argued that before being ordered to report for their preinduction physicals, the defendants had applied for expatriation to Japan, "thereby rendering [themselves] not acceptable for service in the Army of the United States as a matter of law."[13]

This full-barrel attack on the indictment was too much for Chester Monette, one of the two defense attorneys Judge Goodman had initially appointed and still nominally a part of the defense team. Rising to speak before the motion was argued, Monette announced that he wished "to withdraw from the case on the ground that his advice to the defendants had been disregarded."[14] Monette's advice to the Nisei, of course, had been to plead guilty. Judge Goodman's law clerk surmises that Monette must have understood at that point that the judge was inclined to dismiss the charges against the defendants, and he "probably . . . thought it was wrong for them to win." Perhaps Monette simply did not want to be known in his small town as the lawyer who helped the Japs beat the draft. In any event, Monette wanted out of the case, and Judge Goodman permitted him to withdraw.

By this point in the week, Emmet Seawell, the assistant United States attorney handling the case for the government, also realized that things were not going well. At oral argument on the motion to quash, Judge Goodman pursued him on the defendants' due process claim. In light of the defendants' confinement behind barbed wire at Tule Lake, Goodman wished to know, how could any of the defendants be seen as free agents who were capable of being drafted, or of making a willful choice as to whether to comply with the draft, or even of entering a voluntary plea to the charges in the indictment? Seawell, evidently flummoxed by the unexpectedly tough questioning, responded that "he had applied to the United States Attorney General Biddle's office at Washington, D.C., for a ruling on the matter and expected to have it . . . by Saturday morning."[15]

When that "ruling" came, however, it was not of much help to Seawell; Tom Clark, the assistant attorney general who responded to Seawell's request for assistance, was "not certain that [he] thoroughly underst[ood] the question propounded by the court" and did not deal with any constitutional objections to the prosecution. As Clark understood the problem, Judge Goodman was concerned that by virtue of being in custody, the defendants "were not free agents and could not report for induction"—in other words, that the barbed wire fence of the Tule Lake Relocation Center prevented them from taking the physical step of leaving camp to join the army. This, of course, was not Judge Goodman's point; he was concerned with the defendants' "free agency" in a far broader and more philosophical sense. But Clark's response was, in any event, insipid. First, he pointed out that the defendants were charged not with failing to report for induction, but with failing to report for their preinduction physicals. Thus, he argued, any objection the defendants might have to induction into the army would not cancel their obligation to be medically screened for their fitness to be inducted. Second, and even more simplistically, Clark pointed out to Seawell that the War Relocation Authority was only too happy to relinquish custody of internees so that they could leave camp for military service. Thus, he argued, "the fact that they are in custody" did not, as a matter of fact, "inhibit[them] from reporting for induction." Finally, Clark prodded Seawell to have Judge Goodman follow the lead of Judge T. Blake Kennedy from the Heart Mountain case: "No such question as this," Clark reminded Seawell, "was raised in the case involving the 63 Japanese found guilty in the Heart Mountain War Relocation Center case who were sentenced to serve three years several weeks ago."[16]

Plainly, Judge Goodman did not see the case as Judge Kennedy had, and he was prepared to hand the government a defeat. He and his law clerk were, however, concerned that "something terrible might take place" if he ruled in the defendants' favor because "there was such terrible prejudice in the community." Indeed, they were a bit frightened for their own safety—scared that "they might be lynched." As a result, Judge Goodman left the resolution of the Tule Lake resisters' dismissal motion to the very last minute of their week in Eureka—a special Saturday morning session. Judge Goodman and his law clerk toiled late into Friday night, struggling to produce an opinion that would support the dismissal of the government's charges. They had not been much helped by the dearth of legal research materials in Eureka. But by Saturday morning, they had managed to cobble together an opinion dismissing the charges on due process grounds. Judge Goodman read it from the bench as a car containing his packed suitcase idled outside the courthouse, waiting to take him and his clerk back to San Francisco.

Goodman began with a brief review of the circumstances that led to the defendants' incarceration at Tule Lake. He explained that the Nikkei had been evacuated from their West Coast homes in the spring and summer of 1942, temporarily detained in assembly centers near their homes, and then moved to permanent relocation centers away from the coast. He also explained that once the government decided to segregate loyal from disloyal internees in 1943, the Tule Lake camp had been "chosen as a concentration center for those whose disloyalty was determined either by the government or by their own declarations or because of their expressed desire to be repatriated to Japan."

He then described the facts of the case involving the lead defendant in the case, Masaaki Kuwabara, whose circumstances were in all important respects identical to those of the other twenty-six Tule Lake resisters. Kuwabara had been evacuated from his home in California to the Santa Anita Assembly Center and from there had been taken to the WRA relocation camp at Jerome, Arkansas. In 1943, in the wake of registration, Kuwabara had been "removed as a disloyal Nisei to the Tulelake [*sic*] Center and continuously thereafter . . . forcibly detained therein." "It is not controverted," Goodman reported, "that defendant admits disloyalty, claiming that discrimination against him as an American citizen and his consequent detention at Tulelake [*sic*], motivated him to such state of mind." Neither, said Goodman, was it "questioned that Tulelake [*sic*] Center is an area surrounded by barricades and patroled by armed guards and that immediately without the barricades, military forces of the United States are present and available to assure against departure of any of the persons confined in the Center." Kuwabara, Goodman explained, had been classified by the Selective Service System as 1-A while detained at Tule Lake and ordered to report for a preinduction physical examination on May 3, 1944. "Defendant failed to obey the order to report for preinduction physical examination," concluded Goodman, "and the indictment followed."

Goodman then proceeded to evaluate Kuwabara's arguments in support of the motion. He rejected Kuwabara's claim that the Selective Service System had incorrectly classified him as 1-A; these sorts of matters were not properly raised as a defense to a criminal prosecution for failure to comply with an order to report for a physical, but were to be litigated in a habeas corpus action after a draftee's induction.[17] He also set aside Kuwabara's argument that his attempt at expatriation relieved him of the duty to respond to the draft. Expatriation, he said, was not available to Kuwabara so long as he was a resident of the United States.[18]

His analysis then led him to the ultimate question: "Is defendant deprived of his liberty without due process of law in this proceeding by virtue of the circumstances of his confinement at Tulelake [*sic*]?" Judge Goodman refused to pass judgment on the question of whether the underlying removal and internment of the Nikkei from the West Coast were constitutional; "resolution of that question [was] neither necessary nor proper for the determination of the motion." The president, reacting to "[c]ertain dangers vitally imminent to the security of the West Coast," had authorized the removal and internment program, and his war powers, said Goodman, "may be sufficient constitutional justification therefor."

"No such dangers, however," Goodman observed, "are the basis for the prosecution of defendant for refusing to be inducted, or for refusing to undergo preinduction physical examination." Kuwabara's case, in other words, was different from *Hirabayashi v. United States*[19] and *Korematsu v. United States,*[20] cases in which the federal courts either had passed or were about to pass upon the legality of the removal and internment program. In those cases, Goodman seemed to suggest, the government had its full war powers to rely upon, but those powers did not support the prosecutor's judgment to prosecute Kuwabara and his twenty-six fellow resisters for refusing to show up for their physicals.

Goodman then moved to the heart of his analysis. "The defendant cannot be denied the protection of the guaranty of due process because of . . . war or danger to national security but only upon a valid declaration of martial law." Applying the test of due process, Judge Goodman had little trouble concluding the government's conduct was fundamentally unfair:

> It is *shocking to the conscience* that an American citizen be confined on the ground of disloyalty, and then, while so under duress and restraint, be compelled to serve in the armed forces, or be prosecuted for not yielding to such compulsion.

Goodman cited no authority to support this proposition. He did, however, look for support to the Selective Training and Service Act itself, which, in its prefatory Declaration of Policy, announced "that in a free society the obligations and privileges of military training and service should be shared generally in accordance with a fair and just system of selective . . . service." "Certainly," argued Goodman, "'fair and just' compulsory military training in a 'free society' is wholly inconsistent with the instant proceeding."

Goodman rejected the government's contention that the "question of 'due process' [was] not reachable" in a criminal prosecution, "but only by writ of habeas corpus after compliance with the order of the local [draft] board." Of course, Goodman had agreed with precisely that proposition when he rejected Kuwabara's argument that he had been incorrectly classified into the 1-A category. But this constitutional claim, Goodman reasoned, was different because it was "clear to [him] that defendant is under the circumstances not a free agent, nor is any plea that he may make, free or voluntary, and hence he is not accorded 'due process' in this proceeding."

Just as Judge Kennedy had concluded his opinion convicting the Heart Mountain resisters with a personal aside about the duties of loyal citizens, Judge Goodman took the opportunity at the end of his opinion to share a somewhat more personal view: "The issue raised by this motion . . . must be resolved in the light of the traditional and historic Anglo-American approach to the time-honored doctrine of 'due process.' It must not give way to overzealousness in an attempt to reach, via the criminal process, those whom we may regard as undesirable citizens." Behind this defense of the Tule Lake "undesirables" can be seen the passionate views of an immigrant's son on the role of tolerance in good American citizenship.

When Judge Goodman finished reading his opinion, the courtroom fell silent. Tom Noda recalls that he and his fellow defendants remained subdued and quiet, avoiding the emotional outburst that often accompanies courtroom victories. It was not that the Tule Lake resisters were unhappy with the outcome, Noda recalls. It was rather that none of them really "cared whether we went to prison or not because it wouldn't have made much difference." Incarceration was nothing new to these twenty-six internees. Noda himself had been behind barbed wire in a

Pomona racetrack horse stable in the spring and summer of 1942, in a tarpaper Heart Mountain barrack from the fall of 1942 until the summer of 1943, and in segregation at Tule Lake since the summer of 1943. Noda understood that by beating the draft charges, all he had won was an escorted automobile ride back to confinement at Tule Lake. As courtroom victories go, this was a decidedly Pyrrhic one.

The prosecutor, Emmet Seawell, could not have been surprised by the outcome. By midweek, when Judge Goodman brought Blaine McGowan into the case and permitted the first twelve defendants to withdraw their guilty pleas, Seawell must have known that Judge Goodman was thinking of handing the government a defeat. Indeed, Seawell recognized by Thursday that his case was in deep enough trouble to warrant an urgent plea for help to the Justice Department in Washington. Still, once Seawell had a chance to hear and digest Judge Goodman's opinion dismissing his indictments, the prosecutor was not impressed. In a letter to Assistant Attorney General Tom Clark, Seawell confided that "Judge Goodman's reasoning, together with his opinion, have never coincided with my idea of what the law on the subject should be." "As a matter of fact," Seawell added, "I have great difficulty in reconciling Judge Goodman's opinion with any principles of law I am familiar with."[21]

Seawell's reaction was more than just sour grapes from a disappointed loser. As an application of settled legal doctrine, Judge Goodman's opinion was decidedly weak. Its due process holding rested on two distinct propositions, one of which concerned the status of the defendants and the other the nature of the government's actions. First, responding to the government's assertion that the Tule Lake resisters' objections to being drafted must await a habeas corpus action after their induction, Judge Goodman held that the very pendency of the criminal charges against them violated their due process rights: the defendants were "under the circumstances not . . . free agent[s], nor [was] any plea that [they might] make, free or voluntary, and hence [they were] not accorded 'due process'" in the criminal proceeding itself. Goodman's reasoning here was rather obscure, but he appeared to be concluding that the entire effort at prosecuting Kuwabara and the other resisters was void from the start because of the restraint and duress under which they were being held at Tule Lake. Their free will was so overborne by their captivity that they were simply incapable of entering any sort of voluntary plea or otherwise responding to the government's charges as free agents.

Judge Goodman offered no support for this due process theory, and it is not at all clear that he could have. Surely, the residents of Tule Lake were answerable in court for other kinds of criminal conduct. To take an extreme example, if a Tule Lake internee were accused of murdering an abusive camp guard, the accused would not be heard to contend that he was entirely out of the reach of the courts on account of his captivity. By the same token, if an internee were accused of evading the draft because of an allegedly overwhelming fear of dying in battle—a fear that undoubtedly motivated at least some young men, including many noninternees, to refuse the draft—then the fact of his captivity at Tule Lake would not strip him of the capacity to enter a free and voluntary plea to that charge in court. If a resident of Tule Lake was able to enter a free and voluntary plea to a murder charge or to a charge of evading the draft out of cowardice, then he must also have been in a position to enter a free and voluntary plea to a charge of evading the draft out of disloyalty. This is not to say that the circumstances of an internee's confinement at Tule Lake were totally irrelevant to the due process question; it is simply to say that those circumstances could not have removed an internee entirely from the reach of the criminal provisions of the Selective Training and Service Act.

Judge Goodman's second due process theory was quite different. Here Judge Goodman held that the government's decisions first to confine the Tule Lake resisters on grounds of disloyalty and then to force them into the military or prosecute them for resisting that force violated the Due Process Clause and required the dismissal of the indictments because those decisions were "shock[ing]" to his "conscience." This was a considerably more direct rationale for dismissing the indictments than his first due process theory, as it mapped more closely into the moral claim that the resisters were pressing—namely, that there was something innately and deeply disturbing about conscripting people from out of internment camps.

As intuitively appealing as this holding may have been, however, it was not an application of settled legal principles. Indeed, nearly the opposite was true: by invoking this particular due process theory, Judge Goodman stepped into an area of pitched legal battle. The Constitution has two Due Process Clauses—one in the Fifth Amendment, which forbids the federal government from taking away a person's life, liberty, or property without due process of law, and the other in the Fourteenth Amendment, which forbids state governments from doing the same. As might be imagined, the core concern of due process has always been process—the mechanisms by which government goes about its dealings with, and especially the deprivations it imposes upon, its citizens. Thus, by 1944 it was well settled that due process requires government to afford various sorts of procedural safeguards before subjecting people to certain kinds of deprivations. A government that wishes to punish people for smoking pipes must first publicly announce that pipe smoking is illegal; a government that wishes to enjoin a landowner from making some noxious use of his property must give him an opportunity to be heard on the question before the injunction takes final effect.

Somewhat oxymoronically, the Court has held that due process is also concerned with *substance*. That is, the Due Process Clauses guarantee more than just process: they also make it either impossible or extremely difficult for government to subject people to certain sorts of deprivations, no matter how much it first offers in the way of procedural safeguards. For example, a government cannot authorize the cutting off of a batterer's hands as a civil remedy for the tort of battery, even if it offers the batterer all of the procedural protections known to our legal system. This remedy would violate the batterer's right to *substantive* due process. It would strip him of a freedom to bodily integrity, a basic "liberty" of the kind mentioned in the Due Process Clause, that is off-limits to government. The trouble with this branch of due process doctrine, of course, is that the Due Process Clause says nothing about chopping off hands, nothing even of "bodily integrity"; all it speaks of is "liberty." It is therefore up to judges to determine the scope of the word "liberty" and to say what is and is not included in that term. This is the doctrine that has brought the federal courts some of their most agonizing modern debates: Is a woman's decision to terminate a pregnancy one of the "liberties" insulated from government interference by the Due Process Clause? The wish of a terminally ill patient to seek life-ending drugs? The desire of two men, or of two women, to marry, or to have sex?

These are the substantive due process battlegrounds with which we are familiar today, but in the 1940s the Court was deep in debate on a slightly different question of substantive due process—whether the Due Process Clause authorized judges to review criminal convictions for conformity with vaguely defined notions of "fundamental fairness." Much of this debate played itself out in the context of the Fourteenth Amendment's Due Process Clause—the clause that applied the guarantee of due process to state governments. The question was whether that guarantee took the specific provisions of the Bill of Rights that unambiguously constrained the federal government in criminal cases—the right to counsel, the privilege against self-incrimination, the protection against double jeopardy, and all of the other provisions of the first eight amendments to the Constitution—and applied those provisions against the states as well. One position, articulated most forcefully by Justice Hugo Black, was that the word "liberty" in the Fourteenth Amendment's Due Process Clause referred to nothing more and nothing less than those protections already enumerated in the Bill of Rights. The other position, articulated most forcefully by Justice Felix Frankfurter, was that the word "liberty" in the Fourteenth Amendment guaranteed "fundamental fairness" in criminal trials and consistency with "fundamental principle[s] of liberty and justice which inhere[ ] in the very idea of free government,"[22] but not necessarily each and every one of the protections in the first eight amendments. On this view, a court's role was to determine whether a particular government practice in a criminal case "constitute[d] a denial of fundamental fairness, shocking to the universal sense of justice."[23]

This dispute was not merely an arcane disagreement about the meaning of the word "liberty" in the Fifth and Fourteenth Amendments. It was a dispute about the proper role and power of judges. Justice Black complained that a judicial inquiry into the "fundamental fairness" of a criminal trial was too loose, open-ended, and dependent upon the personal preferences of the judge making the assessment. He accused the Court of arrogating for itself (and other federal judges) a "boundless power under 'natural law' periodically to expand and contract constitutional standards to conform to the Court's conception of what at a particular time constitutes 'civilized decency' and 'fundamental liberty and justice.'"[24] Defending the "fundamental fairness" method, Justice Frankfurter responded to Justice Black's attack. "Judicial review of th[e due process] guarantee," he conceded, "[inescapably] imposes upon this Court an exercise of judgment upon the whole course of the [criminal] proceedings in order to ascertain whether they offend those canons of decency and fairness which express the notions of justice of English-speaking peoples." And those standards, he admitted, are "not authoritatively formulated anywhere as though they were prescriptions in a pharmacopeia." "But," he insisted, "neither does the application of the Due Process Clause imply that judges are wholly at large. The judicial judgment in applying the Due Process Clause must move within the limits of accepted notions of justice and is not to be based upon the idiosyncrasies of a merely personal judgment."[25]

It was into this doctrinal maelstrom that Judge Goodman plunged when he dismissed the indictments of the Tule Lake resisters on the basis that they were "shocking to his conscience." He did not support his holding with citations to any relevant precedent, and the most immediate reason for this was undoubtedly that he and his law clerk had nowhere to do any careful legal research in the small town of Eureka. But even if he had had the finest law library in the country, he would not have found much firm support for his opinion. For one thing, the due process doctrine he invoked was still just in the process of being born. Later the Supreme Court, in the case of *Rochin v. California*, began to explain more clearly how a criminal conviction could shock the conscience enough to violate due process. In *Rochin*, the practice of obtaining evidence by forcibly pumping a criminal suspect's stomach was sufficiently shocking to the consciences of six of the Court's nine justices to lead them to overturn the criminal conviction that had been obtained on the strength of that evidence. The stomach pumping, according to Justice Frankfurter, did more than just "offend some fastidious squeamishness"; it was a method "bound to offend even hardened sensibilities" and "too close to the rack and the screw to permit of constitutional differentiation."[26] In 1944, however, this invocation and elaboration of the "shocks the conscience" test were still eight years away, and no other decision of either the Supreme Court or any federal appellate court offered much guidance.

More important—and more distressing—the situation in the *Kuwabara* case simply did not lend itself very well to the due process doctrine Judge Goodman invoked. Goodman did not specify whether it was the government's decision to draft the interned Nisei or the prosecutor's decision to indict them for resisting that was shocking to his conscience. But either way, the judge was pushing due process review into wholly uncharted territory. Judge Goodman did not maintain that the federal government lacked the raw power to apply the draft laws to American citizens interned on suspicion of disloyalty. Indeed, he could not have sustained such a view because the federal government certainly has that raw power; indeed, it has the power to draft even *resident aliens* into the U.S. military.[27] That greater power to draft resident aliens surely must include the lesser power to draft citizens whose loyalty it questions. And this is especially true in light of the fact that the army, by drafting the arguably disloyal, would not necessarily commit itself to deploying this manpower in ways that would endanger national security or create agonizing dilemmas of conscience for the draftees. The army could, if it wished, assign all such draftees to a potato-peeling squad in the kitchens of military hospitals. Of course, to say that the government had the raw *power* to draft the Tule Lake resisters is not to say that drafting them was wise, kind, considerate, or even fair. The country was, however, at war, and the Due Process Clause offered slim support for the federal judiciary to second-guess the personnel judgments of those responsible for manning the war effort.

Similarly, the Justice Department's decision to prosecute the Tule Lake resisters for draft evasion—however morally offensive—was probably not meant to be measured against the conscience of a federal judge on a motion to dismiss an indictment. The enforcement of the criminal law is perhaps the most central function of the executive branch of our government, and the judiciary has long recognized that it is ill-suited to sit in judgment of the executive's enforcement decisions. As far back as 1868, the Supreme Court recognized that "public prosecutions, until they come before the court to which they are returnable, are within the exclusive direction"[28] of the Justice Department. In more recent years—ironically, in a case involving a young man who refused to register for the draft in the early 1980s—the Supreme Court made clear that "so long as the prosecutor has probable cause to believe that the accused committed an offense defined by statute, the decision whether or not to prosecute, and what charge to file or bring before a grand jury, generally rests entirely in his discretion."[29] Emmet Seawell, the assistant United States attorney in the *Kuwabara* case, unquestionably had probable cause to charge the Tule Lake resisters with committing an offense defined by the Selective

Training and Service Act of 1940. However blind to the Nisei's plight the prosecutor's decision may have been, it was undoubtedly a judgment for him to make as an official of the executive branch, without regard for the contrary dictates of a federal judge's conscience.

To be sure, Judge Goodman's decision in *Kuwabara* was a courageous one, the only one of its kind from among all of the prosecutions brought against the Nisei draft resisters during 1944. The opinion struggles to contain its author's moral outrage at the government's audacity in deporting the Nisei from their homes, warehousing them in camps, drafting them into the army, and then prosecuting those who refused. Sadly, though, the Due Process Clause and its "conscience-shocking" test did not really open a proper vent for that outrage.

Interestingly, the situation did offer Judge Goodman such a vent, but he did not use it. The judge chose to dismiss the charges outright by granting the pretrial dismissal motion that Blaine McGowan had filed. That was not the only way of handing the Tule Lake resisters a victory. He could just as easily have denied the motion, tried the case, and then acquitted the defendants on all charges. Of course, the defendants had a right to a jury trial, and they would have had to waive that right and agree to a bench trial in order to put Judge Goodman into the position of rendering a verdict. But Blaine McGowan, having been brought into the case by Judge Goodman for the specific purposes of withdrawing the guilty pleas that some of the defendants had already entered and of filing a motion to dismiss the charges, would surely have understood that his clients' best strategy would be to seek a bench trial before his old law school friend rather than a jury trial before twelve Eurekans. Emmet Seawell would have been powerless to stand in the way of this strategy because the law at the time allowed a criminal defendant to waive a jury trial even over the prosecutor's objection.

In important ways, this might have been a safer plan for Judge Goodman. First, and at the most practical level, this strategy would have insulated his ruling from review and reversal by the court of appeals. The Constitution's Double Jeopardy Clause prevents the government from ever taking an appeal of a verdict acquitting a defendant of criminal charges. An acquittal is, quite simply, final—one of the very few absolutely final decrees known to our legal system. The grant of a pretrial motion to dismiss criminal charges, on the other hand, is *not* final. The government may appeal such an order without violating the defendant's double jeopardy rights, and if the government succeeds in getting the order reversed, the defendant may be tried on the charges. By ruling as he did, Judge Goodman therefore exposed the Tule Lake resisters to the possibility that they might someday be tried for draft evasion. He did not supply them with the ironclad victory that was within his power to grant.

The option of trying and acquitting the defendants would have been safer for a second reason as well: it would have been at least somewhat more consistent with settled law. Because they never had to go to trial, the Tule Lake resisters never had to specify a theory of defense to the charges. But there is little question that their defense would have sought to focus on the many deprivations and cruelties to which the government had subjected them and their families since late in 1941 and on the barrenness, isolation, and vulnerability of their lives at Tule Lake. These aspects of the defendants' situation would have leant strong atmospheric support to the notion that they were all under some subtle form of duress, some sort of inappropriate government pressure, at the time they were ordered to report for induction into the army. Their mistreatment at the hands of the government might also have permitted defense counsel, borrowing from the law of entrapment, to suggest that the crucial element of criminal intent—their willful design to evade the draft—was in a basic way manufactured by the government, and not a product of their own free choice. Of course, neither of these arguments would have met the legal criteria for a proper defense of duress or entrapment. But they might have cast enough of a cloud over the government's theory of willful draft evasion to conjure up a reasonable doubt in the factfinder's mind. And a reasonable doubt was all that Judge Goodman needed to acquit.

Arguably, Judge Goodman would not even have needed to entertain a reasonable doubt about their guilt in order to acquit them after a trial. Because acquittals may never be appealed, American juries have long enjoyed a power known as nullification—the ability to acquit a technically guilty defendant for whatever reason they please. Defenders of the nullification power see it as a protection against government oppression and tyranny, a safety valve that permits the people either to come to the rescue of a defendant who technically violated a law, but does not deserve to be punished as a criminal, or to send the prosecutor a message that it condemns the government's conduct. It is, in a sense, the jury's counterpart to the due process doctrine of fundamental fairness applied by judges—an opportunity for citizen jurors to make clear that the government's effort to punish a particular defendant is shocking to their consciences. Of course, the Tule Lake resisters could never have hoped to assemble a nullifying jury from the citizenry of Eureka during wartime. At a bench trial, however, they surely could have hoped for a nullifying verdict from Judge Goodman. There is, to be sure, precious little law on the question of whether nullification is a prerogative of *judges* as well as juries, and there was even less in 1944 than there is now. But regardless of whether or not Judge Goodman would have had the *right* to nullify, he surely would have had the *power* to do so.

Goodman was a careful and intelligent judge who undoubtedly knew of these safer options. Yet he chose instead to dismiss the indictment on the far shakier grounds of due process. Should he be faulted or praised for choosing the riskier course? The answer to this question must take account of the terrible dilemma that faced him. At times, judges must administer a system of law that they find immoral, yet that has the approval of positive law. Before the Civil War, antislavery judges in the North were called upon to apply the fugitive slave laws and, to their revulsion, return human beings to their owners. Today judges deeply opposed to capital punishment are called upon to preside over trials and appeals in which the state is seeking to take a defendant's life. Judge Goodman found himself in a somewhat similar position when he arrived in Eureka to dispose of the case of the Tule Lake resisters.

Had Judge Goodman channeled his outrage at the government's mistreatment of the Tule Lake Nisei into an acquittal on their draft evasion charges, he would have more ably protected the defendants. But in doing so, he would have lost a precious opportunity to add his voice to the then-ongoing judicial conversation about the lawfulness and morality of the internment program. An acquittal is typically the most cryptic of pronouncements—two simple words, "not guilty," that keep hidden the reasoning that produced the verdict. As a judge, Goodman would presumably have had the prerogative to issue an opinion explaining his verdict, although this would have been a highly unusual step. Unappealable, and quite possibly unexplained, Judge Goodman's "not guilty" verdict would have accomplished virtually nothing: it would have done nothing more than return the twenty-seven Nisei to their Tule Lake barracks. However, by granting the motion to dismiss and exposing his outraged judgment to review by a higher court, Judge Goodman invited further attention to the plight of the Nisei resisters.

It was not an inauspicious moment for such a gambit. As Judge Goodman read his opinion from the bench in that small Eureka courtroom in July of 1944, government lawyers in Washington and civil liberties lawyers along the West Coast toiled away on the briefs they would soon file in the U.S. Supreme Court in the cases of *Korematsu v. United States* and *Ex parte Endo.* These were the blockbuster cases that had been working their way toward the High Court almost since the inception of the government's internment program. Everyone understood that these were the cases in which the Court would determine the legality of that program. In July of 1944, the constitutionality—and, indeed, the basic fairness—of the Japanese American internment was an issue that was very much in play. With his *Kuwabara* opinion, Judge Goodman seized the opportunity to add his voice to the debate.

In addition, the due process doctrine of "fundamental fairness" was itself very much in play in the summer of 1944. It was the subject of fierce debate on the Supreme Court, and its contours had yet to be clearly sketched out. To be sure, Judge Goodman's application of the doctrine was unprecedented, but so was the government conduct to which he applied it. Never before had the United States tried to force into the line of fire a group of young men it had corralled and confined on suspicion of disloyalty to the United States. Never before had the government taken from a person virtually all of the benefits of his citizenship on account of his ethnic origin and then sought nonetheless to impose on him citizenship's greatest burden. And to the extent that history offered anything like precedents for the government's drafting of the Nisei, they were precedents that the government would undoubtedly have been loathe to cite—the Confederacy's impressing of slaves into menial labor during the Civil War, perhaps, or the government's drafting of Native Americans from off of reservations during World War I.

Ultimately, Judge Goodman's invocation of the "shocks the conscience" test probably did little to blunt the charge of the doctrine's opponents that the test left judges—as Justice Frankfurter denied—"wholly at large," striking down government action "upon the idiosyncrasies of a merely personal judgment." After all, Judge T. Blake

Kennedy and Judge Chase Clark also presided over trials of Nisei resisters, and their consciences had been anything but shocked. Still, Judge Goodman could not abide the unfairness he saw in the government's program, and the then-nascent "shocks the conscience" test offered him a chance both to speak his outrage and even possibly to shape, ever so slightly, an emerging constitutional doctrine. For a judge facing the dilemma of administering a system of law he found immoral, he resolved the dilemma in a highly visible, intentionally debatable, and therefore wholly admirable way.

Word of Judge Goodman's opinion dismissing the charges spread quickly, and it produced an enormous swirl of confusion. In Assistant Secretary of War McCloy's office, the staff were dumbfounded. In a telephone conversation about how to respond to the decision, McCloy's executive officer, Colonel Harrison Gerhardt, described the *Kuwabara* decision as "as far off the beam as I've ever heard one." For Gerhardt, Judge Goodman's mistake was to conclude that, by virtue of their segregation at Tule Lake, the resisters had been determined "disloyal" for the purposes of the draft. Plainly, he reasoned, that was not the case; if the military had cleared them for induction, then they could not have been "disloyal" for Selective Service purposes. More important, he ventured a guess that most of the Tule Lake defendants were not disloyal as a matter of fact: many of them, he suspected, had gone to segregation at Tule Lake in order to remain with their parents rather than because of any marked disloyalty of their own.[30] In this, of course, Gerhardt was quite right: Tom Noda and Jimi Yamaichi, both Tule Lake resisters, went there mostly out of a sense of obligation to their parents, in order to keep their families together. Thus, as a practical matter, the actual loyalties of many of the Tule Lake resisters were probably quite similar to those of the resisters from Minidoka, even though the Tule Lake defendants had followed their parents in answering "no, no" to the loyalty and military service questions on their registration forms in early 1943 and had filed requests for expatriation at an earlier date. Colonel Gerhardt simply could not believe "that [a] federal judge could be that naive about this thing."[31]

The War Relocation Authority had a somewhat different reaction to Goodman's opinion. Even if Colonel Gerhardt was right that Judge Goodman had been "naive" in failing to recognize that the situation of the Tule Lake resisters was not really so different from the situation of resisters at other camps, the WRA was desperately afraid that the reasoning of *Kuwabara* might spread to other camps and convince other young Nisei not to comply with the draft. The WRA's task was therefore to persuade camp residents that the reasoning of *Kuwabara* was peculiar to Tule Lake. On August 1, 1944, WRA Director Dillon Myer sent an urgent teletype to all of his project directors, indicating that the WRA had "not yet received a copy of the decision but from newspaper accounts it appears that the judge was influenced by the fact that Tule Lake is a segregation center for disloyal evacuees."[32] Once the WRA had a chance to review the *Kuwabara* opinion, that preliminary understanding matured into the WRA's official explanation. The result in *Kuwabara,* according to the WRA, was entirely a product of Tule Lake's unique status as a segregation camp from which no internee was free to leave. Because internees at the other nine relocation centers were able to apply for various sorts of temporary and even indefinite leaves, especially for permanent resettlement in the interior, the WRA took the position that Judge Goodman's due process reasoning would not apply at any other camp.

One problem with this account, which the WRA conveniently overlooked, was that it did not comport with Judge Goodman's own understanding of the reach of his decision. Shortly after news of Judge Goodman's *Kuwabara* decision became public, H. J. Jepsen, an attorney in the WRA's San Francisco regional office, received an inquiry from officials at Minidoka about the effect of *Kuwabara* on other camps. Jepsen took it upon himself to telephone Judge Goodman in his San Francisco chambers and ask him about the opinion. Judge Goodman told him that the reasoning of *Kuwabara* was *not* in fact confined to Tule Lake, but would apply at other camps as well.[33]

This was an entirely plausible reading of the opinion, even if it was not the only interpretation. To be sure, Judge Goodman had emphasized in *Kuwabara* that the Tule Lake resisters were confined because the government deemed them disloyal. The internees at the other nine camps were not confined under a specific charge or finding of disloyalty, and that would seem to set the Tule Lake resisters apart from the resisters from other camps. However, the resisters at other camps were fenced behind the same kind of barbed wire as the Tule Lake resisters, with the same army's weapons and searchlights pointed at them, and it was the duress inherent in their captivity, more than their suspected disloyalty, that seemed to drive Judge Goodman's reasoning. Whether the reasoning of the *Kuwabara* opinion might apply to the resisters at other camps was therefore at the very least an open question. Thus, when Jepsen passed along Goodman's comments to the camp administration at Minidoka, they caused quite a stir. Jepsen was quickly reprimanded for placing the phone call in the first place, and the WRA chose not to allow Judge Goodman's views on the general applicability of *Kuwabara* to influence its own assessment that the decision was about Tule Lake and Tule Lake only.

With all of this displeasure and confusion in various government quarters over Judge Goodman's *Kuwabara* opinion, an appeal to the U.S. Court of Appeals for the Ninth Circuit might have been expected. The military and the WRA were plainly unhappy with the decision; indeed, at Minidoka, the camp administration went so far as to prepare a press release for distribution in the camp newspaper that criticized the *Kuwabara* opinion and confidently asserted that "[t]here can be no doubt but that the decision of Judge Goodman will be appealed by the Government in order to determine whether the appellate courts will agree with him."[34] This was a sensible prediction; by the time of *Kuwabara*, the government had already won similar draft evasion cases against Nisei resisters in federal courts in Wyoming, Idaho, Colorado, Arizona, and Utah.

Yet, oddly, the government never appealed its loss in *Kuwabara*. The Justice Department's files on the *Kuwabara* case no longer exist, so it is impossible to know the full story of why the government declined to appeal. It appears, however, that once the government lost in the district court, the military decided that drafting Nisei out of the Tule Lake Relocation Center had been a mistake. In the exchange of memoranda between Attorney General Francis Biddle and Assistant Attorney General Herbert Wechsler that began this chapter, there was an important mention of Judge Goodman's *Kuwabara* opinion. Responding to Biddle's inquiry as to whether the Heart Mountain case did not "involve the constitutionality of the whole [internment] program," Wechsler explained that it might: "No doubt," he wrote, "reliance on appeal [of the Heart Mountain case] will be placed on a decision of the District Court for the Northern District of California sustaining a demurrer to an indictment of a number of Japanese-Americans in similar circumstances [to those of the Heart Mountain resisters] on the ground that it was a denial of due process of law to draft a citizen while he is being deprived of his liberty in a relocation camp." That decision, of course, was *Kuwabara*. Wechsler explained to the attorney general that

> [t]he Criminal Division recommended and the Solicitor General determined to take no appeal in that case principally, I believe, because of the extraneous fact that the defendants involved would not actually be accepted by the Army and had been ordered to report by mistake.[35]

In other words, the government's decision not to appeal *Kuwabara* was, in effect, a confession that Tom Noda, Jimi Yamaichi, and their twenty-five Tule Lake colleagues should never have been drafted in the first place.

It is a bit difficult to believe that the Tule Lake prosecutions were a mistake from the start. A number of surviving documents establish that the cases were brought only after careful deliberation by the WRA, the Justice Department in Washington, and the United States Attorney's Office in Sacramento.[36] On the other hand, another military decision in the wake of *Kuwabara* tends to confirm that the army wanted no parts of the Tule Lake Nisei. In the late summer of 1944, after Judge Goodman's ruling, the California Selective Service Board decided again to reclassify all Tule Lake Nisei into the 4-C category, thus making them categorically ineligible for the draft. In a letter to the home office of the WRA in October of 1944, Manzanar's project attorney complained that this change in policy had been based on what he called Judge Goodman's "mistaken" ruling, which in turn was based on a belief that all Nisei at Tule Lake were disloyal. That belief, the project attorney argued, was erroneous because there were many young people at Tule Lake who were not actually disloyal.[37] Of course, the project attorney was correct about this. But right or wrong, the change in policy reflected a decision by the army that the Tule Lake Nisei should not be put in the position of having to step out of the crosshairs of a U.S. Army sentry's rifle and into the U.S. Army.

Or so it seemed. But even this position was not one that the government was willing to apply fairly and consistently. In mid-1946, the draft evasion convictions of three Nisei resisters from the Poston Relocation Center in Arizona came up for review in the U.S. Court of Appeals for the Ninth Circuit.[38] The case of one of those resisters, Hideichi Takeguma, was quite similar to those of the Heart Mountain resisters. Takeguma had never requested expatriation to Japan, but had refused to report for induction because of his ill treatment at the hands of the federal government. The Ninth Circuit had no trouble concluding (as the Tenth Circuit had concluded in the Heart Mountain appeals) that this defendant had no valid objection to his induction. Breezily, the court held that "[t]here is nothing whatever to any claim that the mere removal from the Pacific area (or confinement to any location), harsh as it was, should act to relieve anyone from the necessity of serving in the military forces. This disposes of Hideichi Takeguma's case."

But the case of one of the other Poston resisters, Kingo Tajii, should not have been quite as easy for the court. Tajii registered for the draft in June of 1942, but requested expatriation to Japan—just as the Tule Lake resisters had done—in August of 1943, a few months after the fiasco of the loyalty questionnaires. He alleged that he had been given a leave clearance hearing at Poston and had been told that he "would be transported to Tule Lake Relocation Center unless that place was overcrowded by others from Poston seeking expatriation." Evidently, Tule Lake *was* overcrowded because Tajii remained at Poston rather than being transferred to Tule Lake. He was, however, placed on Poston's "stop list"—that is, he was forbidden from leaving the camp for any reason—and was in all other respects identically situated with the resisters from Tule Lake.

If it had been a mistake for the military to draft the Tule Lake Nisei—if, as Herbert Wechsler said, the Tule Lake Nisei were unacceptable to the military—then the sensible thing for the Justice Department to do in Kingo Tajii's case would have been to confess error and abandon the prosecution. By the army's standards, Tajii was precisely as unacceptable a candidate for military service as Tom Noda and Jimi Yamaichi. Yet the Justice Department did not confess error in Tajii's case; it litigated the case aggressively and procured from the Ninth Circuit a pronouncement that Tajii was not relieved of his duty to comply with the draft.

Notably, the government got more than that; it also obtained a repudiation of *Kuwabara* itself. The Poston resisters, not surprisingly, had relied on Judge Goodman's reasoning in their argument to the Ninth Circuit. The government had argued in response, as it had argued in every post-*Kuwabara* case, that the situation at the Tule Lake Segregation Center had been unique, a world apart from the situation at an ordinary relocation center. The Ninth Circuit conceded that there were certain distinctions between Tule Lake and Poston, but none that made a difference for the purposes of the law. The Poston resisters—even those in the same shoes as the Tule Lake resisters—were properly convicted, said the court, and "[w]herein the reasoning of the *Kuwabara* opinion differs with that of this opinion, it may be taken that we are not in accord therewith." Thus, in retrospect, the government's litigative mistake in the *Kuwabara* case may not have been the initial decision to bring charges against the Tule Lake Nisei who resisted the draft. The mistake may have been the decision not to appeal Judge Goodman's decision to the Ninth Circuit. Had the government done so, the *Takeguma* case shows that the appeal would have been successful, and then the government would have won the right to dragoon into the military even young men like Kingo Tajii whom the army itself claimed to want no parts of.

EIGHT

INCARCERATION REDUX

On October 6, 1944, thirty of the convicted Minidoka resisters boarded a small ferry in Steilacoom, Washington, for a quick trip to the federal penitentiary at McNeil Island. McNeil Island was an old fortress of a prison that sat on a small piece of land in the Puget Sound about four miles west of Tacoma and about fifty miles southwest of Seattle. When the Minidoka resisters arrived, it had been in operation nearly seventy years and had seen its share of colorful inmates, including the murderer Robert Stroud, who would later gain fame as the Birdman of Alcatraz.[1] Among the grim group on the ferry was Gene Akutsu. As he moved across the cold waters of the Puget Sound toward the island jail, the young man could not help but note the irony that two and one-half years earlier the government had forced them from this region as suspected subversives. Now it was forcing them back as convicted felons.

The Minidoka resisters were not the first Nisei to take the ferry ride to McNeil. Just under three months earlier, on July 10, 1944, the younger thirty-three of the sixty-three Heart Mountain resisters convicted by Judge Kennedy in Cheyenne had arrived to serve their sentences. (The other, older thirty of the Heart Mountain resisters had been sent to the federal prison at Leavenworth, Kansas.) And the Minidoka resisters would also not be the last Nisei to ride the ferry. On July 27, 1945, twenty-two more Heart Mountain resisters would arrive. These were young members of the FPC who had decided to resist the draft after the first group of sixty-three had been convicted, while their case was on appeal. Once the court of appeals affirmed the convictions of the sixty-three, this additional group of twenty-two submitted to conviction and sentence, and was bundled off to join the others at McNeil. Among this group of late arrivals was George Nozawa.

As Nozawa looked across the water from the boat, he saw the same sobering sight that had greeted all of the Nisei resisters who had gone before him. Beneath gray skies, a narrow, scrub-lined beach gave way to broad grass fields and, behind them, low, forested hills marked by the raw gashes of clear-cutting. Standing ostentatiously near the water's edge was a cluster of boxy, multistoried, cement-colored buildings, bordered along the back by a cliff. As the ferry steamed closer, Nozawa saw bars on the windows. A tall brick smokestack jutted upward from a small building near the larger cluster, and next to that spread a large field where thin grass stretched to cover countless dusty bare spots. Small, identically clad figures moved about on the field, some in aimless paths and others in bursts of swarming movement that suggested a ballgame of some kind. Only after a time did his eyes settle on the features of the island jail that most reminded him of the Wyoming "home" he had left behind—the fencing that ringed the complex and the six guard towers perched at points around the perimeter.

The launch carrying the resisters docked at a pier that was unremarkable except for the armed guards waiting to welcome them and the guard tower that loomed above in case any of them wished to make a swim for it. Nozawa and the others were then marched up an access road along the side of one of the large boxy buildings he had seen from the water, toward a guarded entry gate. At eye level were the barred windows of a basement laundry facility, where Nozawa could see prisoners laboring among steel machines belching steam. As the Nisei walked along, they soon caught the attention of the laundry workers, who quickly gathered inside the barred glass to examine the new crop of inmates. Nozawa imagined how a group of young Japanese-looking men must look to a group of prisoners during wartime and braced himself for abuse. And soon a catcall did begin to make itself heard from inside the laundry. Songlike, and broken by fits of rueful laughter, the voices chanted, "You'll be *sor*ry . . . You'll be *sor*ry . . . You'll be *sor*ry." Nozawa was startled, realizing that this was probably the chant with which the denizens of the laundry greeted all new arrivals at McNeil from their basement outpost. He felt a wave of relief. He had been expecting to be called "Jap" and far worse. Perhaps, the young Nisei thought, he was entering a world where his Japanese ethnicity would not matter as much as it had for the last several years.

Just over a year earlier, Yosh Kuromiya had taken the same ferry ride and walked up the same path, along with the rest of the first Heart

Mountain group. There he remembers spotting something quite unexpected. Just outside the door they were approaching, Kuromiya saw what he remembers as "a little old Japanese man" in inmate attire hunched over some bushes with a pair of pruning scissors in his hand. The Issei looked up at the line of new Nisei inmates, and his eyes went wide. He straightened up, his arms dropped to his sides, and he watched in amazement as the thirty-three Japanese faces passed by, most of them looking down at the ground, but a few looking his way with a slight nod and a quick smile. The Issei broke into a broad grin, and Kuromiya remembers thinking that the old inmate must have been overjoyed that he "finally had someone he could relate to." But Kuromiya and his fellow resisters quickly disappeared through the doorway, and they would not see this lonely Issei man again for quite some time.

Once inside McNeil's doors, all of the Nisei resisters were put through the same routine. After some paperwork, they were stripped bare and issued prison attire—blue denim shirts and pants. They were then placed in a quarantine facility for nearly a month. The purpose of the quarantine period was to put the new inmates through a rigorous battery of medical and psychiatric tests, as well as to teach them the prison's rules and regulations. In addition to the physical and mental examinations, each of the new inmates had something euphemistically called an "interview" with the warden, which was actually more a stern lecture from the warden than it was a conversation.

George Nozawa appreciated the thoroughness of the quarantine and its array of exams and "interviews"; he thought it helped guarantee that the prison ran well and safely. Quarantine did, however, make for several weeks of virtual solitude. Each of the Nisei was kept for the entire quarantine period in an individual cell. The only contact he could have was with the resisters in the two adjacent cells, and even that needed to be in whispers. Yosh Kuromiya recalls that "you had to be quiet; you couldn't make any noise at all." "At one point," he remembers, "I was whistling to myself—not that loud, either—and the guard came and told me to shut up." Their lone sources of entertainment were a cart that rolled through daily with newspapers, books, and magazines, and the views of the Puget Sound that they could see through barred windows opposite their cells. It was a rough period, but a temporary one.

The resisters were then moved from quarantine to the most secure building at McNeil, a huge structure that the inmates called "mainline" or "the Big House." The main part of the Big House looked like something out of a James Cagney film—a cavernous vault of a building with five long tiers of cells stacked upon one another like so many cages. To this day, George Nozawa says that he cannot walk into a pet store without shuddering at the sight of the piled-up animal cages. The Nisei resisters were housed in ten-man cells on the top floor. From their cells, they looked out through bars across a narrow balcony that ran the length of the building. All that kept an inmate from plunging off the balcony to the concrete prison floor some sixty feet below was a slender black railing. Revealing what may have been his own frame of mind at the time, Yosh Kuromiya recalls that "you'd look over the side and think, if you wanted to end it all, it would be very simple. Just lean over a little too far, and you've had it."

Accommodations in the ten-man cells were spartan. A row of bars ran along their front. Metal-framed bunk beds ran along the two side walls, their thin mattresses covered with a single blanket. Along the back wall was a toilet and a large washbasin with two sets of faucets. Above the washbasin were two small square mirrors and a set of shallow cubbies into which inmates could place their toiletries. Next to the washbasin was a mop. Below the mirrors hung ten little hooks for prison-issued drinking mugs. Several coat hooks adorned the back wall. There were no windows.

Although they did not know what was in store for them when they got there, the two sets of Heart Mountain resisters ultimately spent relatively little time in these cells in the Big House. After a few weeks there, they were released from the Big House and shuttled a couple of miles down the road to the minimum-security Federal Prison Camp on McNeil Island, which was known simply as "the Farm." The Minidoka resisters, however, spent eighteen months—the lion's share of their entire prison terms—in the Big House. Only at the end of April of 1946 were they "paroled" out to the Farm, where they mingled for about two months with the Heart Mountain resisters before the Heart Mountain group was released. None of the resisters knows why it was the Minidoka group who had to endure a year and a half in the Big House. They speculate, however, that the Minidoka resisters were seen as the bigger troublemakers. Consistently with the policy of the FPC, the members of the Heart Mountain group had all maintained their loyalty during the draft controversy and had insisted that they were willing to serve in the army if their civil rights were first restored. Most of the Minidoka resisters, on the other hand, had filed petitions for expatriation to Japan and had said that they were unwilling to serve. Of course, in staking out these positions, both groups were responding to the identical pressures. Yet the response of the Minidokans was evidently deemed more culpable than that of the resisters from Heart Mountain, and for this the Minidokans paid with eighteen months in the Big House.

Days in the Big House were a long series of comings and goings, each preceded and followed by a counting. Inmates were counted before leaving for breakfast and upon their return, counted before leaving their cells for work or recreation and upon their return, counted before leaving for lunch and dinner and upon their return, and counted again before the lights were turned out. Prison rules were enforced quite rigorously in the Big House. Inmates were permitted to write just one letter each week, and only to a recipient on an approved list. Every Wednesday evening after supper, each inmate received a single sheet of ruled paper and a pencil. If he wished to write a letter, he was allowed to do so only in English, and only on the ruled lines. The next morning he was expected to place his letter on a table for mailing and return the pencil. Excessive noise, disrespect for the guards, and even unbuttoned shirt collars at mealtimes were not tolerated. Mealtimes were, however, nothing to get dressed up for. The food was adequate, but the inmates were forced to stand in long lines for it and then sit in cramped rows of eight along narrow tables with attached metal benches, all facing the same direction so that the guards in the balcony above could see their faces. And the dining room was not the only site of long lines. The Big House had a single shower area, and it was in the basement. As a result, inmates could take showers only during tightly scheduled times and had to stand in long "bath lines" for the privilege.

Amusement in the Big House was somewhat hard to come by. Each ten-man cell had a single radio with ten sets of headphones, one of which ran to each of the cell's ten bunks. The reception, however, was quite variable, and usually poor. The Minidoka resisters played a lot of cards, but had to use some ingenuity to do so. The prison administration had forbidden the possession or use of playing cards in order to keep the inmates from illicit gambling. The Nisei, however, devised a system for altering dominoes so that they could use them as playing cards. Four different-colored dots marked the four suits, the white dots on the dominoes indicated the number of the card, and a system of markings converted certain of the dominoes to jacks, queens, and kings. The Minidoka resisters spent long hours playing poker and other games in their cells, with their "hands" of dominoes arranged in front of them like mah jongg tiles.

They even managed to organize a league so that Nisei players from different cells along the fifth-floor hallway could play against each other in championship rounds. This took some doing because inmates were not free just to wander down the corridor at their leisure and while away some time playing "cards" in someone else's cell. Quite the opposite was true: the whole purpose of the countless countings was to make sure that each inmate was always present and in his proper place. The way the Minidoka resisters got around this was by cheating at counting time. On an evening when a championship game was scheduled between players from different cells, the players would come back from dinner and gather in front of the cell where the game was to be played, even if this was not their cell. A corresponding number of nonplayers from that cell would report to the other cell, so that the right number of Nisei ended up standing in front of each cell. The guards would count the Nisei and get the right numbers, never noticing that some of the men they were counting did not belong where they stood. "We all had black hair," one of the resisters laughingly recalls by way of explaining why they never got caught. To the guards, they all looked more or less alike.

Life on the Farm, where the Heart Mountain resisters served most of their time, was quite different from life in the Big House. The Farm was just that—a functioning farm, tended by the inmates, that produced food for the institution. There were fields of vegetables—a familiar sight for many of the Nisei who had grown up in families of truck farmers—as well as pens of pigs and chickens, and even a sizable fruit orchard. All of the Farm's inmates lived together in a huge dormitory that slept over four hundred men. They were allowed to express preferences for various sorts of work. Many simply set to work at farming, as they had done before the war. Yosh Kuromiya worked in the machine shop. George Nozawa did clerical work in the parole office for much of his time and then worked on the poultry farm. Mits Koshiyama drove a truck. Fred Iriye, a Heart Mountain resister admired by many of his colleagues for his wisdom and level-headedness, worked as an electrician at the prison's power plant.

Security at the Farm was low, so for the first time since the summer of 1942, the resisters found themselves in a facility that was not surrounded by barbed wire and guard towers. The views of the Puget Sound were stunning. Mits Koshiyama often got permission from his civilian supervisor on Sunday mornings to drive a truck to a nearby cove, there to sit quietly and take in the scenery. And it was not just the security that was looser on the Farm; so was the overall attitude. Rules that were enforced vigorously in the Big House were enforced at most in the breach on the Farm. Inmates could go to dinner with their collars unbuttoned. The countings continued, but not so many times a day. On occasion, a mischievous Nisei would even playfully tamper with the count by getting counted, slipping around the back of the group to the far end, and then getting counted again. This, of course, made for too many inmates, and the frustrated guard would have to start the count all over again. Life on the Farm was, in other words, rather relaxed. The resisters spent many hours sprawled across one another's bunks, joking and playing cards, and many hours on the ballfields.

It was on the Farm that the Nisei resisters came to know the little Issei man that Yosh Kuromiya had spotted outside the main door trimming the bushes the day they arrived at McNeil. His name was Mikame. Mikame's story was like that of any of the resisters' fathers, at least at its outset. He had come to the United States from Japan in the 1890s and had immediately looked for work so that he could send money to his family back in Japan. His search for work had taken him to the canneries of the southeastern Alaska Territory. There he became infatuated with a married woman—his head so visibly over his heels that some of his fellow Issei cannery workers began to tease him. One once suggested to him that the only way to win his love's heart was to get rid of her husband. And so he did, bludgeoning him to death. This landed him in prison with a life sentence.

By the time the Nisei draft resisters arrived at McNeil Island, Mikame was a man of sixty-some years who had spent forty of them in jail. Because of his advancing age and his impeccable behavior—he was "obviously not a violent person, just a harmless little guy," Yosh Kuromiya recalls—he was sent from the Big House out to the Farm at about the same time as the Heart Mountain resisters. And there Mikame mixed happily, albeit reservedly, with the young men who could have been his sons. Rejecting Japanese formality, the Nisei christened him "Mickey"—all of them, that is, except for young George Nozawa, who "could not bring himself" to use the nickname and instead addressed the older man as "Mikame-san," as befitted an Issei elder. Nozawa remembers Mikame-san as a thin man with salt-and-pepper hair who "wouldn't talk too much unless you pressed the issue." While working in the prison's parole office, Nozawa once saw the Issei described in a document as an "illiterate immigrant," and this incensed the younger man. Mikame-san was in fact a "walking dictionary," always quick to volunteer the toughest missing word when one of the Nisei got stuck on a crossword puzzle and always ready with a sound recommendation in the prison library. He was, however, quite reserved in his dealings with the resisters. Nozawa remembers that Mikame-san never asked the young men anything about their backgrounds, or about their lives in camp, or about their families. This reticence was, of course, to some extent the Japanese way. But for Nozawa it also seemed a way for the older man to protect himself. "He knew," says Nozawa, "that one day we all would leave, and he would not." He did not wish to grow too attached to these young men or to the brief season of joy and comfort they undoubtedly brought into his lonely life.

While the Heart Mountain resisters took under their wing this man who was, in a sense, one of their own, they also mixed with other groups of inmates at McNeil, and this exposure shattered their prewar, and naturally quite negative, impressions of criminal convicts. In the mess hall, on the work details, and especially on the ballfields, the Nisei overcame their isolation and came to embrace—and to be embraced by—their fellow inmates. Although they feared physical and verbal abuse because of their Japanese appearance, they got none. They learned that even the men around them who had committed serious crimes were human beings with assets as well as demerits. "If you sat around with these guys," Heart Mountain resister Tak Hoshizaki remembers, "you really learned something."

The Nisei's jail experience also shattered some of their own preconceptions about race. Growing up in either white or Japanese neighborhoods, the resisters had precious little experience with black people. At McNeil, though, they came to know their black colleagues—in some cases, quite well. During his time in the Big House, Yosh Kuromiya shared a cell for a time with a boyish-looking African American named Lucky Stokes, who had been a championship lightweight boxer. Much to the Nisei's surprise, the boxer approached Kuromiya soon after he arrived and said, "Any time any of these white guys ever threaten you or give you a bad time, just come to me and I will take care of you." Kuromiya never needed Stokes's protection, but the two stayed friendly and exchanged addresses "on the outside" before leaving McNeil. Another black inmate popular among the Nisei was known to them by an amalgam of his prison number and his name—"609 Jackson." A short man with strong hands, 609 Jackson was an outstanding piano player and gave several of the resisters lessons on an old piano that sat unused in a building on the Farm. These sorts of interactions, and the talking and storytelling that went with them, opened the Nisei's eyes to what they had in common—the bitter experience of race discrimination in America. "I never thought about black people's situation," confesses Tak Hoshizaki, "until I heard their stories at McNeil—no money, no jobs, discrimination."

Their time in prison also opened their eyes, or rather their minds, to political influences with which they were quite unfamiliar. Two groups (in addition to the Nisei) were incarcerated at McNeil for noncompliance with the draft. The members of one of those groups, the Jehovah's Witnesses, generally kept to themselves and held themselves apart from (or perhaps, as Yosh Kuromiya recalls, slightly above) the rest of the prison population. But there was also a sizable number of conscientious objectors consisting of two subgroups—members of the Society of Friends, or "Quakers" as they are commonly known, and men who refused to be drafted out of political commitments that ranged from pacifism to anarchy.

The conscientious objectors, or "CO's" as they were called, were an intelligent, well-educated, and, in many cases, accomplished contingent. Among them was the Reverend Glenn E. Smiley, a Methodist minister who, a decade later, would introduce the philosophy of Mahatma Gandhi to a young Martin Luther King Jr. and then share a seat with him on the first integrated bus in Montgomery, Alabama. Another prominent conscientious objector at McNeil was Gordon Hirabayashi, a Nisei from Seattle who, in 1942, had refused on constitutional grounds to be deported to an assembly center, had taken an unsuccessful challenge all the way to the U.S. Supreme Court, and then, due to his Quaker faith, had refused to be drafted. The erudition of the CO's sometimes made them a rather conspicuous group at McNeil. On one occasion, guards arrived at the Farm's main building for their morning shift to discover, in large blue chalk lettering on the front of the white building, an inscription that mocked the Farm's warden, Mr. Stevens: DRAFT DODGER STEVENS WOULD BE A CO IF HE HAD A CONSCIENCE. Warden Stevens immediately forbade all of the conscientious objectors from going off to their work detail that day and ordered them into his office, one by one, for questioning. When Reverend Smiley asked Stevens why he was so sure that one of the CO's was responsible for the graffiti, the warden responded grimly, "Because you are the only bastards on the Island who can spell 'conscience.'"[2]

Intellectuals that they were, the conscientious objectors organized a reading and discussion group on the Farm and welcomed any interested Nisei to join them. Tak Hoshizaki was one who joined the group and grew quite close with many of the objectors, so close that he was asked to be the pitcher for the Quaker baseball team. Some of these resister-objector friendships endured long after the time at McNeil was over. When Yosh Kuromiya married in 1948, it was Reverend Smiley who performed the wedding ceremony.

The days and the weeks turned to long months for the Heart Mountain and Minidoka resisters at McNeil Island. On December 18, 1944, the Supreme Court held it illegal for the War Relocation Authority to continue to detain loyal American citizens of Japanese ancestry at Heart Mountain, Minidoka, and the other relocation centers. Still the Nisei resisters sat at McNeil Island. On January 2, 1945, the military formally reopened the West Coast to loyal Nikkei, and still the Heart Mountain and Minidoka resisters sat at McNeil Island. As the nation celebrated victory over Japan on September 2, 1945, the resisters still sat at McNeil. On October 28, 1945, Minidoka closed its gates for good, and Heart Mountain followed two weeks later. Still the draft resisters from those two camps sat at McNeil.

In some ways, the resisters' lives grew a bit more difficult as the year 1945 wore on. A year earlier the young men had left their families in the camps as both captives and wards of the government. While they resented their families' situation deeply, they also took a measure of comfort from it: they knew, at least, that in their absence their parents and siblings would have food to eat and a roof over their heads. With the closing of the camps, however, their families began to return to the West Coast communities from which they had been uprooted. Most of them had lost nearly everything, and few really had anything like a home to return to. Housing was scarce, jobs were scarce, and prewar careers, businesses, and property were lost. And the young and able-bodied resisters, stuck on their island jail, could do nothing to help.

For the Minidoka resisters, at least, these developments did bring one small change to their lives: they began to have occasional visitors. With their families' Idaho exile at an end, they returned to the Seattle area and found themselves just forty miles from their incarcerated sons. Nao Akutsu traveled every other Sunday, without fail, to visit her two sons Jim and Gene. (Visits were permitted only on two Sundays each month.) To get there, she had to take a series of buses from Seattle through Tacoma to the small town of Steilacoom, just across the water from McNeil Island. From there, at an appointed time, she would take a small launch to the island and make her way to the visiting room in the basement of the prison's administration building, where she would await one of her two sons. Eventually, Jim or Gene—whichever son she had not seen the previous time—would make a faint appearance behind a thick mesh screen and across a table, and mother and son would talk for a while under the eyes and ears of prison guards. After a brief visit, and without so much as a simple caress, she would make the long return trip to Seattle, to endure two more weeks of separation from her children.

The families of the Heart Mountain resisters, however, were hundreds of miles away in northern and southern California, trying to settle back into their former communities, and had neither the time nor the money to visit their sons at McNeil. George Nozawa, for example, learned of his family's return to California in a letter from one of his sisters. The letter informed him that his father, his two sisters, and his brother-in-law were all living together in a rented one-room building on the property they had farmed before the war. This was the building that they and their neighbors had filled with their belongings and locked just before being shipped off to the assembly center in 1942. But in the interim, the building had been looted. With everything of value gone and nothing in the bank, the Nozawas were working seven days a week to make ends meet.

George Nozawa had little choice but to sit out his jail term while his family struggled to get by. But things got even harder in December of 1945, a few months after his family's return to California. One day, as he sat at his desk in the parole office on the Farm, someone approached and handed him a telegram. It was from his sister and said, simply, "Father passed away this morning. Details later." Nozawa was stunned; he had not known that his father was ill. His boss, an assistant parole officer at McNeil, had taken a liking to the young Nisei and instructed him to wire his sister to hold up the funeral. "Give us a couple of days," he said, "and we'll get you out of here on parole." Nozawa, however, quickly realized that the telegram had arrived a day late; it had been directed first to the Big House and had sat there for a day before someone forwarded it to him at the Farm. The disruption to his family, Nozawa feared, would be enormous if he were to ask them to delay the funeral. More important, Nozawa decided that he did not want the parole he was being offered. In solidarity with his fellow resisters, he wanted to serve out his term just like the rest of them and did not want even the appearance of special treatment. He therefore politely declined the offer of parole, missed the funeral, and never had the chance to bid his Issei father farewell.

Nozawa would soon come to suspect, however, that all of the Nisei resisters actually were getting special treatment from the parole office—although not even faintly favorable treatment. One day, at his desk in the Farm's parole office, Nozawa came across a copy of a memorandum that grabbed his attention. The document, dated June 1, 1944, was from James V. Bennett, the director of the federal Bureau of Prisons, and was directed to all federal parole officers. It directed any parole officer deliberating on the possible parole of a Japanese American internee to solicit the comments of Dillon Myer, the director of the War Relocation Authority, before granting release on parole. In a letter that Bennett attached to his memorandum, Dillon Myer had asked for the right to comment on pending parole applications because the WRA was, in his words, "extremely anxious that [the Nisei draft resisters] not be returned on parole to the relocation centers." Myer knew that so long as the Nisei were excluded from the West Coast, many paroled resisters might wish to rejoin their families, even if that meant returning to camp, and others simply might have no other place to go. "You can readily see," Myer explained, "that if they were returned to the centers without serving substantial sentences, other evacuees desirous of evading Army service might conclude that refusal to report would result merely in a slight slap on the wrist which would in fact be preferable to Army service from their point of view." Just as Myer had prevailed on the federal criminal justice system to help him weed out from his camps those he saw as troublemakers by arresting them early, he tried to exert the same influence at the other end of the process by incarcerating them beyond their earliest parole dates.

By midsummer of 1946, even without parole, it was finally time for the first of the Heart Mountain resisters to be released. The second Heart Mountain group followed in late December of 1946, and the Minidoka group in April of 1947. And by and large, their experiences in jail had not been excruciating. This was especially true for those who spent the majority of their time on the Farm rather than in the Big House. They remember the island as a beautiful place and their jail time as calm, orderly, and quiet. For those like Yosh Kuromiya who enjoyed quiet contemplation, the Farm offered that. For those like Tak Hoshizaki who wanted time for study and intellectual discussion, the Farm offered that, especially because of the companionship of the conscientious objectors. And for those like George Nozawa or Mits Koshiyama who needed camaraderie, the occasional ballgame, and steady work, the Farm offered that as well. The Nisei resisters were, of course, well adjusted to confinement by the time they got to McNeil Island, and many of them found that life on the Farm was not so different from life in camp. They had the support of their cohorts and respect from the other inmates. The food, they say, was a good deal better than the WRA's fare at the relocation centers. And perhaps most important, unlike at Heart Mountain and Minidoka, the resisters' time at McNeil was infused with a sense of purpose: they knew exactly why they were incarcerated. They served their time, many of them now say, without bad or guilty feelings.

The rough edges of their memories, however, may have been polished a bit by the passage of time. In fact, as the Nisei resisters left McNeil Island, some of them wrestled with difficult emotions in addition to the joy they felt at regaining their freedom. George Nozawa, for example, struggled over having to leave behind the man he called Mikame-san. As his time at McNeil grew short, Nozawa sensed the older man pulling away from him, cutting conversations short or avoiding them entirely. On his last morning at McNeil, Nozawa sat nervously on the end of his bunk for the routine postbreakfast count of inmates. He knew that Mikame-san would have to file by on his way out to the poultry farm, and the Nisei could not find in himself the words to say goodbye. When Mikame's crew was called out to leave for work, Nozawa stared at the floor, not daring to look up as the older man walked by. Yet even with his eyes averted, he could sense that Mikame-san was also avoiding eye contact, hurrying his step a bit to get past Nozawa's bunk. As he walked by, Nozawa briefly thought of reaching out and stopping Mikame-san, but the moment passed, and the Issei marched away into what Nozawa feared would be a long ending to a lifetime of loneliness. Nozawa, for his part, gathered his few belongings, straightened the uncomfortable suit the prison had issued him for his trip home, and went to the dock for the quick ferry ride back across the waters of the Puget Sound.

The first group of Heart Mountain resisters had made that boat trip several months earlier, decked out in smiles and the same uncomfortable suits, but the joy of their trip was also tinged with sadness. Just two days before their release date, as the resisters wrapped up their work on the Farm and prepared to leave, Fred Iriye gave the inmate who was to replace him as electrician a careful tour of the power plant, explaining to him exactly what the job entailed and showing him how to do various tasks. Those who knew Iriye say that it was just like him to be offering such a detailed lesson to his replacement; he was, they say, conscientious, hardworking, and earnest. Iriye was in fact perhaps the best liked and most respected of the Heart Mountain resisters, a young man whose intellect, athletic abilities, and leadership skills had often left Yosh Kuromiya wondering, self-mockingly, just what had "led Iriye to associate himself with such an undistinguished bunch" as the members of the FPC. And, in fact, Iriye did not accompany his fellow resisters two days later on their ferry ride to freedom. As Iriye explained a task to his replacement, he reached up to touch an electrical switch, believing it dead. It was not. The young man was jolted with a massive burst of electricity and died on the spot.

A few days later there was a memorial service in Los Angeles for Fred Iriye, and the Heart Mountain resisters from southern California, just arrived from McNeil Island, gathered to attend it. Iriye's family members, themselves recently returned from captivity at Heart Mountain and struggling to put their lives back together, were devastated by his death and sat together at the front of the church, dazed. As Yosh Kuromiya entered the church for the memorial service in the company of his fellow resisters, the family's eyes turned to them, and Kuromiya sensed in their gaze the conviction that Iriye's death was *bachi*—a Japanese word with origins in the Shinto religion that means a divine punishment for immoral and disrespectful behavior. Kuromiya felt that in some unarticulated way the mourning family believed that the young resisters of the FPC had sinned in their resistance and that Iriye's death was retribution for his and their arrogance. Kuromiya was overcome with the desperate desire that one of the resisters would rise at the service to deny this unspoken charge of *bachi,* to refute the idea that Iriye's death was punishment, to make clear that Fred Iriye was, in a very real sense, a war casualty. "Fred wouldn't win any medals," Kuromiya thought, "but he died for a reason—for something he believed in."

Yosh Kuromiya did not rise to speak at the ceremony, however, and neither did any of his fellow resisters. Instead, after the service ended, the group silently filed from the church and dispersed across the southern California landscape from which they had been evicted five years earlier, never again to gather as a group. But the accusation that Yosh Kuromiya saw in the eyes of the Iriye family was an omen of things to come for all the Nisei draft resisters in their postwar lives. As they returned from jail and began the task of piecing their lives back together, they soon found themselves in the long shadow cast by the heroic returning veterans of the 442nd Regimental Combat Team and in the accusing glare of a large segment of the Japanese American community.

NINE PARDON?

When George Nozawa returned to Mountain View, California, upon his release from McNeil Island with the second group of Heart Mountain resisters, he found a very different home from the one he had known before the war. The farm to which he returned was the same, but his family had been reduced to the status of subtenants in a one-room outbuilding. His sisters and his brother-in-law worked long days, six and sometimes seven days a week, and had little time to offer him an elaborate welcome. His father was gone.

Gone, too, were all of the family's prewar valuables, lost to the greedy pre-evacuation buyers and the thieves who had stolen their stored belongings while the Nozawas were in camp. When the government offered to compensate the Nikkei for the internment-related losses they could document, George Nozawa contacted an attorney and submitted an itemized claim for compensation to the Department of Justice. The claim was almost pathetic in its modesty. Included were line items for a "1932 Graham Paige sedan, 1942 value of $200.00, sold at evacuation for $75.00," a "Model T Ford truck, running well, value of $100.00, sold at evacuation for $15.00," a "Frigidair, 6 cubic feet, used but good, value of $75.00, sold at evacuation for $25.00," and a "balloon tired bicycle, value of $20.00, sold at evacuation for $5.00." To these losses, Nozawa added claims for various evacuation-related expenses, including suitcases, duffle bags, footlockers, "materials for partitions in barrack," hot plates, and "extra winter clothing for Wyoming winters not usable when returned to California." In all, the Nozawa family's request from the government totaled $1,047.85. Five years later, in 1952, the Justice Department's Claims Division finally got around to ruling on the Nozawas' claim. It disallowed most of what they had asked for and issued George Nozawa a check in the amount of $432.00 for his family's internment-related losses.

The Akutsu brothers, Jim and Gene, returned from McNeil Island along with the rest of the Minidoka resisters in April of 1947. They were greeted with heartache. Jim and Gene found their parents living in a makeshift hostel in downtown Seattle and their father, Kiyonosuke, scrambling to set up a new shoe repair business around the corner from where his thriving prewar shop had been. Their mother, Nao, was a ruined soul. She had waited with determination for years in camp to see her family reunited and, once back in Seattle, had made the lonely trip to McNeil Island by ferry twice each month to spend a few hours across a wire screen from one or the other of her sons in the prison's visiting room. But now, with her family finally reunited, the trauma of her wartime experiences caught up with her and consumed her. She fell into deep depression, plagued, her son Gene remembers, by a constant feeling that "there was a train going through her head." Six months after her boys came home from McNeil, she succumbed to the pressure and died.

As for the Tule Lake resisters, they were spared the experience of hard time in a federal penitentiary. This is not to say, however, that they were spared a hard time. The fruit of their courtroom victory in Eureka was a chauffeured trip back to the barracks, barbed wire, and guard towers of the Tule Lake Segregation Center. There they stayed until, at the earliest, the fall of 1945, when the federal government announced that it would begin deporting those internees who had filed requests for repatriation (in the case of Issei) and renunciations of U.S. citizenship and requests for expatriation (in the case of Nisei). By the end of 1945, these internees numbered more than twenty thousand—nearly one in six of the entire internee population. Almost five thousand of them ended up leaving a camp in the United States for Japan.[1]

Among those who left was Tom Noda, the Tule Lake resister who had answered "no, no" on his registration form back in 1943 and who had demanded expatriation. The Japan that Noda found was, of course, a shattered, starving, shellshocked nation, still reeling from its catastrophic loss to the Allies and the devastation wreaked by two atomic bombs. Although General Douglas MacArthur was busy implementing a top-down, American-style overhaul of Japanese society,

Noda's American ways did not serve him well in Japan. "The whole place was blown up," Noda recalls. "You went to Tokyo and there was no Tokyo there. And so they didn't care too much for us Nisei back there after the war." Ironically, Noda exiled himself from the United States because he was seen as Japanese rather than American, only to find that in Japan he was seen as American rather than Japanese. "We were men without a country," he says of the expatriated Nisei.

Noda remained in Japan for several years, eventually finding work —ironic work, given his wartime draft resistance—as a Japanese language interpreter for the U.S. Army in court-martial proceedings. After several years, though, Noda returned to the United States, and when he did, he returned as an American citizen notwithstanding his earlier renunciation of his citizenship. This, too, was due to Judge Louis E. Goodman. Late in 1945, when the government announced its plan to begin deporting Nisei renunciants to Japan, many of them thought better of their decision to abandon this country and brought suit, as a class, to void their renunciations as the product of coercion and duress. Their case was assigned to none other than Judge Goodman of the Northern District of California, who, after taking evidence about conditions at Tule Lake and the circumstances under which the renunciations had been made, granted the plaintiffs' request for an injunction barring their deportation.

Relying on—indeed, borrowing from—his earlier opinion in *Kuwabara,* Judge Goodman held that it was "shocking to the conscience that an American citizen be confined without authority and then, while so under duress and restraint, for his Government to accept from him a surrender of his constitutional heritage." The evidence, he held, supported a presumption that all of the renunciations by Tule Lake Nisei had been coerced from internees acting in "fear, anxiety, hopelessness, and despair."[2] Goodman did leave the government ninety days to rebut the presumption as to any individual renunciant by offering proof that he had renounced his citizenship freely and voluntarily. The effect of his order, however, was to suspend the deportations and restore the citizenship of thousands of Tule Lake Nisei. The government appealed his order and managed to persuade the U.S. Court of Appeals for the Ninth Circuit that the presumption ought to run in the government's favor rather than the renunciant's. Thus, the Ninth Circuit reversed Judge Goodman's order in part, holding that each individual renunciant had the burden of proving that he had renounced his citizenship under duress and coercion.[3] Back in the district court, however, thousands of renunciants, represented by, among others, A. L. Wirin, eventually filed affidavits alleging duress and coercion, and virtually everyone's renunciation was ultimately voided.

Judge Goodman's forgiving mood was not shared by much of postwar Japanese America. After the victories in Europe and the Pacific, the highly decorated Nisei troops of the 100th Infantry Battalion and the 442nd Regimental Combat Team came home to a well-deserved hero's welcome from the Japanese American community. Their matchless and well-publicized bravery in combat had been the public relations bonanza for the Nisei cause that the JACL, Assistant Secretary of War John McCloy, and WRA Director Dillon Myer had hoped it would. It was the battle-weary face of the Nisei GI, and not the prison-weary face of the Nisei resister, that most of the Nikkei wanted America to see.

The JACL, for its part, reaped the benefit of its years of cooperation with the government and its support for the draft, and entered the postwar period as the essentially unquestioned leader of, and spokesman for, the Japanese American community. When the organization gathered in 1946 for its first national convention of the postwar era, its members' anger at the Nisei draft resisters and the Tule Lake renunciants—two groups they myopically saw as indistinguishable—quickly boiled over.[4] Within moments of President Saboru Kido's calling the very first session to order, delegates raised the question of what the JACL's official attitude should be toward the Tule Lake renunciants and "the Heart Mountain Fair Play Committee who advised Nisei not to respond to their draft calls." Delegates complained that these elements were "creating an embarrassing situation in Northern California and other sections," causing confusion among caucasians as to which Nisei were loyal and which were not. Others alleged that some were belittling the sacrifices made by Nisei veterans. The resisters "have been understood to claim," some delegates complained, "that they enjoy every privilege and advantage that other Japanese enjoy today without having 'risked anything' for the United States. They have created an intolerable situation which may result in ill will for loyal Japanese Americans."

The rage of the JACL delegates extended beyond the Tule Lake residents and the draft resisters to the lawyer who had represented them.

A. L. Wirin had served for some time as counsel to the JACL, even while doing the same for the American Civil Liberties Union (ACLU) and maintaining his own private practice. When Wirin represented the Nisei resisters and the Tule Lake renunciants, he did so privately. But at the 1946 JACL convention, some delegates were not in the mood for seeing nice distinctions between the work Wirin did on his own and the work he did for organizations. They openly criticized "[t]he fact that A. L. Wirin, counsel for J.A.C.L. as well as the A.C.L.U., often acted in behalf of the Tulelake [*sic*] and the Heart Mountain group."

The most vocal opponents of the Tule Lake renunciants and the draft resisters at the JACL convention were, perhaps not surprisingly, the veterans of the 100th and the 442nd. They made "strong representations . . . that no sympathy whatsoever be shown toward the Tulelake [*sic*] and other such groups" and urged "that they be made to face the consequences of their former attitude." The veterans complained that "such actions as those taken by the Tuleans and Heart Mountain 'draft dodgers' made their role even more difficult in the Army and tended to negate in part their achievements." Some delegates worried that "within a few years when public good will is the lot of all Japanese, these Tuleans would reap the benefits of this public attitude and . . . there would be no distinctions made between those who stood for principle and those who wavered." Because the "'troublemakers' would always be in the forefront of [the] anti-America and anti-J.A.C.L. movements," some argued, "steps ought to be taken to curb them now." Some "recommended that J.A.C.L. go on record favoring their deportation immediately," and "[o]thers recommended that released Tuleans be required to carry on their persons at all times special identification." These delegates meant business: the misbehaving Nisei were to be either banished from the United States entirely or, if permitted to remain, marked as card-carrying pariahs.

In the debate that ensued, somewhat calmer heads ultimately prevailed. Opinion ran against the proposal that the JACL petition the government to require former Tuleans to carry identification cards. The delegates came to understand that "[a]sking for such discrimination might result in all Issei and Nisei being required to carry some kind of identification papers," or at least being "continually embarrassed by being asked to show whether they were from Tulelake [*sic*] or not." The delegates ultimately determined that the "troublemakers" would be barred from membership in the JACL; that would be punishment enough. And, finally, the convention decided to spare A. L. Wirin from punishment for representing those the JACL opposed. The delegates were reminded that Wirin "served without compensation and that he had often carried on many cases in behalf of the Japanese community at his own expense." They were also urged not to let their anger displace their common sense: "Attorneys of Mr. Wirin's calibre are few and far-between," and the JACL had been "fortunate to secure his services." The delegates thus "agreed that Mr. Wirin be retained in his present capacity and . . . used as National Headquarters [saw] fit and proper."

If Wirin was chastened by nearly getting fired at the JACL's 1946 national convention, he did not show it. Early in 1947, just a few months after the JACL's convention, Wirin decided to try to clear the names and records of the Nisei draft resisters by petitioning for amnesty. President Truman had set up a board to review the cases of World War II draft violators for possible amnesty and had asked former Supreme Court Associate Justice Owen J. Roberts to head it. In March of 1947, Wirin appeared as a witness before the amnesty board and presented a formal request for amnesty on behalf of the Nisei resisters. Wirin explained to the Roberts board the resisters' reason for refusing the army's call: they felt they had been unlawfully imprisoned and unjustly treated and did not believe that they were required to honor their obligations as American citizens while America was breaching its obligations to them.

The Roberts board recommended pardons for the Nisei resisters.[5] Deeming them "closely analogous to conscientious objectors, and yet not within the fair interpretation of that phrase," the board "fully appreciate[d] the nature of their feelings and their reactions to orders from local Selective [Service] Boards." Those "feelings and reactions," said the board, stemmed from the fact that "prior to their removal from their homes, they had been law-abiding and loyal citizens." The board recognized that the resisters "deeply resent[ed] classification as undesirables" because "most of them remained loyal to the United States and indicated a desire to remain in this country and to fight in its defense, provided their rights of citizenship were recognized." For this reason, the board decided to "recommend[ ] pardons, in the belief that they will justify our confidence in their loyalty."

President Truman accepted the board's recommendation. On Christmas Eve of 1947, he announced that he was granting the Nisei resisters a full pardon, including restoration of all their political and civil rights. For one of them, the pardon had an immediate and significant impact: it released him from jail. One of the small handful of draft resisters from the Topaz Relocation Center in Utah, Joe Nakahira, had received the longest jail term of any of the resisters from any of the camps—five years. He was the only resister still in jail at Christmas in 1947, and therefore the only resister for whom the pardon worked an immediate change in circumstances.

For the rest of the resisters, however, the pardon changed little. They had all served out their terms before the end of 1947, and nothing could give them back their time. The pardon undoubtedly made it easier for some of them to find work, as they no longer had criminal records to report on job applications. Yosh Kuromiya recalls that when he learned of the pardon, he "realized [he] didn't have to worry that much about jeopardizing myself or those around me, should it be discovered that I was a convict." But beyond that, he says, the pardon "really didn't have that big an impact." Kuromiya had had a great deal of time on the Farm at McNeil to reflect on his experience, and by the time he found out about the pardon, he "had pretty much resolved all of the questions and conflicts [him]self."

Truman's pardon of the Nisei draft resisters placed the JACL in something of an awkward spot. On the one hand, the organization's instinct was to respect and support the American government, even when that government took action with which it disagreed. On the other hand, the discussions at its 1946 convention revealed a deep well of anger at the resisters. The JACL therefore reacted to the pardon mutedly, "welcom[ing]" Truman's action, while simultaneously blaming the resisters. An editorial in its newspaper, the *Pacific Citizen,* acknowledged that the resisters' "action was a direct byproduct of a series of undemocratic actions, including the curfew, mass evacuation, and mass detention." This was the reason that "all who are cognizant with the situation" should "welcom[e]" the pardon. On the other hand, the editorial reminded its readers, the resisters' position had not been "upheld by the courts and all of them were convicted of refusal to comply with the Selective Service Act and served prison terms." It continued:

> The action of this group, coming at a time when Americans of Japanese ancestry were being subjected to racist attacks by organized anti-evacuee groups on the Pacific coast, was inexpedient from the standpoint of its effect on public attitudes and threatened to disrupt the government's program of moving all of the evacuees out of the relocation centers in to normal homes and communities.

The resisters, said the editorial, did "establish[ ] a principle," but "in doing so they endangered the future security and welfare of thousands of their fellow citizens." The JACL newspaper predicted, somewhat ominously, that "[t]he problem posed by the action of these draft resisters probably will be one which will remain long in controversy."[6]

The author of that editorial surely could not have imagined that the controversy would still simmer fifty-five years later. But it does. For about thirty years, the resisters' story remained buried. The resisters themselves quickly fell silent. Many did not speak of their wartime protest even with their own children. To some extent, say the resisters, this silence was a cultural phenomenon: it is not the Japanese way to dwell on unpleasantness or on aspects of family history that might be interpreted, or even misinterpreted, as shameful. The years of silence were also the resisters' busiest and most productive years, when they were raising their families and working long hours to make better lives for their children. They had little time, they say, to tell their story, and their attention was elsewhere. Many of the Nisei resisters also report that even when their children—the "Sansei" generation—came of age, they showed little interest in their fathers' opposition to the draft. There were exceptions, of course. Yosh Kuromiya told his children what he had done during the war when they were quite young, and the story became such an item of family lore that one of his daughters presented him one Father's Day with a little round wooden figure dressed as a prisoner, complete with black-and-white-striped clothing and a ball and chain dangling from his foot. Most of the resisters' children, however, asked few questions about the internment and the draft, and so the story went untold.

By the 1980s, however, times both in America and in the Japanese American community had changed in ways that invited a few of the resisters to break their silence. The nation had come through the civil rights revolution of the 1960s, a time when it became more widely acceptable to speak out against racial inequality and government oppression. The country had also endured the agony of Vietnam and had struggled to come to terms with the draft resistance that that war had spurred. A young black boxing champion named Cassius Clay had very publicly resisted the draft for Vietnam and had been celebrated rather than vilified by many in his racial community, and even by many outside it.

The makeup of the Japanese American community had also changed by the 1980s. The Nisei generation was entering its retirement years. Sansei were beginning to occupy positions of prominence and leadership, and many of these third-generation Japanese Americans, more comfortably assimilated than their parents, looked at their parents' wartime experiences through the lenses of the civil rights movement and Vietnam rather than those of the New Deal and total war. Japanese Americans were walking the halls of power, and one of them, Senator Daniel K. Inouye of Hawaii, a wounded veteran of the 442nd Regimental Combat Team, had played a prominent role in uncovering presidential misconduct as a high-profile member of the Senate's Watergate committee. The community was pressing on Congress a demand for monetary redress that would culminate in the passage of the 1988 Civil Liberties Act and a $20,000 payment to each surviving internee.[7]

It was in this time of debate about redress that a few of the Heart Mountain resisters began to find the courage to speak publicly about their wartime experiences. And as the Japanese American community began to focus its attention on this hidden chapter of the story of the internment, certain Nisei veterans' groups slowly began to explore the possibility of making peace with the resisters, even while the JACL hesitated. By the 1990s, several Nisei veterans' groups decided to adopt formal resolutions of reconciliation, recognizing the good faith and courage of the resisters' position. In August of 1998, for example, the board of directors of the 442nd Veterans Club of Oahu, Hawai'i—the largest World War II Japanese American veterans' organization—passed a resolution recognizing the members of the Heart Mountain Fair Play Committee for their "unswerving effort to uphold the Constitution of the United States, the restoration of their civil rights and their fight for justice and democracy." The veterans' club encouraged all Nisei who fought with the 100th and the 442nd to "extend their hands of friendship and goodwill to the members of the Fair Play Committee, their families and supporters."[8]

The Hawai'i veterans' call for reconciliation did not, however, reach the ears of some JACL members on the mainland. Some years earlier the organization had managed to pass a resolution on the resisters, stating that it "regret[ted] any pain and bitterness caused by its failure to recognize this group of patriotic Americans." From the perspective of many of the resisters, however, and even of some within the JACL, this did not go far enough. The JACL, in their estimation, had caused pain and bitterness not merely by failing to acknowledge them in the postwar years, but also by working to discredit them during the internment itself. An apology was in order, many of them said. Some within the JACL, primarily Sansei interested in healing the wounds of their parents' generation, began to press for a JACL resolution of apology to the resisters.

In July of 2000, they finally got such a resolution from the JACL at its national convention, but it took some doing and opened some raw old wounds. Apology supporters spent much of the 1990s lobbying their various regional JACL districts to support a resolution of apology. In order to take effect through this district-by-district approach, the resolution needed the unanimous approval of all eight of the JACL's regional districts. By mid-1999, supporters of the apology had secured passage of the resolution in five of those districts. In September of 1999, however, the Central California District Council, based in Fresno, rejected the resolution, thereby killing it. Fred Hirasuna, a veteran of the 442nd and an outspoken critic of the Fair Play Committee, celebrated the resolution's defeat: "I believe this move by the Heart Mountain resisters was entirely uncalled for. It was not the time and not the place for that kind of move." "This was wartime," Hirasuna emphasized, "and wartime ignores a lot of so-called constitutional rights." According to Hirasuna, draft resistance was harmful to the cause of Nisei assimilation. "We knew we had to get back into American society after the war, and to get back into American society meant we should cooperate with this country in the war against Japan because Japan at the time was the enemy. By cooperation," said the veteran, "I mean we should forget, for the time being, our constitutional rights."[9]

Supporters of an apology regrouped in the wake of their defeat in the Central California District and decided to take the issue to the JACL's National Council at its biennial convention in Monterey, California, in July of 2000. Under the JACL's constitution, the National Council had the power to set national policy by a vote of a majority of its members. In this setting, the resolution passed with the support of exactly two-thirds of the ninety-six council members casting votes. The vote split largely along generational lines, with most of the younger members supporting the measure and many of the older ones opposing it.[10]

When it became clear that the resolution would pass, a group of Nisei veterans stormed out of the room, furious at the notion that the JACL would apologize to the resisters. One longtime JACL member, Tom Masamori, ripped off his JACL name tag and replaced it with a tag identifying him as a "former JACL member." In a letter to the editor of the JACL's newspaper the following week, Masamori charged that by choosing to apologize to the Nisei resisters, whom he called "draft dodgers," the JACL had also chosen to "insult[ ] the veterans." The organization, he said, was "ignoring the fact that over 850 young boys were killed serving this nation at the same time the resisters were staging their protests. The last sleep the soldiers had was in a cold, muddy foxhole and their last meal was most likely a tasteless 'K' ration. The resisters slept on a bed, protected from the elements and given a warm meal. At least we veterans will never forget our fallen comrades," Masamori concluded, "even if JACL does."[11] In the meantime, the JACL's newly elected president set about the task of controlling the damage from the resolution's passage, urging members of the organization's national board to "make a concerted one-on-one effort to mend the rifts" within the JACL. The JACL's national executive director confessed that he expected "attrition in JACL membership in reaction to th[e] resolution's passage."[12] Sadly, even as the Nisei generation that fought on the battlefields of Europe and in the courtrooms of the American West now dies out, the rancor and bitterness of their own internal disagreement live on.

A good part of what fuels the lingering distrust of the Nisei resisters is the belief that they refused to comply with the draft law for ignoble reasons: laziness, cowardice, or even out-and-out disloyalty to the United States. Karl Kinaga, a veteran of the 442nd and longtime Japanese American community leader, puts it bluntly: some of the resisters, he contends, simply "didn't want to get shot at," and some resisted because their pro-Japanese fathers directed them to do so.[13] Others make the point a bit more indirectly by focusing on the timing of the protest. "They had the right to object to the draft for civil rights," says veteran Fred Hirasuna, but "if they were truly sincere . . . , they should have come out at evacuation time and said, 'We won't go.'" Waiting to protest their internment until their draft notice arrived in the mail, Hirasuna argues, made their choice suspect.

A related point, which prosecutors regularly urged in court in 1944, but which one seldom hears today, is that the resisters' challenge was entirely unnecessary—and therefore of questionable motivation—because the courts were already well on their way toward deciding the constitutionality of the internment when the resisters took their stand. Throughout 1944, even the most proadministration of the internment camp newspapers covered the progress of the pending *Korematsu* and *Endo* cases toward their final resolution in the U.S. Supreme Court—a final resolution that came before the year 1944 was out. Did the resisters really need to press an issue in federal district courts when that issue was months or possibly even weeks away from resolution in the highest court in the land? Carl Sackett, the Wyoming prosecutor of the Heart Mountain resisters, pressed the point even further: Why did *eighty-five* young men need to contest the issue by resisting the draft? If the purpose was to create a legal test case, wouldn't *one* resister have sufficed?

In truth, these charges of improper motivation may not be completely groundless; the historical record leaves ample room to question the motives of at least some of the resisters. Many of the resisters from camps other than Heart Mountain took the public step of filing petitions either to renounce their American citizenship or for expatriation to Japan. On their face, these documents certainly revealed a level of disgust with the U.S. government that called into question the continued loyalty of those who filed them.

The allegations of bad faith resonate even among the Heart Mountain resisters, who were, as a group, the most self-avowedly "loyal" of all the Nisei who refused to comply with the draft. Yosh Kuromiya was distressed, for example, when a number of his fellow resisters from Heart Mountain acceded to a ploy proposed by their attorney, Samuel Menin, whereby the defendants would shave their heads before trial to complicate the government's task of proving their identity. This attempt at beating the charges on a technicality "appalled" Kuromiya, who thought, "We went through all this trouble to get ourselves in the position where we could challenge the constitutionality of this whole thing. So now we are going to get ourselves off the hook? Just so they can send us back to camp and do it right next time? And make sure that we are properly identified?" This tactic made Kuromiya wonder what the "real motives" of some of his fellow resisters were at that point.

Kuromiya was similarly distressed when, after losing before Judge Kennedy, a number of his co-defendants expressed reservations about appealing Kennedy's judgment. Some of those who hesitated were undoubtedly deterred by the cost of an appeal; Kuromiya had no quarrel with them. He did, however, have a problem with "some of the guys [who] didn't care whether we appealed or not." Kuromiya had gone into the litigation assuming that he and his fellow resisters "might have to go all the way to the Supreme Court if necessary. We didn't expect the lower courts to be able to handle the constitutional issues." But to Kuromiya's astonishment, "there was quite a lot of controversy over whether we should continue with the appeal or not. Some of the guys said, 'Why bother? We're safely put away now. We are probably here for the duration. So why sweat it?' " This kind of thinking made Kuromiya worry that he was "in the wrong bunch."

The idea of resisting the draft on constitutional grounds must have appealed to some of the Nisei for the wrong reasons. For those who were especially frightened by the prospect of death or injury in battle, a constitutional challenge to the draft undoubtedly provided a convenient cover—a brave mask to pull over the face of cowardice. So, too, for the handful of Kibei among the resisters from the various camps whose childhood training and experience in Japan produced a feeling of loyalty to the emperor that genuinely conflicted with, or even overrode, their loyalty to the Constitution. For them, draft resistance on constitutional grounds may have provided a mask of patriotism to pull over the face of confused or even lapsed loyalty.

In the main, however, the Nisei resisters were a group of young men who, at least until their deportation and incarceration on racial grounds, had more or less the same feelings of affection for and devotion to the country of their birth as any other of their generation. It is true, as Fred Hirasuna charges, that they came to their protest late, but that does not mean that their protest was feigned. At the time of their eviction from the West Coast, the draft resisters were just as cowed by the government, and just as dazed by the enormity of what was being demanded of them, as the rest of the affected Nikkei. And even that moment did not clearly present an opportunity for individualized resistance. They were evicted en masse, as a nameless and faceless horde, by a military order that was posted in public places and addressed to "all persons of Japanese ancestry" living in a particular area. And from the moment they entered the barbed wire confines of the assembly centers until they received their draft notices, circumstances presented no obvious opportunity for individual acts of resistance. The draft was the first moment when the government addressed an order to each resister as an individual—the first moment when each Nisei stood genuinely face to face with his government. It would also be the last such moment because in this face-to-face exchange the government was ordering each Nisei to surrender his individual rights and identity to the anonymity and subservience of military life. Even with other legal challenges to the internment pending, the draft was an entirely sensible moment for a young Nisei to give voice to his outrage.

The government's decision to draft the Nisei from behind barbed wire created a dilemma for them, and each of the resisters resolved that dilemma in his own way. The Heart Mountain group, guided by a handful of older and more thoughtful men, carefully separated the question of loyalty from the question of compliance with the law. They loudly proclaimed their loyalty, while using the draft as a vehicle for venting their disgust with their mistreatment at the hands of the government. Many of the resisters from other camps, who were acting more or less alone and without the guidance of an organization such as the Fair Play Committee, were not so careful and allowed their anger at the government to influence not only their response to the draft, but also their continued sense of belonging in American society. At bottom, though, virtually all of the resisters were reacting to the same camp conditions, and the same state-sponsored racial discrimination. It is difficult to say that those young men who were more skillful at confining their rage to the draft alone were ultimately so different from those whose anger tainted, even if just temporarily, their belief that they were still welcome in the land of their birth.

In addition, by focusing on the cowardly and the disloyal among the resisters, their critics have diverted attention from two other sets of resisters whose actions radiated good faith. Among the resisters were a considerable number of young men who chose to resist the draft even though they had illnesses or physical disabilities that would have instantly disqualified them from serving. Frank Yamasaki, one of the Minidoka resisters, received his draft notice shortly after being released from a sanatorium where he was being treated for tuberculosis. So, too, did Kenji Shinta, one of the Heart Mountain resisters, who had been in and out of sanatoriums for years before World War II. Shinta was so unwell in the mid-1940s that he was medically barred from working while at McNeil Island. He grew so sick while there that he had to be transferred to a federal prison with a superior medical facility well before his release date. He lived to see the end of his prison term, but not his thirtieth birthday. Had these young men been cowards or had they lacked the will to take up arms against their parents' homeland, they could have avoided military service simply by showing up for, and failing, their preinduction physicals. That would have been the easy way out. (Indeed, that would have been the smartest strategy for *any* of the resisters—even those who did not have serious illnesses—if their goal was merely to avoid serving.) Yet these men did not do that; they chose instead to resist the draft and fight for the recognition of their rights in court. Thus, while we might speculate that the ranks of the resisters included a few cowards and traitors, we can be sure that their ranks also included young men of principle like Frank Yamasaki and Kenji Shinta.

We also know that those ranks included young men like Tak Hoshizaki, one of the Heart Mountain resisters. Hoshizaki, a model airplane enthusiast, had at one time dreamed of flying a plane for the U.S. Army. But after being deported from the West Coast, interned at Heart Mountain, and told that he would be permitted to serve only in a racially segregated infantry battalion, Hoshizaki decided to pay his $2 to join the Fair Play Committee. He refused to report for his physical, was convicted by Judge Kennedy along with the sixty-two other Heart Mountaineers, and served nearly three years at McNeil Island. A few years after his release from McNeil, Hoshizaki again received a draft notice, this time for service in the Korean War. Without hesitating, Hoshizaki complied with the draft.

A cynic might say that his decision to comply with the draft and serve in Korea was evidence that his World War II prosecution served its purpose and showed him the error of his more youthful ways. But that was not what prompted Hoshizaki to make a different decision the second time the military called him for duty. What prompted him was a crucial change in circumstances. When first drafted, Hoshizaki was a prisoner, confined at Heart Mountain and stripped of his civil rights because of his ancestry. The second time, he again felt like an American citizen. He had received a presidential pardon for his earlier act of protest, had regained a measure of financial stability, and was deeply involved in the study of botany at a fine state university in California. There was no occasion for protest in 1952, and so Hoshizaki complied. So, too, did five other Heart Mountain resisters of World War II who were young enough to be eligible for the draft during the Korean War. Plainly, these young men were not cowards. They were men of conscience who, when called from behind barbed wire to fight for their country in Europe, chose first to fight for their rights in a U.S. courtroom.

It was undoubtedly difficult for much of the Japanese American community, or indeed much of the nation as a whole, to appreciate draft resistance as an act of conscience while war still raged in the Pacific. For most of the Nisei resisters, however, that was what it was—a patriotic decision. The resisters' patriotism was the patriotism of protest, a model of Americanism with a pedigree at least as pure—and at least as ancient—as the First Amendment's guarantee of the right "to petition the government for a redress of grievances."

Admittedly, wartime is a tenuous moment for this model of good citizenship, focusing as it does on the rights of the individual rather than the power and safety of the community. But in this instance, inconvenient timing did not make for questionable citizenship. To be sure, the resisters appealed to a very different model of American patriotism than did both the JACL, which preached the patriotism of compliance, and the government, which chose to punish deviations from compliant Americanism with hard time in jail. But as between the resisters' emphasis, on the one hand, and that of the JACL and the government, on the other, the resisters' was the more distinctively American. Ironically, the Nisei of the Japanese American Citizens League, desperate to prove their unvarnished Americanism, took the unmistakably Japanese mantras of their Issei parents—*shikata ganai* and *gaman suru* ("it can't be helped" and "just bear it")—and turned them into arguments for unquestioning compliance with government authority. And the government, for its part, stood ready to prove that the nail that sticks up gets hammered—just as Japanese culture had always said it would.

If the resisters' punishment was designed to teach them something about Americanism, it failed. The resisters emerged from their courtroom experiences schooled in the ways of legal realism: they simply cannot be persuaded that American criminal justice is a product of much more than the views and prejudices of the judge deciding the case. This was, of course, the lesson of their experience. For the identical offense, the Nisei resisters saw most of their ranks condemned in the courtrooms of callous racists like T. Blake Kennedy and Chase Clark, even while a small group of them was exonerated in the courtroom of a compassionate outsider like Louis Goodman. And to those convicted, federal judges meted out sentences ranging from just a few months' imprisonment all the way up to five years. One federal judge, having the luxury of imposing sentence long after the war was over and the relocation centers were closed, chose to sentence the resisters before him to no jail time at all and a fine of just one cent.[14] For Frank Emi, one of the leaders of the Fair Play Committee, these variations "made [him] think, 'Gee, what in the hell is the matter with this justice system? It doesn't make sense. The charge is the same, identical.'"[15]

Yet one finds a surprising lack of bitterness against the government among the surviving Nisei draft resisters of World War II. Most of them went on from their prison experiences to lead industrious lives, to find steady blue-collar (and, in some cases, white-collar) work, to raise their children in relative comfort, to own their own homes, and to join the great American middle class. Many of the surviving resisters are still quite reluctant to speak about their experiences. Yet those who do speak do not speak ill of America. If anything, they emerged from their experiences with a heightened commitment to the American emphasis on individual freedom and a keener perception of the subtleties of American race discrimination. As they age into their seventies and eighties, many remain vigilant, scouring the political landscape for infringements of the rights they themselves lost and fought in court to reestablish. They also remain proud of the choice they made from behind barbed wire as young men. "I lost my citizen's rights," says Yosh Kuromiya, "the day I allowed myself to be put into camp. I regained them the day I challenged the Selective Service law."[16]

Afterword

As I searched for photographs to include in this book, I came across a series of images taken in the Heart Mountain poster shop in January of 1943. The poster shop was a tidy, somewhat cramped studio in one of the barracks, filled with drafting tables at which earnest-looking young Nisei men and women sat, hard at work. My attention was drawn to one shot of three young internees around a drafting table. One of them was hunched over the work surface, his hand poised above a poster he was preparing for a rubber-saving campaign. Across the top of the poster, at an angle and in stylish lettering, were the words "Drive for Uncle Sam!" Just beneath those words, Uncle Sam himself looked sternly out, his tall top hat decorated with stars and a bold stripe. As the designer worked, two other Nisei poster shop employees looked on. One of these, a young man of perhaps twenty, with a paintbrush tucked behind his right ear and a few strands of thick, slicked-back hair falling over his eyebrow, looked very much the part of the serious young artist.

He also looked vaguely familiar to me. Then I remembered that Yosh Kuromiya, one of the Heart Mountain resisters whom I had come to know well, worked at Heart Mountain's poster shop before deciding to resist the draft. I made a copy of the photograph and mailed it to him at his home in southern California. "Could this suave young artist be you, Yosh?" I asked him teasingly.

"Yup, that's me!" was his response, which reached me by return mail. "It sure brings back memories," he added. "Those were happier days when we thought we were doing our share in the war effort—patriotic posters for the War Department." The photograph had been taken a good six weeks before the fiasco of registration, and over a year before the announcement of the reopening of the draft. "Never thought our government would let us down," Yosh wrote.

"But," he continued, "if the draft issue had never come up, I probably would have remained as nonchalant as I appear in the pictures. Even while we were getting screwed, I probably would never have considered the constitutional issues that seriously. There may never have been a confrontation." Then his thoughts took a more personal turn. "I also wouldn't have met you, and you wouldn't have anything to write about,—and our dear Constitution would have remained in the closet gathering dust." I flushed a bit as I read this, sensing both his fondness for me and his assumptions about my views on the merits of the resisters' constitutional arguments.

I put the letter down and thought for a while about my work on the project that has become this book. The fondness he expressed in the letter was something I felt for him, too—and not just for him, but, to varying degrees, for all of the Nisei men whose stories I had listened to, and whom I had come to know. I had sat with them for hours, talked with them. I had lunched with them, sometimes on sandwiches and soda, other times on teriyaki and tea. I had gone to dinner with them and, in some cases, met their children—attractive Sansei of my own generation, people with whom it looked like I could have gone to college or law school.

I had been welcomed into their homes, many of which reminded me, in small ways, of my father's parents' home: comfortable homes, American homes, with the slightly worn and outdated furnishings of an older generation, but laced throughout with traces of a foreign culture. At my grandparents' home, it was the German books on the bookshelves, the Swiss confections on the table, the European objets d'art on the breakfront. In the Nisei homes, it was the small and precious figurines on the shelves, the little wooden Buddhist shrines, the carefully arranged rock gardens or small fruit trees in the backyards.

I had looked at old documents and photographs with these men, sat quietly as their eyes welled with tears, flashed with anger, and sparkled with amusement at the memories my questions called forth. In those memories, I had at times heard hints of my own family's memories, even though my father was an immigrant from the West and theirs were immigrants from the East. Perhaps these men had sensed some of this in me. Perhaps it had helped them trust me enough to speak across the generational and cultural gaps between us.

But along with my fondness for these men came a worry—a worry that Yosh Kuromiya touched in his letter's easy reference to "our dear

Constitution." In interviewing the draft resisters from Heart Mountain, Minidoka, and Tule Lake, I had quickly learned that they saw their legal case as open and shut, a "no-brainer" in the current vernacular. In their view, they were the victims of a civil rights violation of breathtaking scale, and they were entitled to resist the draft in order to establish that. On the first point, of course, I agreed with them wholeheartedly: their eviction and internment were among this country's most shameful and egregious human rights violations. And I went into the project expecting to agree with them wholeheartedly on the second as well. I certainly shared their moral outrage at the government, not just for evicting and interning them, but also for having the audacity to draft them and then to punish them when they refused. It was that sense of moral outrage, and a matching sense of disbelief, that had prompted me to try to discover the story behind the photograph of the sixty-three young Nisei in Judge Kennedy's courtroom.

As I learned their story, though, and thought carefully about their legal position, I struggled to match my sense of moral outrage with a corresponding conviction that the law was on their side. I had every confidence that they had been horribly mistreated by the government, but less confidence than I expected that the government could not constitutionally draft them out of the camps. To me, it just seemed—and still seems—a much closer question than I had anticipated, for the reasons I outline in chapter 7 of this book. I am attracted to the argument that the Constitution's Due Process Clauses will not abide the government's decision to strip citizens of so many of the basic rights and benefits of citizenship, while demanding that they make citizenship's greatest sacrifice. But the law in 1944 did not establish this proposition, and neither does the law today.

On balance, I prefer the creativity, sensitivity, and courage of Judge Goodman's substantive due process approach to the cold and cranky views of Judge Kennedy and Judge Clark. Yet Judge Goodman's creativity also worries me. Is due process flexible enough to support this sort of judicial review of government decisions about military manpower and prosecutorial discretion? If a judge can strike these sorts of decisions down on the ground that they "shock the conscience," whose conscience will be the benchmark? I would be far happier, I think, to live under a government that is checked by Judge Goodman's conscience than by Judge Kennedy's. But, of course, I do not get to choose.

On the other hand, I am at least as hesitant, maybe more so, about the notion of stripping judges of a discretionary power to veto egregious abuses of government power. If our legal system cannot allow judges this sort of reviewing power because it is not "law," then how can it ever hope to respond effectively to a unique case of moral outrage like that of the Nisei draft resisters? Would we want to live in a world that sets law and morality into such separate spheres in tough cases?

I hope that if I were a judge, I would have the courage to do what Judge Goodman did—to press on the boundaries of the law in order to see just how much "give" there really is, to keep a public focus on the government's conduct rather than sweeping it under the rug, and, perhaps most important, to right what struck me as a deep moral wrong. I am left at the end of this project not knowing for sure whether I would have had that courage.

Neither do I know, ultimately, whether I would have had the courage to do what Yosh Kuromiya did. This, I think, is a question that resonates deeply among Americans who grew up during and after the Vietnam War. When American forces were pulled out of Vietnam in 1973, my older brother was fourteen, and I had already sensed my parents' unease about the prospect of his reaching draft age while American troops were in combat overseas. In the neighborhood, kids played games about the Vietnam War. To me, everything about going to war sounded terrifying, from basic training to the trenches. I could not imagine myself surviving such experiences. As I got older, I learned more about that war and came to the conclusion (as did so many of my generation) that the war was deeply wrong. But beneath that conviction was the sense that it was also deeply scary. Fortunately, I have never been called upon to tease apart philosophy from fear.

The Nisei draft resisters were called upon to do just that. Undoubtedly, some of them resisted from mixed motives, although I have been struck over and over again by the intense and compelling good faith of the ten resisters from Heart Mountain, Minidoka, and Tule Lake whom I interviewed for this book. But if I had been one of them, would I have had the courage to do what they did? To be, as the saying went, the nail that stuck up? And if I had, would I have been sticking up for principle, or just for myself?

Some object to the claim that what Yosh Kuromiya and his fellow resisters did was courageous. This has been the position of many of the vocal Nisei veterans and many in the JACL since the war ended: the courageous and patriotic choice was the decision to comply with the draft. And they are right, in part. Who could deny that those who fought, and those who died or were wounded, were both courageous and patriotic? But the resisters' critics are also partly, and importantly, wrong. *Both* choices—wholehearted, willful compliance and wholehearted, willful defiance—were patriotic and courageous. What distinguished one choice from the other was not patriotism, but its pedigree. Both the patriotism of duty and that of protest have proud antecedents in this nation's history. Of course, the patriotism of duty has a powerful Japanese history as well, and that is one of the many ironies in the government's demand of compliance.

On November 9, 2000, a new public monument was dedicated in the nation's capital—the National Japanese American Memorial to Patriotism. It is a monument in the best Washington, D.C., tradition, or at least the best post-Vietnam Washington, D.C., tradition: a grassy, tree-lined triangle containing an austere, marble-walled space shaped roughly like the numeral "9." At the memorial's center stands a commissioned sculpture of two Japanese cranes pressed tightly together, their left wings raised together as they struggle to free themselves of the barbed wire that pins their right wings closely to their sides. A simple five-line *tanka* poem graces one of the memorial's central panels:

> Japanese by blood
> Hearts and minds American
> With honor unbowed
> Bore the sting of injustice
> For future generations.[1]

Alongside this poem are inscribed the names of the nearly eight hundred Nisei soldiers killed in action during World War II, as well as the names, locations, and populations of the ten WRA relocation centers. These—the veterans and the internees, joined together in their experiences of suffering "the sting of injustice"—are the honorees of the Japanese American Memorial to Patriotism.

Yet this memorial honors not just people; it also honors an idea. That idea is the fully assimilated Americanism of Japanese America, and the memorial presents the Nisei combat soldier as the agent of that assimilation. Much of the memorial's power and pathos comes from its juxtaposition of the names of the nearly eight hundred fallen Nisei soldiers with the words of JACL leader Mike Masaoka, identified on the memorial neither as the leader of the JACL nor (of course) as the collaborator that he was with many of the wartime government's anti-Nikkei policies, but rather as a staff sergeant of the 442nd Regimental Combat Team: "I am proud that I am an American of Japanese ancestry. I believe in this nation's institutions, ideals, and traditions; I glory in her heritage; I boast of her history; I trust in her future." To much the same effect is a section of marble wall inscribed with the words President Harry Truman spoke to the soldiers of the 100th and the 442nd upon their return from Europe: "You fought not only the enemy, but you fought prejudice—and you won. Keep up that fight, and we will continue to win—to make this great republic stand for just what the Constitution says it stands for: the welfare of all of the people all of the time."

There is much here to celebrate. But there is also something sad, even tragic. What, ultimately, does this monument say to its visitors, the countless American tourists who wander through it? It teaches the lesson of the *tanka* poet: Bear the sting of injustice for future generations. Endure the unendurable, and you will be rewarded. Assimilate through silent suffering. *Gaman suru.* Perhaps this is part of what has led white America to look upon Japanese Americans as a "model minority": when the nation punished them with its racism, they endured it.

The Nisei draft resisters did not simply endure it, and in large and small ways, they have paid the price of their heresy ever since. There will never be a monument to the Japanese American draft resisters of World War II in our nation's capital, or for that matter, anywhere else. Yet these young men were patriots; in their willingness to risk the condemnation of their community, they showed courage. They were the nails that stuck up. True to the prediction of their Japanese forebears, they got hammered. Perhaps now, fifty-five years later, we can begin to hear in that hammering the construction of a truly American identity.

Notes

Chapter One

1. My account of the Minidoka induction ceremony comes from War Relocation Authority, Minidoka Relocation Center Community Analysis Section, Field Report No. 303, National Archives, RG 210 (National Archives microfilm M1342, Reel 24), and from a letter from Minidoka Project Attorney Frank S. Barrett to WRA Solicitor Philip M. Glick, 27 June 1944, National Archives, RG 210, Entry 16, Box 262, File 37.109 #10, March to July 1944.

2. John L. DeWitt, quoted in "West Coast War Probe," *San Francisco Chronicle*, 14 April 1943.

3. See Sheldon Goldman, *Picking Federal Judges: Lower Court Selection from Roosevelt through Reagan* (New Haven, Conn.: Yale University Press, 1997).

4. 347 U.S. 483 (1954).

5. *United States v. Kuwabara*, 56 F. Supp. 716, 719 (N.D. Cal. 1944).

6. The story of at least some of the Japanese American draft resisters is briefly summarized in Roger Daniels, *Concentration Camps U.S.A.: Japanese Americans and World War II* (New York: Holt, Rinehart & Winston, 1971), 123–39, and in Page Smith, *Democracy on Trial: The Japanese American Evacuation in World War II* (New York: Simon & Schuster, 1995), 335–41.

Chapter Two

1. For background on the Issei, see Yuji Ichioka, *The Issei: The World of the First Generation Japanese Immigrants, 1885–1924* (New York: Free Press, 1988); Roger Daniels, *Asian America: Chinese and Japanese in the United States since 1850* (Seattle: University of Washington Press, 1988), 100–154; Eileen Sunada Sarasohn, ed., *The Issei: Portrait of a Pioneer* (Palo Alto, Calif.: Pacific Books, 1983).

2. See *Ozawa v. United States*, 260 U.S. 178, 192–97 (1922).

3. U.S. Constitution, amend. 14.

4. For background on the Nisei, see Bill Hosokawa, *Nisei: The Quiet Americans* (New York: Morrow, 1969), 154–69; David Yoo, *Growing Up Nisei: Race, Generation, and Culture among Japanese Americans of California, 1924–49* (Urbana: University of Illinois Press, 2000); James Hirabayashi, "Nisei: The Quiet American? A Re-evaluation," *Amerasia Journal* 3 (Summer 1975): 114–29.

5. This and all other quotations from individual draft resisters come from their interviews with the author, as listed in the book's Acknowledgments, except where indicated otherwise.

6. For background on the Kibei, see Minoru Kiyota, *Beyond Loyalty: The Story of a Kibei* (Honolulu: University of Hawaii Press, 1997).

7. This recollection is in an unpublished, untitled manuscript by Yosh Kuromiya, on file with the author.

8. Frank F. Chuman, *The Bamboo People: The Law and Japanese-Americans* (Del Mar, Calif.: Publisher's Inc., 1976), 74–89.

9. See the Quota Immigration Act of 1924, ch. 190, § 13(c), 43 Stat. 153, 162 (known unofficially as the Japanese Exclusion Act).

10. Monica Sone's story is in her wonderful autobiography, *Nisei Daughter* (Seattle: University of Washington Press, 1979), 133.

11. Hosokawa, *Nisei,* 191–92.

12. Tokie Slocum was born Tokutaro Nishimura in Japan in 1895. He was brought to the United States as a young child and raised by a white family by the name of Slocum.

13. See Act of May 9, 1918, ch. 69, 40 Stat. 542. Congress amended this provision in 1919 to allow naturalization of "[a]ny person of foreign birth who served in the military or naval forces of the United States during the present war" and who was honorably discharged. Act of July 19, 1919, ch. 24, 41 Stat. 163, 222.

14. See *Toyota v. United States,* 268 U.S. 402 (1925).

15. Bill Hosokawa, *JACL in Quest of Justice* (New York: Morrow, 1982), 52–53.

16. The resolution is quoted in ibid., 43.

17. See Chuman, *Bamboo People,* 166.

18. Act of June 24, 1935, ch. 290, 49 Stat. 397.

Chapter Three

1. Jack Tono, in *And Justice for All,* ed. John Tateishi (New York: Random House, 1984), 168.

2. For a complete account of the FBI's post–Pearl Harbor sweep, see Louis Fiset, *Imprisoned Apart* (Seattle: University of Washington Press, 1997). See also Commission on Wartime Relocation and Internment of Civilians, *Personal Justice Denied* (Washington, D.C.: Civil Liberties Public Education Fund; Seattle: University of Washington Press, 1997), 54–55. The Issei were not the only foreign nationals picked up by the FBI in the wake of Pearl Harbor; many German and Italian aliens were also arrested.

3. Frank Emi, interview, in *Japanese American World War II Evacuation Oral History Project,* pt. 4, *Resisters,* ed. Arthur Hansen (Munich, Germany: K. G. Saur, 1995), 361.

4. Biddle is quoted in Page Smith, *Democracy on Trial: The Japanese American Evacuation in World War II* (New York: Simon & Schuster, 1995), 99–100. Biddle's background and role in the Japanese American internment are ably

chronicled in Peter Irons, *Justice at War: The Story of the Japanese American Internment Cases* (Berkeley: University of California Press, 1983).

5. Roger Daniels, *Prisoners without Trial* (New York: Hill & Wang, 1993), 30.

6. General DeWitt derived his power to issue his directives from Executive Order 9066, signed by President Roosevelt on February 19, 1942. The order "empowered the Secretary of War or his delegate to designate military areas to which entry of any or all persons would be barred whenever such action was deemed militarily necessary or desirable." Commission on Wartime Relocation and Internment of Civilians, *Personal Justice Denied,* 100–101. The story of the rancorous debate between the military and the Justice Department over the necessity and legality of what became Executive Order 9066 is well told in Peter Irons, *Justice at War.*

7. Helen Murao, in *And Justice for All,* ed. John Tateishi (New York: Random House, 1984), 41–42.

8. It offended Minoru Yasui, a Nisei attorney from Oregon, enough to make him get himself arrested for violating the curfew in order to test its legality in court. His case went to the U.S. Supreme Court, along with the companion case involving another resisting Nisei named Gordon Hirabayashi. See *Yasui v. United States,* 320 U.S. 115 (1943); *Hirabayashi v. United States,* 320 U.S. 81 (1943). The Court unanimously upheld DeWitt's curfew order.

9. The removal of the West Coast Japanese was unprecedented in the size of the territory it sought to clear and the numbers of people it sought to move. Sadly, though, it was not unprecedented in its overtly ethnic targeting. About eighty years earlier, during the Civil War, General Ulysses S. Grant gave Jews twenty-four hours to evacuate Tennessee and parts of Arkansas and Kentucky. Some twenty-five hundred Jews were forced to flee northward and remained away until President Abraham Lincoln overruled Grant's order. See Eric L. Muller, "All the Themes but One," *University of Chicago Law Review* 66 (1999): 1395–1433.

10. Executive Order 9066, 3 *Code of Federal Regulations, 1938–1943,* 1092–93.

11. J. L. DeWitt, *Final Report: Japanese Evacuation from the West Coast, 1942* (Washington, D.C.: U.S. Government Printing Office, 1943), 34.

12. Ibid.

13. Frank J. Taylor, "The People Nobody Wants," *Saturday Evening Post,* 9 May 1942, 66.

14. See Bill Hosokawa, *JACL in Quest of Justice* (New York: Morrow, 1982), 156; Roger Daniels, *Asian America: Chinese and Japanese in the United States since 1850* (Seattle: University of Washington Press, 1988), 218–24.

15. Saboru Kido, "Living with JACL," *Pacific Citizen,* 12 January 1962.

16. Milton Eisenhower, speech at Conference on Evacuation of Enemy Aliens, 14–21, Salt Lake City, Utah, 7 April 1942, University of California at Berkeley, Bancroft Library, Japanese Evacuation and Resettlement Study, C1.03, 67/14C, File 1 of 3.

17. See Smith, *Democracy on Trial,* 173–74; Richard Drinnon, *Keeper of Concentration Camps* (Berkeley: University of California Press, 1987), 69.

18. Eisenhower, Salt Lake City speech. "Evacuation" and "evacuees" were the government's words for the Nikkei who were forcibly removed from their West Coast homes for the interior. They are misleading words: to "evacuate" someone is to save him from something threatening, such as a flood. The Nikkei were not "evacuated" from the West Coast; they were "removed" or "evicted" or "deported."

19. Chase Clark, speech at Conference on Evacuation of Enemy Aliens, 26, Salt Lake City, Utah, 7 April 1942, University of California at Berkeley, Bancroft Library, Japanese Evacuation and Resettlement Study, C1.03, 67/14C, File 1 of 3. Clark's comment about the necessity of "concentration camps" came in a radio address he delivered shortly after the Salt Lake City conference. Chase Clark, radio address, 40, University of California at Berkeley, Bancroft Library, Japanese Evacuation and Resettlement Study, C1.03, 67/14C, File 1 of 3.

20. Eisenhower, Salt Lake City speech, 40.

21. See Drinnon, *Keeper of Concentration Camps,* 8.

22. Commission on Wartime Relocation and Internment of Civilians, *Personal Justice Denied,* 175–78.

23. Amy Uno Ishii, interview, in *Japanese American World War II Evacuation Oral History Project,* pt. 1, *Internees,* ed. Arthur Hansen (Munich, Germany: K. G. Saur, 1991), 66.

24. Ibid., 67.

25. Ibid.

26. Yosh Kuromiya, "The Heart Mountain Fair Play Committee (A Resister's Account)" (Alhambra, Calif., 2 July 2000). For a fine description of the internment camp newspapers (and their general progovernment slant), see Lauren Kessler, "Fettered Freedoms: The Journalism of World War II Japanese Internment Camps," *Journalism History* 15 (1988): 70–79.

27. Murao, in *And Justice for All,* 50.

28. Memorandum from John L. DeWitt to Chief of Staff, U.S. Army, 7, 27 January 1943, National Archives, RG 107, Entry 180, Box 22, ASW 342.18, Enlistment, Japanese Americans ("unknown or doubtful"); DeWitt, *Final Report,* 34 ("racial strains").

29. Minutes of the Special Emergency National Conference, Japanese American Citizens League, 119, 17–24 November 1942, Salt Lake City, UCLA Library, Department of Special Collections, Collection 2010, Box 296.

Chapter Four

1. Franklin Delano Roosevelt to Henry Stimson, 1 February 1943, National Archives, RG 107, Entry 180, Box 47, ASW 342.18, General—Enlistment.

2. Kiko Hori Funabiki, "World War II Resisters" (Letter to the Editor), *Pacific Citizen,* December 1985.

3. Mike Masaoka and Bill Hosokawa, *They Call Me Moses Masaoka* (New York: Morrow, 1987), 119.

4. Minutes of the Special Emergency National Conference, Japanese American Citizens League, 36, 17–24 November 1942, Salt Lake City, UCLA Library, Department of Special Collections, Collection 2010, Box 296.

5. Ibid., 36–40. The text of the resolution is reproduced as supplement number 35 in the Supplement to Minutes of the Special Emergency National Conference, Japanese American Citizens League, 17–24 November 1942, Salt Lake City, UCLA Library, Department of Special Collections, Collection 2010, Box 296.

6. Minutes of the Special Emergency National Conference, JACL, 76. In fact, the notion of permitting or requiring the Nisei to serve in the military was an idea that had been circulating within the military, but gaining little ground, since shortly after President Roosevelt signed Executive Order 9066. See Roger Daniels, *Concentration Camps U.S.A.: Japanese Americans and World War II* (New York: Holt, Rinehart & Winston, 1971), 145–47.

7. Kai Bird, *The Chairman* (New York: Simon & Schuster, 1992), 18.

8. Ibid., 168; see also William Scobey to Colonel Booth, 20 February 1943, National Archives, RG 107, Entry 180, Box 22, ASW 342.18, J.A. Volunteers (Gen & Alphabet).

9. Poston internees to the President of the United States, 6 January 1943, National Archives, RG 107, Entry 183, Box 48, ASW 342.18, JA INDUCTION, Feb. 1, 1943–Dec. 31, 1943.

10. Commission on Wartime Relocation and Internment of Civilians, *Personal Justice Denied* (Washington, D.C.: Civil Liberties Public Education Fund; Seattle: University of Washington Press, 1997), 188.

11. Elmer Davis to the President of the United States, National Archives, RG 407.

12. Henry Stimson to George C. Marshall, National Archives, RG 407.

13. John L. DeWitt to Chief of Staff, U.S. Army, 27 January 1943, Tab A, National Archives, RG 107, Entry 180, Box 22, ASW 342.18, Enlistment, Japanese Americans.

14. M. G. White to John J. McCloy, 22 May 1943, National Archives, RG 107, Entry 180, Box 22, ASW 342.18, Enlistment, J.A. (Divisions). See also Daniels, *Concentration Camps U.S.A.*, 147.

15. John L. DeWitt to Chief of Staff, U.S. Army, 27 January 1943, National Archives, RG 107, Entry 180, Box 22, ASW 342.18, Enlistment, Japanese Americans.

16. The Masaoka-McCloy discussions are described in Bird, *The Chairman,* 168, and in Masaoka and Hosokawa, *They Call Me Moses Masaoka,* 123–26.

17. M. G. White to John J. McCloy, 19 April 1943, National Archives, RG 107, Entry 180, Box 22, ASW 342.18, Enlistment, Japanese Americans.

18. Allen W. Gullion to the Assistant Chief of Staff, G-2, 2 November 1943, National Archives, RG 165, Entry 43, Box 445, Decimal 291.2, Japanese, 1 June 42–31 Dec. 43.

19. The WRA, recognizing its mistake, quickly modified the title of the

form to the slightly less threatening "Information for Leave Clearance." See Page Smith, *Democracy on Trial: The Japanese American Evacuation in World War II* (New York: Simon & Schuster, 1995), 293.

20. John Hall to General Surles, 20 January 1943, National Archives, RG 107, Entry 180, Box 47, ASW 342.18, General—Enlistment.

21. Program, Dinner Party for Volunteers and 150 Guests, 24 February 1943, National Archives, RG 107, Entry 183, Box 50, ASW 342.18, Log—Colorado River.

22. James M. Sakoda, "Minidoka: An Analysis of Changing Patterns of Social Interaction" (Ph.D. diss., University of California, 1949), 113.

23. Stanley D. Arnold to John M. Hall, 12 February 1943, National Archives, RG 107, Entry 183, Box 51, ASW 342.18, Log—Minidoka.

24. Franklin D. Roosevelt to Henry Stimson, 1 February 1943, National Archives, RG 107, Entry 180, Box 47, ASW 342.18, General—Enlistment.

25. Stanley D. Arnold to John M. Hall, 19 February 1943, National Archives, RG 107, Entry 183, Box 51, ASW 342.18, Log—Minidoka.

26. See Sakoda, "Minidoka," 112–13.

27. John M. Hall and Ray McDaniels, telephone conversation, 9 February 1943, National Archives, RG 107, Entry 183, Box 50, ASW 342.18, Log—Heart Mountain.

28. Ray McDaniels and Lieutenant Pierce, telephone conversation, 12 February 1943, National Archives, RG 107, Entry 183, Box 50, ASW 342.18, Log—Heart Mountain.

29. The brief story of the Congress of American Citizens at Heart Mountain is told in Frank Inouye, "Immediate Origins of the Heart Mountain Draft Resistance Movement," in *Remembering Heart Mountain: Essays on Japanese American Internment in Wyoming,* ed. Mike Mackey (Powell, Wyo.: Western History Publications, 1998). See also Report on Registration at Heart Mountain, February 1943, National Archives, RG 210 (National Archives microfilm M1342, Reel 24).

30. Ray McDaniels to John M. Hall, 18 February 1943, National Archives, RG 107, Entry 183, Box 50, ASW 342.18, Log—Heart Mountain.

31. William Scobey to Ray McDaniels, 17 February 1943, National Archives, RG 107, Entry 183, Box 50, ASW 342.18, Log—Heart Mountain.

32. William Scobey and Ray McDaniels, telephone conversation, 17 February 1943, National Archives, RG 107, Entry 183, Box 50, ASW 342.18, Log—Heart Mountain.

33. 50 U.S.C.A. § 33 (West 1928) (repealed 1948).

34. "Robertson Places Responsibility for Enlistments on Block Heads, Life Long Stigma Awaits Nisei Who Have Failed to Shoulder Obligations," *Heart Mountain Sentinel,* 6 March 1943.

35. The numerical results of registration at Heart Mountain are tallied in Final Report of Registration at Heart Mountain, 12 March 1943, National Archives, RG 107, Entry 183, Box 50, ASW 342.18, Log—Heart Mountain.

36. Questions Pertaining to the "Army Induction Message," Questions Pertaining to WRA Form 126-Rev., Questions Pertaining to Form 304-A, National Archives, RG 107, Entry 183, Box 50, ASW 342.18, Log—Tule Lake. Brief descriptions of the immediate reaction to registration at Tule Lake can be found in Harold S. Jacoby, *Tule Lake: From Relocation to Segregation* (Grass Valley, Calif.: Comstock Bonanza Press, 1996), 74–76, and Michi Weglyn, *Years of Infamy* (New York: Morrow Quill Books, 1976), 146.

37. S. L. A. Marshall, Report on the Tule Lake Registration, 17, National Archives, RG 107, Entry 183, Box 50, ASW 342.18, Log—Tule Lake.

38. Jacoby, *Tule Lake,* 76.

39. Deborah K. Lim, "Research Report Prepared for the Presidential Select Committee on JACL Resolution #7," Section II#(5), 1990, *www.resisters.com/Study/LimPartIIE.htm#IIE5.*

40. Weglyn, *Years of Infamy,* 158.

41. On the early experiences of the 100th and the 442nd, see James M. Hanley, *A Matter of Honor* (New York: Vantage Press, 1995), 14–23; Chester Tanaka, *Go for Broke: A Pictorial History of the Japanese American 100th Infantry Battalion and the 442d Regimental Combat Team* (Richmond, Calif.: Go for Broke, 1982), 10–16.

42. Teiko Ishida to Colonel William Scobey, 30 July 1943, National Archives, RG 107, Entry 183, Box 48, ASW 342.18, JA INDUCTION.

43. This exchange between G-1 and McCloy's office is in M. G. White to John J. McCloy, 19 April 1943; William Scobey to John J. McCloy, 20 April 1943; M. G. White to John J. McCloy, 23 April 1943; and M. G. White to John J. McCloy, 26 April 1943, National Archives, RG 107, Entry 180, Box 22, ASW 342.18, Enlistment, J.A. (Divisions).

44. John F. Hall to Colonel Bicknell, 13 August 1943, National Archives, RG 107, Entry 180, Box 22, ASW 342.18, Enlistment, J.A. (Divisions).

45. John J. McCloy to M. G. White, 4 May 1943, National Archives, RG 107, Entry 180, Box 22, ASW 342.18, Enlistment, J.A. (Divisions).

46. M. G. White to John J. McCloy, 22 May 1943, National Archives, RG 107, Entry 180, Box 22, ASW 342.18, Enlistment, J.A. (Divisions).

47. Harrison A. Gerhardt to Director, Bureau of Public Relations, 22 December 1943, National Archives, RG 107, Entry 183, Box 48, ASW 342.18, JA INDUCTION.

48. Ibid.

49. Ibid.

50. Teiko Ishida to John M. Hall, 20 December 1943, National Archives, RG 107, Entry 183, Box 48, ASW 342.18, JA INDUCTION, Feb. 1, 1943–Dec. 31, 1943.

51. John F. Hall to Noel Macy, 1 January 1944, National Archives, RG 107, Entry 183, Box 48, ASW 342.18, J.A. Selective Service, Jan. 1, 1944 thru.

52. Dillon Myer to John J. McCloy, 22 December 1943, RG 107, Entry 180, Box 22, ASW 342.18, Enlistment, J.A. (Divisions).

Chapter Five

1. War Department Bureau of Public Relations Press Branch, Selective Service to Be Reinstated for Americans of Japanese Descent, 19 January 1944, National Archives, RG 107, Entry 183, Box 48, ASW 342.18, JA INDUCTION, Feb. 1, 1943–Dec. 31, 1943.

2. War Relocation Authority, Community Analysis Section, The Reaction of Heart Mountain to the Opening of Selective Service to the Nisei, National Archives, RG 210 (National Archives microfilm M1342, Reel 17).

3. See Harold S. Jacoby, *Tule Lake: From Relocation to Segregation* (Grass Valley, Calif.: Comstock Bonanza Press, 1996), 89–90; Michi Weglyn, *Years of Infamy* (New York: Morrow Quill Books, 1976), 163–73.

4. *Minidoka Irrigator,* 22 January 1944.

5. Kimi Tambara, "On Equal Footing," *Minidoka Irrigator,* 22 January 1944.

6. "Director D. S. Myer Clarifies Nisei Men Draft Situation," *Minidoka Irrigator,* 26 February 1944.

7. Kimi Tambara, "A United Front," *Minidoka Irrigator,* 26 February 1944.

8. *Yasui v. United States,* 320 U.S. 115 (1943).

9. Minoru Yasui, in *And Justice for All,* ed. John Tateishi (New York: Random House, 1984), 80–82.

10. Minoru Yasui, "Nisei and Selective Service," *Minidoka Irrigator,* 11 March 1944.

11. War Relocation Authority, Minidoka Community Analysis Section, Report No. 283, Attachment 1, National Archives, RG 210 (National Archives microfilm M1342, Reel 24).

12. On this first skirmish in the draft battle at Minidoka, see "97 Nisei Draftees Accepted by Army," *Minidoka Irrigator,* 26 February 1944; Clarence T. Arai to Philip M. Glick, 9 March 1944, National Archives, RG 210, Entry 16, Box 262, File 37.109 #10, March to July 1944; "2 Draft Evaders under $2,000 Bond," *Minidoka Irrigator,* 1 April 1944.

13. Ralph C. Barnhart to Philip M. Glick, 24 April 1944, National Archives, RG 210, Entry 16, Box 262, File 37.109 #10, March to July 1944.

14. Jimmie H. Akutsu to the President of the United States, National Archives, RG 210, Entry 16, Box 262, File 37.109 #10, March to July 1944.

15. John J. McCloy to Cordell Hull, 11 May 1944, National Archives, RG 107, Entry 183, Box 48, ASW 342.18, J.A. Selective Service, Jan. 1, 1944 thru.

16. "Two Youths Held on Draft Charge," *Minidoka Irrigator,* 6 May 1944.

17. Kuroki is lionized in Ralph Martin, *Boy from Nebraska* (New York: Harper & Brothers, 1946). A more sensitive and balanced picture of him emerges in Arthur A. Hansen, "Sergeant Ben Kuroki's Perilous 'Home Mission': Contested Loyalty and Patriotism in the Japanese American Detention Centers," in *Remembering Heart Mountain: Essays on Japanese American Internment in Wyoming,* ed. Mike Mackey (Powell, Wyo.: Western History Publications, 1998), 153–75.

18. For an account of Kuroki's visit, see War Relocation Authority, Minidoka Community Analysis Section, Events and Factors Involved in Sgt.

Kuroki's Visit at Minidoka, Document No. 305, National Archives, RG 210 (National Archives microfilm M1342, Reel 24).

19. James Sakoda, quoted in Hansen, "Sergeant Ben Kuroki's Perilous 'Home Mission,'" 159.

20. War Relocation Authority, Minidoka Community Analysis Section, Events and Factors, 8.

21. The noncompliance during the summer of 1944 is recounted in Frank S. Barrett to Philip M. Glick, 10 June 1944; Frank S. Barrett to Philip M. Glick, 27 June 1944; and Frank S. Barrett to Philip M. Glick, 25 August 1944, National Archives, RG 210, Entry 16, Box 262, File 37.109 #10, Aug. to Dec. 1944.

22. Frank S. Barrett to Philip M. Glick, 25 August 1944, National Archives, RG 210, Entry 16, Box 262, File 37.109 #10, Aug. to Dec. 1944. Barrett, Minidoka's project attorney, expressed some doubt about the authenticity of this letter and ordered an investigation. That he never reported that the letter was a fake in any of his subsequent detailed dispatches to his boss in Washington suggests that the letter was authentic. So, too, did Barrett's contemporaneous admission that a request of this kind from the camp to the draft board would not have been unexpected. See ibid.

23. It is not clear why the government deviated from this practice in late April when agents arrested Gene Akutsu.

24. Frank S. Barrett to Philip M. Glick, 4 July 1944, National Archives, RG 210, Entry 16, Box 262, File 37.109 #10, March to July 1944.

25. A. T. Hansen, Further Reactions to Selective Service at Heart Mountain, March 16–April 7, 22, 15 April 1944, National Archives, RG 210 (National Archives microfilm M1342, Reel 17) ("intellectual hobo"); Bill Hosokawa, telephone conversation with author, 22 January 1998 ("latrine lawyer"); A. T. Hansen, The Reaction of Heart Mountain to the Opening of Selective Service to the Nisei, 5, 1 April 1944, National Archives, RG 210 (National Archives microfilm M1342, Reel 17) ("over-radical . . .").

26. Sixty was the estimate of this night's attendance by internee Harry Yoshida in his testimony as a government witness at the trial of the leaders of the Heart Mountain draft resistance. See Record on Appeal in *United States v. Kiyoshi Okamoto et al.*, United States Court of Appeals for the Tenth Circuit, National Archives Branch Depository, Denver, Colo., RG 276, Transcripts of Records on Appeal, 1929–54, Box 386.

27. George Nozawa, unpublished essay on the Fair Play Committee, Mountain View, Calif., n.d.

28. Kuromiya's memories of the Fair Play Committee meetings are in Yosh Kuromiya, "The Heart Mountain Fair Play Committee (A Resister's Account)" (Alhambra, Calif., 2 July 2000).

29. The bulletin is reproduced in Hansen, Reaction of Heart Mountain, 14–15.

30. Indeed, in its very first public pronouncement, the Fair Play Committee had made clear that it was "out to give [the internees] that side [of the draft issue] which the Assistant Project Director and the JACL have not presented."

Fair Play Committee, First Bulletin of the Fair Play Committee, 24 February 1944, attached to stipulation dated 23 October 1944, *United States v. Kiyoshi Okamoto et al.*, United States Court of Appeals for the Tenth Circuit, National Archives Branch Depository, Denver, Colo., RG 276, Transcripts of Records on Appeal, 1929–54, Box 386.

31. The petition is reproduced in Hansen, Reaction of Heart Mountain, 15–17.

32. See Lauren Kessler, "Fettered Freedoms: The Journalism of World War II Japanese Internment Camps," *Journalism History* 15 (1988): 73–74.

33. "Our Cards on the Table," *Heart Mountain Sentinel*, 11 March 1944.

34. See Hansen, Further Reactions, 30–31; James Omura, interview, in *Japanese American World War II Evacuation Oral History Project*, pt. 4, *Resisters*, ed. Arthur Hansen (Munich, Germany: K. G. Saur, 1995), 213–17, 253–54, 257–70, 290.

35. Fair Play Committee, Third Bulletin of the Fair Play Committee, 4 March 1944, attached to stipulation dated 23 October 1944, *United States v. Kiyoshi Okamoto et al.*, United States Court of Appeals for the Tenth Circuit, National Archives Branch Depository, Denver, Colo., RG 276, Transcripts of Records on Appeal, 1929–54, Box 386.

36. Hansen, Reaction of Heart Mountain, 23.

37. Kuromiya, "The Heart Mountain Fair Play Committee (A Resister's Account)."

38. "Wyoming Draft Resistance Has Authorities Stumped," *Rocky Shimpo*, 10 March 1944.

39. War Relocation Authority, Heart Mountain Relocation Center, Minutes of Staff Meeting, 19 February 1944, National Archives, RG 210, Entry 48, Box 158, Staff Meetings (Minutes).

40. War Relocation Authority, Heart Mountain Relocation Center, Minutes of Heart Mountain Community Council Meeting, 22 February 1944, *United States v. Shigeru Fujii et al.*, United States District Court for the District of Wyoming, National Archives Branch Depository, Denver, Colo., RG 21, Criminal Case Files 1890–1943, Entry 9, Box 150.

41. War Relocation Authority, Heart Mountain Relocation Center, Minutes of Staff Meeting, 11 March 1944, National Archives, RG 210, Entry 48, Box 158, Staff Meetings (Minutes).

42. Ibid.

43. Philip Glick to Dillon Myer, 15 March 1944, National Archives, RG 210, Entry 16, Box 94, File 13.607 #11, March 1944; Carl Sackett to Tom Clark, 16 June 1944, National Archives, RG 60, Class 146-28, Box 65, File 146-28-282, Section 5.

44. Hansen, Further Reactions, 6.

45. Frank Emi, interview, *Japanese American World War II Evacuation Oral History Project*, pt. 4, 369.

46. Guy Robertson to Roger Baldwin, 13 April 1944, National Archives, RG 210, Entry 17, Box 4, Chrono. Copies: Outgoing—Sept. 1943–June 1944.

47. Dillon Myer to John Edgar Hoover, 25 April 1944, National Archives, RG 210, Entry 16, Box 94, File 13.607 #13, April to May 1944.

48. For details on Kuroki's visit to Heart Mountain, see Hansen, "Sergeant Ben Kuroki's Perilous 'Home Mission.'"

49. D. Newcomb Barco Jr. to Lawrence M. C. Smith, 24 September 1942, National Archives, RG 60, Class 146-28, Box 64, File 146-28-282, Section 1.

50. Alien Property Custodian to The Japanese Publishing Company, 23 August 1943, National Archives, RG 60, Class 146-28, Box 64, File 146-28-282, Section 3.

51. Memorandum by Helen Chapin, 23 February 1943, National Archives, RG 60, Class 146-28, Box 64, File 146-28-282, Section 2. Omura shared some of his own recollections of his early work for the *Rocky Nippon* and the *Rocky Shimpo* in James Omura, "Japanese American Journalism during World War II," in *Frontiers of Asian American Studies,* ed. Gail Nomura et al. (Pullman: Washington State University Press, 1989), 72–73.

52. Jimmie Omura, "Freedom of the Press," *Rocky Shimpo,* 19 March 1944.

53. Jimmie Omura, "Our Second Reply to Mr. Saboru Kido," *Rocky Shimpo,* 5 April 1944.

54. Malcolm E. Pitts to Dillon S. Myer, 12 April 1944, National Archives, RG 210, Entry 16, Box 94, File 13.607 #12, April to May 1944.

55. Harry F. Tarvin to Malcolm E. Pitts, 6 April 1944, National Archives, RG 210, Entry 16, Box 94, File 13.607 #12, April to May 1944.

56. Omura, interview, *Japanese American World War II Evacuation Oral History Project,* pt. 4, 303.

57. John C. Baker to Charles F. Ernst, 14 April 1944, National Archives, RG 210, Entry 17, Box 4, Chrono. Copies: Outgoing—Sept. 1943–June 1944.

58. For further evidence of the government's involvement in naming Omura's successor at the *Rocky Shimpo,* see Dillon Myer to James G. Lindley, 19 April 1944; Robert Dolins to Leo T. Simmons, 19 April 1944, National Archives, RG 210, Entry 17, Box 4, Chrono. Copies: Outgoing—Sept. 1943–June 1944.

59. Memorandum by J. M. McInerney, May 1944, National Archives, RG 60, Class 146-28, Box 64, File 146-28-282, Section 3.

60. Joe Grant Masaoka and Min Yasui, Visit to Cheyenne County Jail with Japanese American Draft Delinquents, National Archives, RG 210, Entry 16, Box 94, File 13.607 #12, April to May 1944.

61. I have drawn all biographical information on Carl Sackett from the Carl Sackett Collection, Wyoming State Archives, Cheyenne.

62. Carl Sackett to Tom Clark, 27 June 1944, National Archives, RG 60, Class 146-28, Box 64, File 146-28-282, Section 5. The case of which Sackett complained was *Hartzel v. United States,* 322 U.S. 680 (1944).

63. Masaoka and Yasui, Visit to Cheyenne County Jail.

64. Deborah K. Lim, an attorney hired by the JACL in the late 1980s to prepare an investigative report on the JACL's wartime activities, concluded that Masaoka and Yasui did send a copy of their report to the FBI. See Lim, "Re-

search Report," Section IIE(1). I have not been able to corroborate that conclusion in my own research.

65. As unseemly as it may have been for Carl Sackett to use the JACL men as surrogate interrogators of the jailed resisters, it was not unconstitutional at the time. Twenty years later, in the landmark case of *Massiah v. United States*, 377 U.S. 201 (1964), the Supreme Court would condemn this sort of practice as a violation of the defendant's Sixth Amendment right to counsel. In 1944, however, nothing but a prosecutor's own sense of fair play prevented him from using a third party to interrogate an indicted criminal defendant in the absence of counsel.

Chapter Six

1. The Supreme Court heard oral argument in *Korematsu v. United States*, 323 U.S. 14 (1944), on October 11 and 12, 1944. On December 18, 1944, the Court decided the case, upholding the constitutionality of the internment. For more on the story of *Korematsu* and the three other cases on the Japanese American internment that reached the Supreme Court in 1943 and 1944, see Peter Irons, *Justice at War: The Story of the Japanese American Internment Cases* (Berkeley: University of California Press, 1983).

2. Francis Biddle to Herbert Wechsler, 14 October 1944, National Archives, RG 60, Class 146-28, Box 66, File 146-28-282, Section 8.

3. After the war, Wechsler took a position on the faculty of the Columbia Law School. In 1959, he published one of the most important and intensely debated articles in the constitutional law canon: "Toward Neutral Principles of Constitutional Law," *Harvard Law Review* 73 (1959): 1–35.

4. Herbert Wechsler to Francis Biddle, 28 October 1944, National Archives, RG 60, Class 146-28, Box 66, File 146-28-282, Section 8.

5. T. Blake Kennedy to George W. Hewlett, 31 March 1944, T. Blake Kennedy Collection, American Heritage Center, University of Wyoming, Laramie.

6. Kozie Sakai to Frank Emi, 12 June 1944, personal collection of Frank Emi, San Gabriel, Calif.

7. Kozie Sakai to Frank Emi, 13 June 1944, personal collection of Frank Emi, San Gabriel, Calif.

8. Materials on Menin's career can be found in the Samuel D. Menin Collection, Archives/Special Collections, Auraria Library, Denver, Colo.

9. See *United States v. Mammoth Oil Co.*, 5 F.2d 330 (D. Wyo. 1925), *rev'd*, 275 U.S. 13 (1927).

10. Jack Tono, in *And Justice for All*, ed. John Tateishi (New York: Random House, 1984), 171.

11. T. Blake Kennedy, Memoirs, 451, T. Blake Kennedy Collection, American Heritage Center, University of Wyoming, Laramie.

12. Ibid., 615.

13. T. Blake Kennedy, The Race Problem in America, T. Blake Kennedy Collection, American Heritage Center, University of Wyoming, Laramie. This address by Kennedy is undated. However, it appears in his papers together with

other speeches he delivered between about 1906 and the early 1920s, and most likely dates from that period as well.

14. T. Blake Kennedy, Our Immigration Policy, 1924, T. Blake Kennedy Collection, American Heritage Center, University of Wyoming, Laramie.

15. T. Blake Kennedy, Will the New Immigration Policy Improve American Citizenship? T. Blake Kennedy Collection, American Heritage Center, University of Wyoming, Laramie. This address is undated, but from context can be dated to 1927.

16. T. Blake Kennedy, Remarks on Naturalization Day, 3 July 1944, T. Blake Kennedy Collection, American Heritage Center, University of Wyoming, Laramie.

17. T. Blake Kennedy, Remarks on Naturalization Day, 2 July 1945, T. Blake Kennedy Collection, American Heritage Center, University of Wyoming, Laramie.

18. Vern Lechliter, "Mass Trial of Japs Opens in U.S. Court," *Wyoming Eagle*, 13 June 1944.

19. Stipulation as to Statement of Facts and Designation of Parts of Record to Be Included in Record on Appeal, *United States v. Shigeru Fujii et al.*, United States Court of Appeals for the Tenth Circuit, National Archives Branch Depository, Denver, Colo., RG 276, Transcripts of Records on Appeal, Box 378, File 2973.

20. Ibid.

21. Vern Lechliter, "FBI Agents Testify Here in Jap Trial," *Wyoming Eagle*, 14 June 1944.

22. Kozie Sakai to Frank Emi, 20 June 1944, personal collection of Frank Emi, San Gabriel, Calif.

23. "Final Arguments in Trial of 63 Japs Are Heard Here," *Wyoming Eagle*, 20 June 1944.

24. Kozie Sakai to Frank Emi, 20 June 1944, personal collection of Frank Emi, San Gabriel, Calif.

25. See "63 Japs Are Given 3-Year Terms in Pen," *Wyoming Eagle*, 27 June 1944.

26. *United States v. Fujii*, 55 F. Supp. 928, 929–32 (D. Wyo. 1944).

27. Brief of Appellant, *Shigeru Fujii v. United States*, No. 2973, United States Court of Appeals for the Tenth Circuit, Samuel D. Menin Collection, Archives/Special Collections, Auraria Library, Denver, Colo.

28. *Fujii v. United States*, 148 F.2d 298, 299 (10th Cir. 1945).

29. The U.S. Supreme Court declined to hear the case. See *Tamesa v. United States*, 325 U.S. 868 (1945).

30. 50 U.S.C.A. App. § 311 (West 1944).

31. In Memoriam of the Honorable Eugene Rice, 304 F. Supp. 7, 10 (1969).

32. Transcript of Hearing, 5 August 1944, *United States v. Kiyoshi Okamoto et al.*, United States District Court for the District of Wyoming, National Archives Branch Depository, Denver, Colo., RG 21, Entry 9, Box 150.

33. Ibid.

34. Bill of Exceptions, *United States v. Kiyoshi Okamoto et al.*, United States Court of Appeals for the Tenth Circuit, National Archives Branch Depository, Denver, Colo., RG 276, Transcripts of Records on Appeal, Box 386.

35. James M. Omura to Frank S. Emi, 17 April 1944, *United States v. Kiyoshi Okamoto et al.*, United States District Court for the District of Wyoming, National Archives Branch Depository, Denver, Colo., RG 21, Entry 9, Box 150.

36. Bill of Exceptions, *United States v. Kiyoshi Okamoto et al.*, United States Court of Appeals for the Tenth Circuit, National Archives Branch Depository, Denver, Colo., RG 276, Transcripts of Records on Appeal, Box 386. A camp's "stop list" was its list of internees who were forbidden to leave camp for any reason.

37. Carl Sackett to Tom Clark, 2 November 1944, National Archives, RG 60, Classified Subject Files, Box 66, File 146-28-282, Section 8.

38. Defendants' Requested Instruction No. 1, *United States v. Kiyoshi Okamoto et al.*, United States Court of Appeals for the Tenth Circuit, National Archives Branch Depository, Denver, Colo., RG 276, Transcripts of Records on Appeal, Box 386.

39. Carl Sackett to Tom C. Clark, 28 October 1944, National Archives, RG 60, Classified Subject Files, Box 66, File 146-28-282, Section 7.

40. Memorandum by Edward S. Lazowska, 2 November 1944, National Archives, RG 60, Classified Subject Files, Box 66, File 146-28-282, Section 8.

41. Carl Sackett to Tom C. Clark, 2 November 1944, National Archives, RG 60, Classified Subject Files, Box 66, File 146-28-282, Section 8.

42. *United States v. Okamoto,* 152 F.2d 905, 907 (10th Cir. 1945).

43. Carl Sackett to Tom C. Clark, 28 October 1944, National Archives, RG 60, Classified Subject Files, Box 66, File 146-28-282, Section 7.

44. Carl Sackett to Tom C. Clark, 2 November 1944, National Archives, RG 60, Classified Subject Files, Box 66, File 146-28-282, Section 8.

45. See Arthur A. Hansen, "Jimmie Omura's World War II Colorado Campaign: Denver's 'Resettlement Press' and the Japanese American Citizen's League, 1942–1943," in *Nikkei (Dis)appearances,* ed. Louis Fiset and Gail M. Nomura (forthcoming).

46. See James M. Omura, interview, in *Japanese American World War II Evacuation Oral History Project,* pt. 4, *Resisters,* ed. Arthur Hansen (Munich, Germany: K. G. Saur, 1995), 323–26.

47. 325 U.S. 478 (1945).

48. See *United States v. Keegan,* 141 F.2d 248 (2d Cir. 1944), *rev'd,* 325 U.S. 478 (1945).

49. *Okamoto,* 152 F.2d at 908.

50. Carl Sackett to Theron L. Caudle, 28 December 1944, National Archives, RG 60, Classified Subject Files, Class 146-28, Box 66, File 146-28-282, Section 9.

51. Carl Sackett to Theron L. Caudle, 29 December 1944, National Archives, RG 60, Classified Subject Files, Class 146-28, Box 66, File 146-28-282, Section 9.

52. Theron L. Caudle to the Solicitor General, 11 January 1946, National Archives, RG 60, Classified Subject Files, Class 146-28, Box 66, File 146-28-282, Section 9.

53. Mr. Elliff to Mr. Caudle, 30 January 1946, National Archives, RG 60, Classified Subject Files, Class 146-28, Box 66, File 146-28-282, Section 9.

54. Memorandum by Mr. McInerney, 31 January 1946, National Archives, RG 60, Classified Subject Files, Class 146-28, Box 66, File 146-28-282, Section 9.

55. Philip M. Glick to Dillon Myer, 4 March 1943, National Archives, RG 210, Entry 16, Box 237.

56. *Idaho Daily Statesman,* 26 May 1942.

57. "Japanese Face Trial," *Idaho Daily Statesman,* 7 September 1944.

58. Motion to Quash Indictment and to Dismiss Action, *United States v. Jim Hajime Akutsu,* United States District Court for the District of Idaho—Southern Division, National Archives Branch Depository, Seattle, Wash., RG 21, Box 89, File 2974.

59. *Ex parte American Steel Barrel Co.,* 230 U.S. 35, 43 (1913).

60. George K. Kodama to Seattle Draft Board, 12 June 1944, *United States v. George Kodama,* United States District Court for the District of Idaho—Southern Division, National Archives Branch Depository, Seattle, Wash., RG 21, Box 90, File 2984.

61. Frank S. Barrett to Philip M. Glick, 20 September 1944, National Archives, RG 210, Entry 16, Box 262, File 37.109 #10, Aug. to Dec. 1944.

62. "Lawyer Says Jurors May Be Prejudiced," *Minidoka Irrigator,* 23 September 1944; see also Frank S. Barrett to Philip M. Glick, 27 September 1944, National Archives, RG 210, Entry 16, Box 262, File 37.109 #10, Aug. to Dec. 1944.

63. Frank S. Barrett to Philip M. Glick, 27 September 1944, National Archives, RG 210, Entry 16, Box 262, File 37.109 #10, Aug. to Dec. 1944.

64. "Federal Court Hands Nisei Jail Sentence," *Idaho Daily Statesman,* 26 September 1944.

Chapter Seven

1. Eleanor Jackson Piel, interview with author, 7 July 1999, New York City.

2. In addition to the Wyoming and Idaho cases, draft evasion cases were brought against interned Nisei in federal district courts in Colorado, Utah, and Arizona in 1944. Convictions were obtained everywhere.

3. Information about Judge Goodman is sparse. Much of the material in this chapter comes from interviews with the judge's late daughter, Lorraine Bennett; his grandson, Daniel Bennett; and two of his law clerks, Eleanor Jackson Piel and William Wunsch. See Lorraine Bennett, interview with author, 15 October 1998, Menlo Park, Calif.; Daniel Bennett, interview with author, 7 June 1998, Ventura, Calif.; William Wunsch, interview with author, 9 January 1998, San Francisco; Eleanor Jackson Piel, interview with author, 7 July 1999, New York City.

4. Louis E. Goodman, remarks at I Am an American Day, 19 May 1946, Judge Louis E. Goodman Collection, Archives, United States District Court for the Northern District of California, San Francisco.

5. Louis E. Goodman, remarks at Services, Day of Atonement, 24 September 1947, Temple Emanu-El, San Francisco, Judge Louis E. Goodman Collection, Archives, United States District Court for the Northern District of California, San Francisco.

6. "6 Japanese Appear in Court Here on Draft Charges," *Humboldt Standard,* 17 July 1944.

7. The story of this incident is told in Lynwood Carranco, "A Study in Prejudice: The Chinese and Humboldt County, California," in *Redwood Country,* ed. Lynwood Carranco (Belmont, Calif.: Star, 1986), 46–51.

8. "Not Enough Food, Japanese Complain in Jail Here," *Humboldt Standard,* 17 July 1944.

9. See "27 Jap Internees Face Trial Here on Draft Count," *Humboldt Standard,* 14 July 1944.

10. See "Puter to Entertain Court Attaches Here Tonight," *Humboldt Standard,* 17 July 1944; Matthew T. Rice, "Federal Court Attaches, Local Bar Members Attend Annual Dinner," *Humboldt Standard,* 18 July 1944.

11. "12 Japanese Admit Draft Evasion Charges in Federal Court Today; 6 Others Arraigned," *Humboldt Standard,* 18 July 1944.

12. See "Permission to Withdraw Pleas of Guilty Asked by 12 Japanese," *Humboldt Standard,* 19 July 1944.

13. Motion to Quash and Terminate Proceedings, *United States v. Masaaki Kuwabara et al.,* United States District Court for the Northern District of California, National Archives Branch Depository, San Bruno, Calif., RG 21, Subgroup Sacramento, Criminal Case Files, 1916–1963, Box 413, File 8966.

14. "Indictments of 27 Japanese Attacked in Court Here," *Humboldt Standard,* 20 July 1944.

15. Ibid.

16. Tom C. Clark to Emmet J. Seawell, 20 July 1944, National Archives, RG 60, Class 146-28, Box 65, File 146-28-282, Section 5.

17. Judge Goodman correctly cited *Falbo v. United States,* 320 U.S. 549 (1944), for this proposition.

18. On this point, too, Goodman was correct. Federal law at the time allowed a U.S. citizen to expatriate himself only after arriving on foreign soil. See 8 U.S.C.A. § 803(a) (West 1942), *repealed,* 66 Stat. 280 (1952).

19. 320 U.S. 81 (1943).

20. 323 U.S. 213 (1944).

21. Emmet J. Seawell to Tom C. Clark, 16 October 1944, National Archives, RG 60, Classified Subject Files, Box 65, File 146-28-282, Section 7.

22. *Twining v. New Jersey,* 211 U.S. 78, 106 (1908).

23. *Betts v. Brady,* 316 U.S. 455, 462 (1942).

24. *Adamson v. California,* 332 U.S. 46, 69 (1947) (Black, J., dissenting).

25. Ibid., 68 (Frankfurter, J., concurring).

26. *Rochin v. California,* 342 U.S. 165, 171 (1952).

27. See *United States v. Lamothe,* 152 F.2d 340, 342 (2d Cir. 1945); Jamin Raskin, "Legal Aliens, Local Citizens: The Historical, Constitutional, and Theoretical Meanings of Alien Suffrage," *University of Pennsylvania Law Review* 141 (1993): 1391, 1442; Charles E. Roh Jr. and Frank K. Upham, "The Status of Aliens under United States Draft Laws," *Harvard International Law Journal* 13 (1972): 501–17.

28. *The Confiscation Cases,* 74 U.S. 454, 457 (1868).

29. *Wayte v. United States,* 470 U.S. 598, 608 (1985) (quoting *Bordenkircher v. Hayes,* 434 U.S. 357, 364 (1978)).

30. Colonel Gerhardt, Colonel Washburn, and Colonel Sweitzer, telephone conversation, 2 August 1944, National Archives, RG 107, Entry 183, Box 48, ASW 342.18, J.A. Selective Service, Jan 1, 1944 thru.

31. Ibid.

32. Dillon Myer to Project Directors, 1 August 1944, National Archives, RG 210, Entry 16, Box 94, File 13.607 #13, June to Aug. 1944.

33. See Philip M. Glick to Edgar Bernhard, 31 July 1944, National Archives, RG 210, Entry 17, Box 4, Chrono. Copies: Outgoing—July–Dec. 1944.

34. See Frank S. Barrett to Philip M. Glick, 1 August 1944, National Archives, RG 210, Entry 16, Box 262, File 37.109 #10, Aug. to Dec. 1944.

35. Herbert Wechsler to Francis Biddle, 28 October 1944, National Archives, RG 60, Class 146-28, Box 66, File 146-28-282, Section 8.

36. See Emmet J. Seawell to the Attorney General, 29 June 1944, National Archives, RG 60, Class 146-28, Box 65, File 146-28-282, Section 5; Tom C. Clark to Emmet Seawell, 3 July 1944, National Archives, RG 210, Entry 16, Box 94, File 13.607 #13, June to Aug. 1944; Tom C. Clark to Dillon S. Myer, 5 July 1944, National Archives, RG 210, Entry 16, Box 94, File 13.607 #13, June to Aug. 1944.

37. See Project Attorney Campbell to Edwin Ferguson, 6 October 1944, National Archives, RG 210, Entry 16, Box 94, File 13.607 #14, Sept. to Oct. 1944; Edwin Ferguson to Project Attorney Campbell, 13 October 1944, National Archives, RG 210, Entry 16, Box 94, File 13.607 #14, Sept. to Oct. 1944.

38. See *Takeguma v. United States,* 156 F.2d 437 (9th Cir. 1946).

Chapter Eight

1. See Paul W. Keve, *The McNeil Century: The Life and Times of an Island Prison* (Chicago: Nelson-Hall, 1984), 219–24.

2. Glenn E. Smiley, Calendar of Exile, Peace Collection, Swarthmore College, Swarthmore, Pa.

Chapter Nine

1. See Commission on Wartime Relocation and Internment of Civilians, *Personal Justice Denied* (Washington, D.C.: Civil Liberties Public Education Fund; Seattle: University of Washington Press, 1997), 251.

2. *Abo v. Clark,* 77 F. Supp. 806, 811 (N.D. Cal. 1948), *aff'd in part and rev'd in part sub nom. McGrath v. Furuya,* 186 F.2d 766 (9th Cir. 1951).

3. See *McGrath v. Furuya,* 186 F.2d 766, 772–74 (9th Cir. 1951).

4. Minutes of National Convention, Japanese American Citizens League, 28 February to 4 March 1946, Denver, Colo., UCLA Library, Department of Special Collections, Collection 2010, Box 296.

5. U.S. President's Amnesty Board, *Report Granting Pardon to Certain Persons Convected of Violating the Selective Training & Service Act of 1940 as Amended* (Washington, D.C., 1947); President, Proclamation, "Granting Pardon to Certain Persons Convicted of Violating the Selective Training and Service Act of 1940 as Amended, Proclamation 2762," *Federal Register* 12, no. 250 (24 December 1947): 8731.

6. "Christmas Amnesty," *Pacific Citizen,* 3 January 1948.

7. For more on the redress story, see Mitchell Maki, Harry Kitano, and S. Megan Berthold, *Achieving the Impossible Dream: How Japanese Americans Obtained Redress* (Urbana: University of Illinois Press, 1999); William Hohri, *Repairing America: An Account of the Movement for Japanese-American Redress* (Pullman: Washington State University Press, 1988).

8. The resolution is quoted in Kenji G. Taguma, "Hawaii Vets Recognize Nisei Draft Resisters," *Nichi Bei Times,* 19 August 1998.

9. Hirasuna is quoted in Martha Nakagawa, "CCDC Rejects National JACL's Reconciliation Resolution with Resisters of Conscience," *Pacific Citizen,* 3–9 September 1999.

10. Martha Nakagawa, "JACL National Council Approves Apology to Resisters of Conscience," *Pacific Citizen,* 7–13 July 2000.

11. Tom Masamori, Letter to the Editor, *Pacific Citizen,* 14–20 July 2000.

12. Nakagawa, "JACL National Council Approves Apology to Resisters of Conscience."

13. Kinaga is quoted in Norihiko Shirouzu, "Decades on, a Legacy of War Still Haunts Japanese-Americans," *Wall Street Journal,* 25 June 1999.

14. See, e.g., Judgment and Commitment, *United States v. Kiyoshi Miyamura,* United States District Court for the District of Arizona, National Archives Branch Depository, Laguna Niguel, Calif., RG 21, Box 183, C7131–7135. Indeed, Judge David Lyng, the federal district judge who sentenced the Poston resisters to a fine of a penny, had more than just the benefit of hindsight in crafting his sentence late in 1946. He also had the scolding concurrence of Judge William Denman, a judge of the United States Court of Appeals for the Ninth Circuit, on an earlier appeal of a draft evasion conviction and three-year sentence for a Poston resister. See *United States v. Takeguma,* 156 F.2d 437, 442 (9th Cir. 1946) ("I feel that these young men should be considered by the executive as the subject of its clemency. They were United States citizens and only attempted to give up their citizenship after a continued illegal imprisonment by the Federal Government in barbed wire enclosures, guarded by armed soldiers, under conditions of great oppression and humiliation.").

15. Frank Emi, interview, in *Japanese American World War II Evacuation*

Oral History Project, pt. 4, *Resisters,* ed. Arthur Hansen (Munich, Germany: K. G. Saur, 1995), 387.

16. Yosh Kuromiya, letter to author, 29 October 1998.

Afterword

1. Akemi Matsumoto Ehrlich, "Legacy," National Japanese American Memorial to Patriotism, Washington, D.C.

Index